SOUTHEAST ASIA
IN THE NEW INTERNATIONAL ERA

POLITICS IN ASIA AND THE PACIFIC
Interdisciplinary Perspectives

Haruhiro Fukui
Series Editor

Southeast Asia in the New International Era, Clark D. Neher

FORTHCOMING

Emerging Ocean Regimes in the "New Pacific," Biliana Cicin-Sain, Robert Knecht, and William Nester

China and Tiananmen, Lowell Dittmer

Japan's Land Policy and Its Global Impact, Shigeko N. Fukai

Politics and Public Opinion in China, Alan P.L. Liu

Popular Protest and Political Culture in Modern China: Learning from 1989, Jeffrey N. Wasserstrom and Elizabeth J. Perry

SOUTHEAST ASIA
IN THE NEW INTERNATIONAL ERA

Clark D. Neher
NORTHERN ILLINOIS UNIVERSITY

Westview Press
BOULDER • SAN FRANCISCO • OXFORD

Politics in Asia and the Pacific: Interdisciplinary Perspectives

Copyright © 1991 by Westview Press, Inc.

Published in 1991 in the United States of America by Westview Press, Inc., 5500 Central Avenue, Boulder, Colorado 80301, and in the United Kingdom by Westview Press, 36 Lonsdale Road, Summertown, Oxford OX2 7EW

Library of Congress Cataloging-in-Publication Data
Neher, Clark D.
  Southeast Asia in the new international era / Clark D. Neher.
    p. cm. — (Politics in Asia and the Pacific :
interdisciplinary perspectives)
  Includes bibliographical references and index.
  ISBN 0-8133-1179-9. — ISBN 0-8133-1180-2 (pbk.)
    1. Asia, Southeastern—Politics and government—1945-   . 2. Asia,
Southeastern—Foreign relations. I. Title. II. Series: Politics
in Asia and the Pacific.
DS526.7.N45 1991
959.05′3—dc20   91-15136
                                                                                CIP

Printed and bound in the United States of America

The paper used in this publication meets the requirements
of the American National Standard for Permanence of Paper
for Printed Library Materials Z39.48-1984.

10   9   8   7   6   5   4   3   2

CONTENTS

Preface and Acknowledgments   xi
List of Acronyms   xiii

1   Introduction   1

     Notes, 6

2   The New International Era   9

     International Changes, 9
     Domestic Changes in the New International Era, 15
     Notes, 22

3   Thailand   23

     Institutions and Social Groups, 28
     Democratization, 38
     Economic Development, 39
     The Thai State, 41
     Foreign Policy, 48
     Conclusion, 52
     Notes, 53

4   The Philippines   55

     Institutions and Social Groups, 63
     Democratization, 72
     Economic Development, 74
     The Philippine State, 77
     Foreign Policy, 79

Conclusion, 83
Notes, 84

5   Indonesia   87

Institutions and Social Groups, 90
Democratization, 94
Economic Development, 95
The Indonesian State, 97
Foreign Policy, 99
Conclusion, 101
Notes, 101

6   Malaysia   103

Institutions and Social Groups, 108
Democratization, 112
Economic Development, 114
The Malaysian State, 115
Foreign Policy, 117
Conclusion, 118
Notes, 119

7   Singapore   121

Institutions and Social Groups, 123
Democratization, 126
Economic Development, 127
The Singaporean State, 128
Foreign Policy, 130
Conclusion, 131
Notes, 132

8   Negara Brunei Darussalam   133

Institutions and Social Groups, 134
Democratization, 135
Economic Development, 136
The Bruneian State, 136
Foreign Policy, 138
Conclusion, 138
Notes, 139

9   Burma   141

Institutions and Social Groups, 146
Democratization, 150
Economic Development, 151
The Burmese State, 152
Foreign Policy, 154
Conclusion, 155
Notes, 156

10   Vietnam   157

Institutions and Social Groups, 164
Democratization, 167
Economic Development, 168
The Vietnamese State, 170
Foreign Policy, 171
Conclusion, 175
Notes, 176

11   Cambodia   177

Institutions and Social Groups, 183
Democratization, 187
Economic Development, 188
The Cambodian State, 189
Foreign Policy, 190
Conclusion, 194
Notes, 195

12   Laos   197

Institutions and Social Groups, 201
Democratization, 203
Economic Development, 204
The Laotian State, 205
Foreign Policy, 206
Conclusion, 207
Notes, 208

13   Conclusion   209

Bibliography   213
About the Book and Author   219
Index   221

PREFACE AND ACKNOWLEDGMENTS

This book results from information gathered during many trips to Southeast Asia over the past twenty-seven years. I am grateful to the National Science, Ford, and Fulbright Foundations, the United States Information Agency, and the United States–Indochina Reconciliation Project for their generous assistance of the more lengthy stays. I am also indebted to the faculty and staff of Chulalongkorn University, Thammasat University, Chiang Mai University, and Payap University in Thailand and the University of San Carlos in the Philippines for their intellectual and material support of my work at their campuses.

During my career as a student of Southeast Asian politics, I have learned much from colleagues who share my interest. I am especially indebted to M. Ladd Thomas, Dwight King, and Brantly Womack in the Department of Political Science at Northern Illinois University. They have provided generous intellectual and collegial counsel. Roberta Burk and April Davis contributed outstanding administrative support, and Kittipak Thavisri and Warner Winborne provided outstanding research assistance. Both undergraduate and graduate students at Northern Illinois University have contributed to this book as well through their enthusiastic interest in the Southeast Asian region. It is gratifying to have taught these students, many of whom are now among the new generation of scholars of Southeast Asia.

Although I accept responsibility for all errors and misinterpretations, many scholars of Southeast Asia will see their ideas reflected in *Southeast Asia in the New International Era*. Among those scholars who have helped shape my views are David Wilson, Donn Hart, Michael Aung-Thwin, Ansil Ramsay, Prasert Bhandachart, Bidhya Bowornwathana, Kusuma

Snitwongse, Suchit Bunbongkarn, Danny Unger, Gary Suwannarat, David Adams, Sheldon Simon, Chai-Anan Samudavanija, Sukhumbhand Paribatra, Proserpina Tapales, John McAuliff, Anek Laothamathas, and Narong Sinsawasdi.

This book is dedicated to Arlene, Erick, Gregory, and Carol Neher.

Clark D. Neher

ACRONYMS

AFP	Armed Forces of the Philippines
AFPFL	Anti-Fascist People's Freedom League
APU	*Angkatan Perpaduan Umnah*
ASEAN	Association of Southeast Asian Nations
BSPP	Burmese Socialist Program Party
CGDK	Coalition Government of Democratic Kampuchea
CPP	Communist Party of the Philippines
CPV	Communist Party of Vietnam
DAP	Democratic Action Party
DPR	Indonesian Parliament
EOI	export-oriented industrialization
FUNCINPEC	United National Front for an Independent, Peaceful, and Cooperative Cambodia
GNP	gross national product
GRC	Group Representation Constituency
GSP	Generalized System of Preferences
IPR	intellectual property rights
ISI	import-substitution industrialization
KBL	*Kilusang Bagong Lipunan*
KPNLF	Khmer People's National Liberation Front
LPRP	Lao People's Revolutionary Party
MAI	Multilateral Aid Initiative
MBA	Military Bases Agreement
MPR	People's Consultative Assembly
NAP	New Aspirations Party
NDF	National Democratic Front
NEFOs	newly emerging forces
NEP	new economic policy

NGO	nongovernmental organization
NICs	newly industrialized countries
NLD	National League for Democracy
NLF	National Liberation Front
NLHS	*Neo Lao Hak Sat*
NOC	National Operations Council
NPA	New People's Army
NPKC	National Peace Keeping Council
NUP	National Unity Party
ODP	Orderly Departure Program
OLDEFOs	old established forces
PAP	People's Action Party
PAS	*Partai Islam Se-Malaysia*
PAVN	People's Party of Vietnam
PDI	Indonesian Democratic Party
PGNU	Provisional Government of National Unity
PKI	Communist Party of Indochina
PPP	United Development Party
PRK	People's Republic of Kampuchea
PRPK	People's Revolutionary Party of Kampuchea
RAM	Reform the Armed Forces Movement
RBAF	Royal Brunei Armed Forces
SEATO	Southeast Asia Treaty Organization
SLORC	State Law and Order Restoration Council
SNC	Supreme National Council
UMNO	United Malay Nationalist Organization
UNIDO	United Nationalist Democratic Organization
ZOPFAN	Zone of Peace, Freedom, and Neutrality

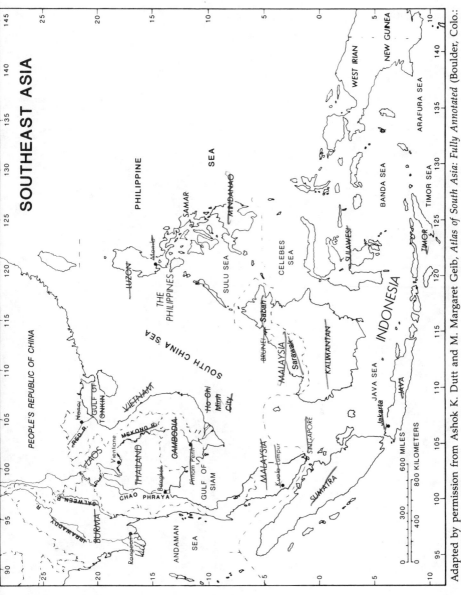

SOUTHEAST ASIA

Adapted by permission from Ashok K. Dutt and M. Margaret Geib, *Atlas of South Asia: Fully Annotated* (Boulder, Colo.: Westview Press, 1987).

1

INTRODUCTION

Writing a book in 1990 about contemporary Southeast Asia can easily be seen as problematic because the region is no longer a primary focus of U.S. political attention. Weeks go by without any major media stories about this region that, just two decades ago, dominated the discussions of government officials and ordinary citizens. Because of the many great changes in the Soviet Union, China, and Europe and the relatively stable, crisis-free environment in much of Southeast Asia, Americans have focused their interest elsewhere. Moreover, the lingering trauma, disillusionment, and cynicism of the Vietnam War period have also kept journalists, political scientists and policymakers from focusing on Southeast Asia.

This relative indifference is all the more frustrating because significant events are occurring in the region, both politically and economically, with serious consequences for the entire world. Periodic spurts of interest in Southeast Asia have accompanied the rise and travails of Corazon Aquino in the Philippines, the remarkable economic growth of Thailand, the brutal crackdown by the military on prodemocracy demonstrators in Burma, the continuing tragedy of Indochinese refugees, and attempts to forge a peace settlement in Cambodia.[1] Nevertheless, despite the region's rising economic importance, Southeast Asia has remained peripheral to U.S. foreign policy considerations.

A new era in international relations has arisen in the last several decades with important repercussions for Southeast Asia. Political, economic, and social forces of unprecedented scope have transformed the entire region. *Southeast Asia in the New International Era* analyzes contemporary politics in the context of these international and domestic political-economic realities from the perspectives of both the Southeast Asians

1

and the international community. Each nation is evaluated in terms of its major institutions, degree of democratization, movement toward economic development, foreign policy, and the role of the state. Thailand and the Philippines are treated the most comprehensively, demonstrating two contending political and economic patterns and reflecting their intrinsic interest and importance to the region as well as the author's specific expertise.

Southeast Asia, a region of remarkable diversity, consists of ten nations with differing histories, cultural traditions, resource bases, and political-economic systems. Except for geographic proximity and a tropical ecology, few characteristics link these nations into a coherent whole. Nevertheless, most of them share certain patterns: a colonial past; a postwar struggle for independence and modernization; religious penetration by Islam, Hinduism, Buddhism, and Christianity (which are in many cases a thin veneer over animism); agricultural economies that have been overtaken by manufacturing in the past decade; reliance on patron-client bonds for achieving goals; and a strong sense of the village as the primary unit of identity.[2]

The most striking similarity among the Southeast Asian nations has been the postindependence movement from diffuse feelings of nationalism into strong nationalist loyalties. The nationalist movement has manifested itself in various ways, but the roots lie in the common colonial history experienced by all these nations as well as their common subjugation by the Japanese during World War II. Many of the problems of economic and political development faced by Southeast Asian leaders today can be traced to common historical colonial patterns.

Colonial rule resulted in the formation of nation-states with viable boundaries. The imperialists guaranteed these boundaries, thus introducing a sense of stability and order to the region. Colonialism was also responsible for the growth of economic structures such as ports, railways, and roads. A money economy was introduced, and large-scale industries were established requiring skilled and unskilled laborers. Because the Southeast Asian peasants found industrial labor antithetical to traditional values, the colonialists imported Chinese and Indians to work in factories, tin mines, and rubber plantations. The Chinese and Indian communities, through their connections with Western imperialism, have thus enjoyed and continue to enjoy economic power in Southeast Asia far beyond their numbers.

Perhaps the most important consequence of colonialism was its direct impact on the rise of nationalism throughout Southeast Asia. The colonial nations became unified territorial states, whereas their predecessors had been nonintegrated dynastic principalities. By the late nineteenth century, the major national boundaries had been demarcated, and the entire area of Southeast Asia, except Thailand, was in European hands. This colonial heritage helps explain the strong nationalism of the Vietnamese manifested in their resistance to French, Japanese, and U.S. attempts to influence their nation. In Vietnam, Laos, Cambodia, Indonesia, and Burma, nationalism as a unifying force was exemplified by their violent struggles for independence in the post–World War II era. In the Philippines, Singapore, Brunei, and Malaysia these struggles were less violent.

Southeast Asian nations (except for Singapore and Brunei) are characterized by the agricultural base that is at the heart of the nations' economic life. The basic economic unit is the family-operated farm, with most of the farm products being consumed by the family itself or being used to pay for the additional farm labor required. The agricultural village is the major unit of identity for the rural population, acting as the educational, religious, cultural, political, economic, and social center.

The hierarchical structure at the village level is found throughout Southeast Asian political life, with a village headman serving as the major focus of power. Essentially, these societies are organized into networks of superior-subordinate (patron-client) ties, which form the basis of the political structures of the society. These patron-client bonds act as an integrating grid of relationships that hold the society together and as linkages between the state and the citizenry. Where there are marked inequalities in wealth, status, and control and where resources are insufficient, those with limited access to the resources form alliances with individuals of a higher socioeconomic level. The relationship is one of mutual benefits in which the patron expects labor, protection, defense, or some other reward in return for dispensing benefits to the subordinate. The mutual interests provide a security the state itself cannot provide.

Because of the great diversity in and among Southeast Asian states as well as the rapid changes they have been undergoing, categorization of these states is difficult and must be complemented by analysis of the unique attributes of each. The diversity and complexity of the region become clear when the region is broken down into four political categories: semidemocratic, military authoritarian, absolute monarchy, and Communist authoritarian. From a political perspective, the semidemocratic nations include Thailand (until the February 1991 military coup d'etat), Malaysia, the Philippines, Singapore, and Indonesia. "Semidemocratic" refers to those nations with a semblance of citizen involvement in choosing governmental leaders, the executive leader not fully accountable to the legislative branch, a high degree of civil liberties—with some exceptions—to ensure "law and order," and autonomous groups representing the interests of the people. Burma is the best example of a military authoritarian government, featuring a dominant role for the military in all phases of political life. Brunei, however, is an absolute monarchy. Finally, Communist authoritarian governments reserve an exclusive role for the Communist party in political life, establish command economies, and have a low level of civil liberties. Vietnam, Cambodia, and Laos fall into this category.

Because of rapid changes experienced by most of the ten nations, as this book will show, such categories sometimes obfuscate as much as they clarify. Until the late 1970s, for example, Thailand fit into the military authoritarian category and could return to it at any time. In 1986 the Philippines ended two decades of authoritarian rule under President Ferdinand Marcos, following the extraordinary rise of "people's power," which brought constitutional government and the Democrat Corazon Aquino into power. Singapore and Indonesia, both with the structural trappings of democracy, are in fact governed by an exclusive elite (civilian in Singapore; military in Indonesia) that periodically suppresses the rights of the citizenry.

The attempt to overthrow the military dictatorship and establish democratic rule in Burma in 1988, which was reminiscent of the people's power revolt in the Philippines, was terminated by the military. Although continuity of political rule has existed in Vietnam and Laos since 1975 when Communist governments were installed, economic liberalization programs, begun in the mid-1980s, have begun to change the structure of these societies. Cambodia, having undergone the horrors of the Khmer Rouge, has moved toward a semblance of normalcy since 1979 when a Vietnamese-installed government overthrew the genocidal regime. Nevertheless, the Communist party controls all aspects of political and economic life in the Indochinese nations.

Brunei, independent only since 1984 and with a population of just over two hundred thousand, is an absolute monarchy; its economy is based on oil revenues, so that Brunei cannot be compared to any of its neighbors in the region. Malaysia, perhaps more than any other Southeast Asian nation, has experienced a long—albeit tenuous—period of semi-democracy and economic stability, although recent events indicate an increase in the politics of confrontation among the leading ethnic groups.

This political categorization, although useful for specific times in history, does not adequately portray Southeast Asian nations at all times, as none of the states fits precisely into the categories. Thus, an alternative listing of political categories could include, first, Leninist single-party dictatorships, using the principle of democratic centralism as found in Vietnam, Cambodia, and Laos. Second, authoritarian-pluralist systems—characterized by an elitist-centered, restrictive political order with social and economic institutions that have various degrees of independence from party or state control—are found in Thailand (under the military), the Philippines (under President Ferdinand Marcos), Indonesia, Burma, Singapore, and Brunei. A third category is a parliamentary-democratic system, featuring support of the government through free, competitive elections with limits on state power. Malaysia, the Philippines (under President Aquino), and Thailand (from 1977 to 1991) meet these criteria.[3]

Also suffering from the problem of imprecision, even this categorization does not adequately distinguish the region's political structures and behavior. The political repression in Burma, for example, is significantly greater than that in Singapore, Indonesia, and Thailand (even under the military). Although Singapore has experienced single-party rule since its independence, its style of government is qualitatively different from the absolute family rule of Brunei or the corrupt cronyism of the Philippines under President Marcos. Similarly, placing the contemporary Philippines in the same category as Thailand and Malaysia blurs these nations' strikingly different political systems. The Philippines relies on the personal charisma of President Aquino for stability and adherence to democratic procedures, whereas Thailand and Malaysia have developed these characteristics without charismatic leadership.

Another way of categorizing the Southeast Asian nations is simply geographic, with mainland Southeast Asia consisting of Thailand, Burma, Laos, Cambodia, and Vietnam and insular Southeast Asia consisting of the Philippines, Singapore, Indonesia, Brunei, and Malaysia. One advantage of this categorization is that it corresponds to religious criteria as well. All of the mainland countries practice Buddhism (with significant variations from country to country), while the peoples of the archipelagic nations practice a form of Islam. The Catholic Philippines is an exception, although important Muslim minorities are found in the southernmost islands. Singaporeans practice Confucianism, Buddhism, Islam, and Christianity.

The notion of an integrated mainland Southeast Asia was advanced in the late 1980s when Thai leaders set forth the idea of *Suwanabhum* (Golden Land), a term encompassing all the mainland nations. Thai leaders attempted to surmount the political differences among the mainland Southeast Asian nations by suggesting that these nations had a common destiny in their common religious beliefs, geographic proximity, and desire for modernization. However, *Suwanabhum* was not accepted by the leaders of most mainland nations, as they rejected the implicit hegemonic designs of Thailand and as such conflicts were felt deeply throughout the region.

Insular Southeast Asia is a problematic category because Malaysia is as much mainland as island, sharing a long border with mainland Thailand. The Philippines, the only Christian nation, is geographically and culturally distant from the rest of the archipelago. Indonesia, with a population of over 180 million—most of which is involved with rice farming—is fundamentally different from Brunei (which has only 200,000 citizens) and from the city-state of Singapore (which has no agricultural base).

The founding of the Association of Southeast Asian Nations (ASEAN) in 1967, initiated by the non-Communist Southeast Asian nations in response to a perceived Communist threat, has led to still another means by which to categorize the Southeast Asian nations. Non-Communist ASEAN includes Thailand, Malaysia, Singapore, Indonesia, the Philippines, and Brunei (which joined in 1984), while Laos, Cambodia, and Vietnam compose the Communist Indochinese nations. Burma, of course, has remained neutral.

Thus far, ASEAN has served economic rather than military purposes. As an alliance, ASEAN has been more passive than active, held together largely by the members' common antipathy toward Vietnam. ASEAN's fame comes not from its cooperative ventures but from the fact that separately, these nations have emerged as among the most economically vital in the world. ASEAN has become a showcase of successful economic development.

Nationalism is the major reason ASEAN has not become a more meaningful alliance. The ASEAN nations are also as much economic competitors as they are collaborators. Similarly, the Leninist nations have rarely worked in concert for common goals. The Communist ideology shared by these nations has not erased three centuries of enmity due to traditional Vietnamese and Cambodian expansionism. For example, Vietnam invaded Cambodia in 1979 following years of border disputes. The attempt by the Communist Vietnamese to forge an Indochina Federation floundered because of the history of intense conflicts and mutual distrust among the three nations.

The difficulty in categorizing the Southeast Asian nations emphasizes the importance of viewing them as highly diverse and worthy of analysis from the vantage point of their unique attributes. Specifically, the chapter on each country will focus on the following factors: political institutions, the process of democratization, economic development (and role in the world economic system), the role of the state, and foreign policy.

Before assessing each Southeast Asian nation's contemporary political status, I will discuss the impact of the new international era on politics in the region.

Notes

1. On June 18, 1990, the military rulers of Burma announced that the country's official name (in English) is Myanmar and that Rangoon's name has been changed

to Yangon. Because this name change may be temporary and has not been accepted internationally, and to reduce confusion when referring to the country and city prior to the name change, this book will use the names Burma and Rangoon. In 1989 the rulers in Cambodia changed the nation's name from Kampuchea to State of Cambodia. In this text, the name Cambodia will be used throughout.

2. A detailed discussion of similarities and differences among the ten Southeast Asian nations is included in the author's *Politics in Southeast Asia* (Rochester, Vermont: Schenkman Books, Inc., 1987). The detailed historical and cultural background discussions included in that volume are summarily repeated in the present volume.

3. For a fuller treatment of these categories, see the essay by Robert A. Scalapino, "Political Trends in Asia and Their Implications for the Region," in *Asia and the Major Powers: Domestic Politics and Foreign Policy*, ed. Robert A. Scalapino, Seizaburo Sato, Jusuf Wanandi, and Sung-joo Han (Berkeley: Institute of East Asian Studies, University of California, 1988).

2

THE NEW INTERNATIONAL ERA

An extraordinary sweep of international change occurred in the 1980s: the transformation of the dominant bipolar world of Communists and non-Communists to a more fragmented and interdependent world of competing multipolar centers of power, with the United States participating more as an equal than as a superpower and the Soviet Union losing its vast empire. The extent of the changes, occurring in rapid fashion, stunned the world and irrevocably recast international relations.

The full dimensions of the change will not be known for decades. However, it is clear that the collapse of the Communist empire, the parallel democratization of previously authoritarian political systems, and the fading of ideological distinctions will have an impact on virtually all of the world's nations, including those in Southeast Asia.

International Changes

As ideological distinctions faded, economic relations with new, emerging centers of power became more important than security ties. The containment of communism was no longer the central goal of the United States or its allies. Instead, trade relations assumed greater importance, with Japan, the European Community, the newly industrialized countries, and China taking center stage. Even the Persian Gulf war had little to do with political ideologies and much to do with the economic security of the United States and its allies.

A major catalyst for these changes has been Soviet President Mikhail Gorbachev, who has acted on the assumption that the Soviet Union will flourish only by a comprehensive reorganization (*perestroika*) and opening (*glasnost*) of Soviet society. *Perestroika* has resulted in the demise of the

Soviet Communist party apparatus, the establishment of new pluralist governmental institutions, a rising nationalism among the union's constituent republics, and the introduction of a market economy. So fundamental are these changes that the Soviet Union faces a long period of destabilizing transition.

These changes also demonstrate clearly that the Soviet economy has all but collapsed. Soviet President Gorbachev decided that the militarization of the country had been a colossal mistake both in terms of the internal economy and external relations throughout the world. He moved to rectify the problem through huge cuts in military expenditures and by diplomatic activity designed to integrate the nation into the world capitalist system.

Glasnost has led to the repeal of the Brezhnev doctrine, which had proclaimed that no nation was free to leave the Soviet sphere of influence or the Socialist camp. Without the threat of Soviet tanks, the nations of Eastern Europe ousted their Communist leaders and moved toward pluralist political systems. *Glasnost* also increased the amount of information available to Soviet citizens. The presumed advantages of centralized planning vanished in the Soviet Union and other politically authoritarian states as the revolution in technology and communications made comparisons between societies possible. State legitimacy, once a function of a prescribed ideology, now depended on improved performance.

For Asia, the ramifications of the changes in the Soviet Union include the Soviet withdrawal of troops from Afghanistan; the cessation of Soviet aid to insurgencies in Southeast Asia, of Soviet economic and trade ties with the non-Communist ASEAN region, and of Soviet criticism of ideological rigidity in Vietnam and the consequent reduction of aid; Soviet pressure upon Vietnam to withdraw troops from Cambodia; Soviet acceptance of a significant U.S. role in Southeast Asia; demilitarization of the Sino-Soviet border; and reduced Soviet use of basing facilities in Vietnam. The Soviet Union has been unable to participate in the growing economic and technological development in Asia.[1]

Symbolic of the decline of Soviet interest in militarily influencing Southeast Asia are the reduced use of Cam Ranh and Da Nang bases in Vietnam and signs that the bases will soon be abandoned altogether. Although the bases were never used to influence the course of events in Southeast Asia, they provided potential Soviet domination over the vital waterways of the Pacific Ocean, South China Sea, and Indian Ocean that are deemed indispensable for U.S. trade, access to oil by Japan, and the security of ASEAN. Soviet withdrawal is a clear sign that these threats are not imminent and that Southeast Asia is not a target of expansionism, either from the Soviet Union itself or from its client-state, Vietnam.

The decision to withdraw support from Vietnam reflects the Soviet view that its alliance with Vietnam has isolated Moscow from Southeast Asia's economically dynamic countries. This alliance has been a major cause of the continued ASEAN alliance with the United States and the improvement of ties between ASEAN and China. President Gorbachev's desire for a more positive relationship with ASEAN explains Soviet support for the Vietnamese troop withdrawal from Cambodia and for an overall, negotiated settlement of the Cambodian civil war.

In 1987 then-Soviet Foreign Minister Eduard Shevardnadze visited several ASEAN capitals, the first such visit by a ranking Soviet leader. This trip enhanced the ASEAN view that the Soviet Union could play a constructive role in Southeast Asia as a balance of power for the other superpowers including China, Japan, and the United States.

Equally as dramatic as the transformation of Soviet domestic and foreign policy are the changes in China since the rise of the more pragmatic post-Mao leadership. During the period of Mao Zedong, China was the Southeast Asian nations' most feared adversary. By the mid-1970s, China had emerged as the major guarantor of Thai security against possible Vietnamese aggression and as an increasingly important trade partner with ASEAN. Aid to Communist insurgencies ceased. Despite the Tiananmen Square massacre in June 1989, which set back political liberalization in China, Chinese leaders regarded their goals in Southeast Asia as coincident with those of the United States. They sought to contain Soviet expansionism, develop closer economic ties with ASEAN, ensure an independent Cambodia that was free from Vietnamese occupation, and keep Southeast Asia from being dominated by any one superpower.

In just one decade after 1975, the Communist powers of the Soviet Union, China, and Vietnam ceased being security threats to Southeast Asia. The advent of *perestroika* and *glasnost* foreclosed the possibility that the Soviet Union would attempt a military move into Southeast Asia. China is also fully engaged in attempts to strengthen its economy by improving trade relations with the world's capitalist countries, including those of ASEAN. Vietnam's withdrawal of troops from Cambodia in 1989, its policy of economic liberalization and renovation (*Doi Moi*), and its precarious economic status preclude military intervention in another region of Southeast Asia.

Since 1970, the economic dynamism of Japan has not only dramatically changed international relations but has refashioned the economies of Southeast Asia as well. Japan has become the most important U.S. ally, and Asia's economic importance to the United States increases each year. U.S. trans-Pacific commerce reached $215 billion in 1989, exceeding U.S. trade with Europe by over 50 percent. Although the Pacific Rim is now the largest overseas market for U.S. agricultural exports, 60 percent of the total U.S. trade deficit of $170 billion is with Asia (and 35 percent with Japan alone).

U.S. relations with Japan best illustrate the enormity of the new interdependence between Asia and the United States. The flow of trade, capital, technology, and people has unalterably transformed both cultures. Japan and the United States together account for about 40 percent of the world's gross national product (GNP). Japan has invested $31 billion in the United States; more than 300,000 Americans now hold jobs in Japanese-owned enterprises, whereas 100,000 Japanese work for U.S. ventures in Japan. Japan's defense budget is the fifth largest in the world, with some $2.5 billion of the total $30 billion allocated for support and maintenance of U.S. forces stationed in Japan. The United States imports about 40 percent of Japan's exports, while in 1987, Japan imported U.S. products worth $28 billion—more than any nation except Canada and more than West Germany, France, and Italy combined. Nevertheless, the United States suffers a $60 billion trade deficit with Japan each year.

Five of the world's seven largest banks are Japanese, and Japanese firms and individuals are buying property and businesses in the United States. Highly educated Asian-Americans, although constituting only 3 percent of the U.S. population, play an increasingly major role in U.S. life in virtually all sectors of the society as the process of de-Europeanization continues. The various aspects of Asian culture exhibited by Asian-Americans, together with the inundation of the United States by commodities from Japan and the "Four Tigers" (Singapore, South Korea, Taiwan, and Hong Kong), have been felt at all levels of U.S. society and have rekindled interest in and concern about Asia. In the mid-1980s, U.S. policymakers realized that the dynamism in Asia, if unattended, could be exerted against U.S. interests.

Despite the fact that Japan attacked and occupied all the Southeast Asian nations in World War II and was demilitarized after its defeat, it still plays a vital role in contemporary Southeast Asia. Ironically, the unrealized goal of Japan's World War II scheme for a "co-prosperity sphere" has been achieved economically in contemporary Southeast Asia. Japan has overtaken the United States as the principal economic partner of the ASEAN nations. Japanese businesses, for example, account for 53 percent of the foreign investment in Thailand, a much larger amount than Taiwan with 12.5 percent and the United States with 5.8 percent. Between 1987 and 1989, 823 Japanese companies invested $5–6 billion in Thailand. Japan has become Thailand's most important aid provider and trade partner. Indeed, all of ASEAN is economically dependent upon Japan as the major source of imports, market for exports, aid provider, and foreign investor.

Japan's economic might has not been paralleled by political or military influence in Southeast Asia, mainly because Japan is sensitive to that region's concerns about too dominant a role for one superpower, although these sensitivities decrease as each year passes and the bitter memories of World War II and Japanese occupation are forgotten. For most Southeast Asians today, Japan represents first-rate consumer goods, such as cars, televisions, videos, and other electronic gadgets. Moreover, as U.S. influence wanes and the danger of Soviet and Chinese military aggression diminishes, Japan will play an even more prominent role in all aspects of the region.

The economic interests of Japan, South Korea, and Taiwan in Southeast Asia stem from the presence of disciplined and cheap labor easily exploited by foreign corporations. The emergence of a new international division of labor with Southeast Asians taking the role of the traditional proletariat has led to an increase in assembly plants and other industries producing goods for export. The East Asian newly industrialized countries (NICs) and Japan have generated significant flows of foreign investment into Southeast Asia in response to their own rising labor costs and exchange-rate fluctuations. This dramatic change has been the engine of development, as the ASEAN nations move toward export-oriented economies and away from import substitution.

Rapid industrialization has come mainly from external pressures rather than indigenous technology. A self-generating technological or research-oriented culture has failed to grow in ASEAN. Thus far, much of Southeast Asia's prosperity depends on external forces well beyond its control: outsiders' capital, technology, management, and markets.[2]

For Southeast Asia nations, this globalization of their economies makes them vulnerable to economic domination by external forces, especially Japan and the East Asian NICs. Downward trends in the world capital markets, slowed world economic growth, the questionable viability of multilateral institutions such as the World Bank, and the rising cry for protectionism in Western nations (including the new European Community) will increasingly have a direct negative impact on Southeast Asia. The Middle East crisis, following the August 1990 Iraqi invasion of Kuwait, is an example of how world events beyond the control of any of the Southeast Asian nations can directly affect these nations' economic stability and growth.

For U.S. foreign policy, Southeast Asia is perceived as peripheral to its central interests in Japan, China, the Middle East, Latin America, the European Community, and the Soviet Union. The primary reason for this low priority stems, paradoxically, from the U.S. perception that the region is politically stable, undergoing democratization, relatively supportive of U.S. interests, and free from major international crises. In contrast to 1975, when U.S. foreign policy in Southeast Asia was paralyzed and in shambles, the present U.S. position is stronger than at any time since the end of World War II. Today it is Vietnam that is isolated, with its economy in chaos and its international and regional influence depleted. Insurgencies have failed throughout ASEAN (the Philippines representing an exception), and both China and the Soviet Union are playing relatively constructive roles (with the exception of China's support for the Khmer Rouge in Cambodia).

Except for the interminable Cambodian imbroglio, which includes big power involvement and therefore potential war spillover, and the controversy over U.S. military bases in the Philippines, U.S. security interests in Southeast Asia are minimal. In accordance with the principle that interests determine commitments, U.S. commitments in Southeast Asia are secondary to those in other areas of the world.

This secondary interest is a complete turnaround from the period 1950–1970, when Southeast Asia was the focus of the U.S. containment policy against a perceived monolithic international Communist threat.[3] During this period, the United States established security treaties with the Philippines, Thailand, and South Vietnam; participated in the Southeast Asia Treaty Organization (SEATO); acquired military base facilities throughout Southeast Asia; and eventually sent 4.2 million soldiers, spent $120 billion, and sustained approximately 58,000 deaths in the attempt to keep South Vietnam from Communist rule.[4]

This period of intense and direct U.S. involvement in Southeast Asia was supplanted in the early 1970s by a more discriminating military policy. As a part of his Guam Doctrine, President Richard Nixon asserted that Asian wars were to be fought by Asians, not by Americans. The United States extricated itself from its Indochina war through a process of "Vietnamization," after which military bases in Vietnam and Thailand were no longer available to Americans. During the latter half of the 1970s, the United States played only a secondary security role in the region.

The Soviet-supported Vietnamese invasion of Cambodia in December 1978 and the subsequent Chinese incursion into Vietnam once again brought warfare to the region. The United States strengthened its military aid programs to its ASEAN allies and joined ASEAN in a common policy against Vietnam. Backed by President Ronald Reagan's fervent conservatism, ASEAN's unity and anti-Communist stance were intensified during this period.

By the end of the 1980s, this intensity had ebbed, a consequence of the changes in the new international era. The Vietnamese withdrew their troops, once numbering approximately 150,000, from Cambodia in September 1989 (with the exception of some 3,000 to 5,000 troops in the western provinces, intended to thwart Khmer Rouge attacks). Thailand, once the frontline state in the Southeast Asian cold war, began buying inexpensive weapons from China and developed economic ties with Vietnam following Thai Prime Minister Chatichai Choonhavan's call for turning "the Indochinese battleground into a trading market." His call for increased trade with Vietnam and his invitations to Cambodian Prime Minister Hun Sen to visit Bangkok reversed Thai foreign policy, which had long opposed the normalization of relations with either Cambodia or Vietnam.

The Soviet Union reduced its military presence at Cam Ranh Bay, moved to improve economic ties with ASEAN governments, and began a policy of rapprochement with China. In an incredibly short time, beginning with Gorbachev's rise to power in the Soviet Union and the subsequent liberalization of foreign policies in China and Vietnam, ASEAN state sovereignty was no longer threatened by the world's major Communist powers. These reduced tensions suggested that U.S. security resources could be reduced correspondingly, although most ASEAN leaders believed a U.S. presence in the area was still warranted. For example, during negotiations between the Philippines and the United States over the future of U.S. bases, ASEAN leaders called for a continued U.S. presence. The classic balance of power theory remained operative in the view of the leaders of both the major powers and the Southeast Asian nations in terms of their desire to keep the Soviet Union, China, Japan, Vietnam, or the United States from becoming *the* regional power. The reduced presence of the major powers allowed the Southeast Asian nations to share defense burdens more than was the case in the past.

A "new nationalism" in foreign policy, characterized by reduced dependence on the major powers, became the theme of both the Communist and non-Communist governments in Southeast Asia. This new nationalism emphasized balanced relationships with all the world's nations, irrespective of ideology, and international interdependence in economic matters such as trade.

Domestic Changes in the New International Era

Coinciding with the remarkable changes in the international sphere have been indigenous developments throughout the region that make the Southeast Asian nations fundamentally different from the 1970s. The clearest illustration of these changes has occurred in the three Indochinese nations of Vietnam, Laos, and Cambodia, where socialist economics has been judged a failure and been replaced by market-oriented economies more similar to those in ASEAN. Ten years of economic decline following the 1975 Communist takeover of all three nations led to similar policies of renovation that ended collectivization, promoted decentralized planning, downgraded agricultural cooperatives, and terminated price controls and subsidies to inefficient industries. Foreign capital was solicited by means of liberalized foreign investment laws, and trade relations with ASEAN and Western capitalist nations were promoted.

These significant changes in Indochina, initiated in 1986, bore fruit in the late 1980s. In Vietnam, for example, farm production rose so that food self-sufficiency was achieved in 1989. Indeed, Vietnam became the third largest exporter of rice in the world, a major achievement because in the preceding decade Vietnam had been forced to import food. Laos experienced similar economic growth after promulgating the "new thinking" (*chin tanakan may*) reforms in 1986.

Cambodia's economy was also opened and decentralized with entrepreneurs who were allowed to run enterprises jointly with the state. Food deficits, the result of low productivity, continued in the 1980s because the populace was still traumatized by the heinous policies of the Khmer Rouge. The entire bureaucracy had been decimated during the period 1975–1979; the nation's infrastructure was almost nonexistent, and a continuing civil war had bled the country of its meager resources. A trade embargo, initiated by the United States, kept investment capital scarce. U.N. development programs were not allowed into Cambodia because the Cambodian U.N. seat was held by the Coalition Government of Democratic Kampuchea (CGDK), a tripartite alliance of rebel forces arrayed against the sitting government in the capital, Phnom Penh. The CGDK included the anti-Communist Khmer People's National Liberation Front (KPNLF), the Sihanoukists led by Cambodia's former ruler, and the Communist Khmer Rouge—the architects of the "killing fields."

Despite dismal economic conditions in Cambodia, there has been some normalization of life since 1979, when the Khmer Rouge was overthrown by the Vietnamese-sponsored Hun Sen government. The omnipresent fear and oppression that led to the deaths of some two million Cambodians from 1975 to 1979 have ended. The cities, once emptied, have repopulated. Nuclear families are living in accordance with Cambodian customs, practicing Buddhism, and educating the youth once again. In 1990 a dubious ceasefire was signed by the warring factions, designed to lead eventually to a freely chosen government. The eleven-year-old Cambodian war, which has pitted the Hun Sen government in Phnom Penh against the three rebel forces, has defied myriad attempts at resolution, at least partially because outside powers—such as the United States, China, Thailand, and Vietnam—have complicated matters by using Cambodia for their own purposes.

Changes in non-Communist Southeast Asia have been very different, but no less important, than those in the Indochinese states. The most obvious change concerns the process of modernization by the six ASEAN nations. Since the 1970s, and except for the Philippines, these states have moved from somnolent, primarily agricultural economies to vibrant, manufacturing-oriented economies with higher economic growth rates than states in any other region of the world.

The rush to wealth among the ASEAN nations has led to both the best and worst aspects of westernization. Improved educational, infrastructural, and health facilities and greater opportunities in every aspect of life have been paralleled by problems of crass materialism, pollution, intolerable traffic conditions, rising crime, corruption, alienation, and an increasing gap between the rich and poor. Capital has poured into the region in unprecedented rates as the ASEAN nations have been assimilated into the global capitalist economy. Only Burma and the three Indochinese nations have been isolated from incorporation into the world political economy.

The phenomenal economic growth rates, as high as 10 percent per year in the late 1980s, have fundamentally changed the ASEAN landscape. The most obvious change is the rapid increase in per capita gross national product (GNP), which has more than tripled in just one decade. Per capita GNP in Thailand in 1977, for example, was $300; in 1990 the figure was $1,200. Similar per capita GNP growth rates for the same years occurred in the other ASEAN nations: Malaysia $660 to $2,053; Indonesia $150 to $520; Singapore $2,120 to $10,521; and the Philippines $310 to $720. (The smaller growth rate for the Philippines was due to economic mismanagement during the Marcos presidency.)

Corresponding figures for Burma, Vietnam, Cambodia, and Laos show minuscule growth in per capita GNP during the same period, around $150 per country. Brunei, because of its oil base, had an anomalous per capita GNP of $17,000 in 1990. For comparative purposes, 1990 per capita GNP in the United States was $21,000, in Japan $22,000, in China $305, and in India $320.[5]

Quality of life indicators have also markedly improved in ASEAN. Since 1970, life expectancy in all of the ASEAN countries has increased by ten years to the mid-60s, while Burmese, Cambodian, and Laotian life expectancies are about 50 years. In Vietnam the figure is 63, up from 43 in 1980. ASEAN literacy rates are all above 90 percent except for Indonesia, which is 60 percent. Annual population growth rates have decreased since 1980 as a result of family planning policies, the rising standard of living, and the availability of birth control devices. Fertility declined more than 20 percent in the ASEAN countries between 1960 and 1987. The average number of children per woman in 1960 and 1987 in each country was:

Singapore 6.3 and 1.6, Thailand 6.6 and 3.5, Malaysia 6.9 and 3.9, Indonesia 5.6 and 3.3, and the Philippines 6.6 and 4.7.[6]

In 1987, the numbers of televisions and automobiles per 1,000 people in Thailand were 106 and 20, respectively; in Indonesia 50 and 6, in Singapore 208 and 194, in Malaysia 172 and 64, in the Philippines 69 and 10, in Vietnam 7 and 4, and in Laos and Cambodia 1 and 1, respectively. These figures are important for understanding differences in these nations in the breadth of information available as well as in the capacity for travel and mobility.

These changes have paralleled the rapid urbanization of the ASEAN nations and the growth of an aware and involved middle class. This group is urban, educated, politically astute, materialistic, and technologically proficient. Although still a minority of the total population, the rising middle class is the most important socioeconomic change from the recent past—just three decades ago in 1960 these countries' populations were 90 to 95 percent peasantry and 5 to 10 percent elite.

Similarly, a skilled blue-collar class has arisen to work in the new industries. This class, which represents the backbone of the export-oriented ASEAN economies, has been at the heart of the rapid economic growth rates. Much of these spectacular growth rates is due to the influx of industrial factories, mainly from Japan, South Korea, and Taiwan, all of which hire indigenous workers to produce products that are then exported throughout the world.

These socioeconomic changes have had both positive and negative ramifications. Life in Southeast Asia is increasingly characterized by higher standards of living, broadened horizons from a wider information flow, better health, higher levels of education, more active and meaningful participation in political affairs, and increased opportunities in virtually every sector of life. At the same time, these societies are now confronted with higher rates of crime, alienation, and corruption—social ills that are characteristic of urban centers. Air pollution, deforestation, traffic jams, and land scarcity are a few of the environmental problems in Southeast Asia. The high levels of economic development are threatened by the assault on the region's natural resources and the governments' inability to build infrastructures sufficient to cope with the economic growth. Gaps between the few rich and the many poor are widening, despite the higher standard of living of all groups.

Although more difficult to specify, internal political changes in Southeast Asia are as important as domestic economic changes. Throughout the region there has been a tenuous, sometimes faltering trend toward pluralistic polities with stronger political institutions and less reliance on personalism. In Vietnam, Laos, and Cambodia, for example, there is more openness in conversations and in the media regarding political issues. In

Vietnam's local-level elections in November 1989, candidates were allowed to campaign with platforms that differed from the Communist party view. Although the Communist party retains its preeminent position, real debates have taken place in the national assemblies of all three nations. Factional struggles between conservatives and reformers have led to changes in party doctrine and governmental policies. Prior to 1986, such conflict and open discussion were not allowed.

In Burma, the move toward pluralistic politics climaxed in the summer of 1988 with massive demonstrations against the military government controlled by former General Ne Win. In an extraordinary outpouring of popular discontent against the government that had led Burma since 1962, thousands of citizens demanded a freely elected, democratic government. The euphoria ended abruptly on September 18, 1988, when Burma's military defense force (*Tatmadaw*) quelled the movement and instituted a period of even greater repression under General Saw Maung, a protege of former dictator Ne Win.

Despite the crackdown against those demanding democracy, the movement led to elections of members of a national assembly on May 27, 1990. In a stunning rebuke of the military rulers, and despite the fact that the most famous dissident leaders were not allowed to contest the election, opposition parties won an overwhelming majority of the seats. In the first multiparty elections in thirty years, the opposition National League for Democracy won two-thirds of the votes whereas the military-backed National Unity Party won only a small percent. However, in the spring of 1991 the fate of the democracy movement was still not clear, as Burma remained isolated from the world.

The movement toward democratization did not reach Brunei, which since its independence in 1984 has remained under the rule of its absolute monarch, Sultan Haji Hassanal Bolkiah Mu'izzaddin Waddaulah. No opposition parties have been sanctioned, and all government leaders must swear allegiance to the sultan. The immense wealth of Brunei, which comes from oil revenues, has allowed the government to set forth a comprehensive welfare and education program that, in turn, has kept anti-government sentiment to a minimum.

The other ASEAN nations have continued their slow evolution toward pluralism, stronger institutions, and civil liberties. The clearest example of the trend is the Philippines, where in February 1986 "people's power" succeeded in ousting the authoritarian government of Ferdinand Marcos and installing the democratic Corazon Aquino as president of the republic. The inability of Aquino to restructure the feudalistic socioeconomic system in the Philippines detracts from her success in revitalizing constitutional rule, free elections, freedom of the press, and autonomous institutions accountable to the public. Although personalism remained an integral part of Filipino politics under Aquino, corruption and cronyism declined compared to the Marcos era.

The Thai political system has been dominated by the military for fifty of the fifty-nine years since 1932 when the absolute monarchy was replaced by a constitutional monarchy. Thailand's government was transformed into a bureaucratic military polity in which succession was determined by coups d'etat rather than by heredity. Since 1970, and especially since the 1973 student-led revolt when democratic procedures were introduced, two important changes have occurred: the widening of the political base with the growth of new interest groups that play important political roles outside the bureaucracy, and the strengthening and legitimizing of such formerly weak institutions as political parties and the parliament. These changes have resulted in the gradual democratization of Thai politics, a shift from personalized, clientelist politics, and the temporary weakening of the military's role in government affairs. The 1991 military coup d'etat reversed the process of democratization, at least for the short run.

The clearest sign of change in contemporary Thai politics is the rise to power of Chatichai Choonhavan, the first elected member of parliament to become prime minister since 1976. Chatichai became prime minister after the July 24, 1988, parliamentary elections when he was elected a member of parliament. As leader of the *Chart Thai* party with the largest plurality in parliament, Chatichai formed a coalition government of five leading political parties. By 1990 the military had lost its monopoly of power in the Thai political system, although an army-led resurgence occurred in 1991 when the military deemed that the government was carrying out policies antithetical to the military's best interests.

Since independence in Malaysia in 1957, pluralist politics have been integral to the way authoritative decisions have been made. Through a system of quasi-separation of powers, competitive elections, and circumscribed civil liberties, the Malaysian government has been relatively accountable to the citizenry. Because of the ethnic communal tensions that pervade Malaysian society, the populace has accepted certain controls on its freedom, designed to assure continued stability and consensus. Malaysia's leaders, including Prime Minister Datuk Seri Mahathir bin Mohamad, have been chosen by regularized elections, all won by the ruling *Barisan Nasional* (National Front) coalition.

Since achieving independence from the Dutch in 1949, Indonesia has relied on the leadership of President Sukarno, who dominated Indonesian politics for nearly two decades until 1965, and President Suharto, who has led the country in the subsequent years. General Suharto, who was elected to his fifth five-year term in 1988, brought the military into a commanding position in Indonesian politics. At the same time, he established a constitutional order that features regular elections, which he and his Golkar political movement have controlled through skillful political management, mobilization of local-level bureaucrats, selected repression of oppositionists, a workable economic program, and unlimited access to revenue for campaign purposes.

President Suharto has attempted to balance the rising demands for more political openness with policies that ensure order, stability, and the continued primary role for the military. The balance is delicate because of the government's grip over mass social organizations and key areas of the economy. Suharto has followed Sukarno's dictum that Western-style democracy is inappropriate for Indonesians, who thrive in a system of consultation (*musjawarah*) and consensus (*mufakat*) in which the leaders make the key decisions for the people. Western-style democracy is viewed by Indonesian leaders as a formula for anarchy, factionalism, and revolts. Just as important, democratization is seen as a sure means for the present leaders to lose their coveted positions.

Singapore, Southeast Asia's most efficiently run government, is a wealthy city-state entrepot that lacks the complexity of its larger, more populated, and more diverse neighbors. It does have the brilliant Lee Kuan Yew, who led the country since its independence from the British until November 1990 when he resigned as prime minister. Within a formal structure of democratic institutions that features free elections and a parliamentary system, Singapore has been run as a one-party system centering around Lee. By circumscribing the freedoms of the opposition and by achieving remarkable economic growth, Lee Kuan Yew obtained the support of the overwhelming majority of the people.

The involvement of large numbers of people in the political affairs of Southeast Asian nations is a fundamental innovation, replacing traditional hierarchical patterns of rule. The leaders of virtually every nation in the region must consider the views of the populace as articulated through votes, demonstrations, interest groups, the media, dissident leaders, disaffected political factions, mobilized ethnic groups, and student associations. Moreover, national leaders must have the foresight to meet the needs of the people before these needs become impossible demands. This requirement for effective leadership in the new Southeast Asia is not only unprecedented, it is an indigenously inspired change from the centralized polities that pervaded the region for centuries. The ideas of majority rule, freedom to oppose leadership, and institutionalized rather than personalistic government are not a traditional part of Southeast Asian political culture. When these changes are viewed in conjunction with the equally momentous movement toward modernization and the international drive toward more open political and economic systems, the transformation of

Southeast Asia in the new international era becomes increasingly intelligible.

The themes touched upon above are treated in more depth in the following country chapters. Each Southeast Asian nation will be analyzed in terms of its political institutions, the processes of development and democratization, policy issues, and the role of the state.

Notes

1. Paul Kreisberg, "Containment's Last Gasp," *Foreign Policy*, no. 75, Summer 1989, p. 153.

2. James Clad, *Behind the Myth: Business, Money and Power in Southeast Asia* (London: Unwin and Hyman, 1989), p. ix.

3. For a detailed discussion of phases of U.S.–Southeast Asian relations, see Muthiah Alagappa, "U.S.–ASEAN Security Relations: Challenges and Prospects," *Contemporary Southeast Asia*, vol. 11, no. 1, June 1989, pp. 1–39.

4. The figures are from Stanley Karnow, *Vietnam: A History* (New York: Viking Press, 1983).

5. All figures are from *Asiaweek*, June 1, 1990.

6. Far Eastern Economic Review, *Asia 1989 Yearbook* (Hong Kong: Review Publishing Company, 1989), p. 23.

3

THAILAND

Thailand has become an exemplary case study of how Third-World countries can develop successfully.[1] The Thai people's capacity to shape their nation into an increasingly developed society, both politically and economically, stems from a history of astute adaptation of those aspects of modernization and development that were appropriate to traditional Thai ways. Throughout their history, as citizens of the only Southeast Asian nation never to be colonized, the Thais never had a foreign culture thrust upon them. Instead, they were able to choose and mold a political system that fits Thai culture.

Thailand's success in developing politically is all the more striking given the fact that for centuries the government was autocratic in form and spirit. Power was the privilege of a small elite as well as of absolute monarchs who were not accountable to the people and whose authority was enhanced by an aura of divinity attached to the highest levels of office. Those who ruled were believed to possess superior ability and moral excellence. Common citizens exhibited little interest in affairs beyond their own villages.

The Sukhothai Kingdom (c. 1238–1350) was the first Thai-controlled kingdom. In this formerly Khmer area, the Thai absorbed the cultures of the Khmers, Mons, Indians, and Chinese and began the assimilation process that is important even today for understanding modern Thai society. Buddhism and Brahmanism were introduced to the Thais during the Sukhothai era. The Sukhothai Kingdom expanded and retracted, depending on the fortunes of military campaigns, until the Ayuthaya period (1350–1767) began.

The Thais adapted much from the Indianized Khmers who had dominated the Ayuthaya period. In particular, the kings were transformed from paternalistic guardians to autocratic god-kings with the attributes of a Brahmanic deity. The perception of the kings as god-kings remains even today as an important element of the veneration shown the king by his subjects. Notwithstanding this aura of godliness, the kings did not enjoy absolute power but were limited by court factionalism and competition for power and by an assumption of kingly virtue.

During the Ayuthayan reign important institutions were established that still influence Thai society. A *sakdi na* (power over fields) system was introduced that provided structure and hierarchy to the social and political relationships of the Thais. Virtually all persons in the kingdom were given *sakdi na* rankings according to the amount of land (or persons) they controlled. The ranking determined the salary of officials, the deference due them, and labor obligations to the state. Although the quantifiable character of the *sakdi na* system ended by 1932, the informal hierarchical character of the society is still a significant element of Thai society.

The destruction of Ayuthaya by invading Burmese in 1767 was a traumatic event in Thai history. The political-social system was torn asunder. Despite the near-total destruction of the kingdom, the Thais displayed remarkable recuperative powers and in a short time resumed life under a new centralized government in Bangkok led by the Chakri dynasty. Many of the Chakri kings were reform-oriented—systematizing administrative structures, freeing the slaves, bringing in highly educated technocrats, and assuring the continued independence of the nation from western colonialists. King Phumiphol Adunyadej is the ninth king of the dynasty.

Even after the 1932 revolt, which overthrew the absolute monarchy and established a constitutional monarchy, politics remained in the hands of a small elite group, now mostly civilian bureaucrats and military generals. The military, which emerged as the dominant institution, has controlled political power in Thailand for about fifty of the past fifty-nine years, since the revolt against the absolute kings. Until recently, politics in Thailand was monopolized by military leaders and a small number of government officials, with no external competition or balance from forces outside the bureaucratic arena. The basis of political power was highly personalized and subject to informal political manipulations and loyalties.

Thailand entered the modern period at the end of World War II in considerably better shape than most of its Southeast Asian neighbors. Having acquiesced to Japanese occupation (thereby having suffered little war damage) and not having fought a debilitating struggle for independence, Thailand was secure and stable. Initially after the war, Thailand seemed headed toward a constitutional system of parliamentary democracy, but the army soon took power.

The most influential of the post-war leaders was Marshal Sarit Thanarat, army commander-in-chief, who became prime minister in 1957, declared martial law, and ruled dictatorially for six years. He was the first prime minister to make economic development the cornerstone of his rule. His successor, Marshal Thanom Kittikachorn, followed in Sarit's footsteps by keeping the military in firm control of every aspect of government and by pursuing economic development. During both administrations, the legislature was impotent, political parties were for the most part forbidden to form, and corruption was rampant.

In response to the low level of political accountability and the high level of corruption, the "great tragedy" of October 14, 1973 (*Wan Maha Wipayok*), occurred when the citizenry rose against the Thanom government and forced the leadership into exile. King Phumiphol Adunyadej, Thailand's revered monarch, appointed the first civilian government since the immediate postwar period. The major causes of discontent included the political and economic mismanagement of the military regime, the perception that the military was increasingly ruling in its own self-interest, factionalism within the military, and the rise of an organized and aroused student population supported by the citizenry and the king.

Democratic-civilian rule lasted only until October 1976, when the military again overthrew the government, proclaimed martial law, and abrogated the constitution. The 1973 revolt had raised the expectations of many Thais that fundamental economic reforms would be carried out. The succeeding three-year period, however, coincided with a worldwide recession and with inflation that temporarily ended the nation's rapid economic growth. Hence, the hopes of many Thais that democracy would improve their lives were dashed by an economic situation over which the new government had no control.

The civilian government was also faced with an international and regional situation over which it had little control. The change to Communist governments in Vietnam, Laos, and Cambodia and the rise in insurgency throughout the Thai countryside shocked many Thais, who felt that only an authoritarian, military-dominated government could deal effectively with these threats. Because Thailand's traditional security ally, the United States, was withdrawing from Southeast Asia, the civilian governments renewed ties with the Communist nations. This destabilizing state of flux added to the uncertainty felt by many Thais.

The military remained the dominant government institution until 1988. Under General Prem Tinsulanond's prime ministership, the kingdom began its transformation to a more democratic society. Prem included civilian technocrats in his cabinet and relied on the freely elected legislature for support of his programs. Despite two coup attempts against him, he remained in power from 1980 until 1988, when he voluntarily stepped down.

The clearest sign of democratization in contemporary Thai politics was the rise to power of Chatichai Choonhavan, the first elected member of parliament to become prime minister since 1976. Chatichai assumed his new position following the 1988 elections when the political party he led received the largest plurality of votes and when Prem refused to accept another term as prime minister. Prem, who had led Thailand since 1980 during a period of stability and economic growth, had been deemed acceptable to both civilian and military forces and had been expected to continue in office. His refusal opened the way for civilian leadership under Chatichai.

The smooth transition from Prem to Chatichai reflected the new optimism about Thailand's evolution toward democracy. Chatichai had assumed power without relying on the support of the army. The constitutional provisions for elections worked well in transferring political power. Thus, the military coup d'etat in February 1991 was a shocking assault on the notion that Thailand had successfully institutionalized democratic-civilian processes.

Chatichai had served as minister of foreign affairs, minister of industry, and deputy minister under previous administrations. Because his reputation was that of a big business playboy, most analysts believed his tenure as prime minister would be short. However, Chatichai initiated a number of highly popular policies, thereby enhancing his *baramee* (charisma) in the minds of the populace.

Chatichai raised the salaries of government officials as well as the minimum wage for laborers, banned the indiscriminate cutting of trees, and stood up to the United States on trade and other economic issues. The decision to ban logging was particularly dramatic because conventional wisdom suggested that neither the cabinet nor the parliament would ever agree to ban an industry in which many of the political and military elites had major economic interests. Although the government has yet to show that it can control illegal encroachment in the remaining forests, the ban was a first step in repairing ecological damage.

In a series of innovative proposals, Chatichai enhanced his rising reputation as a master politician among the populace. His idea to turn the Indochinese battleground into a trading market was especially popular with the business community, which sought to open economic ties with the Vietnamese. His call for increased trade with Vietnam and his invitation to Cambodian Premier Hun Sen to visit Bangkok reversed Thai foreign policy, which had long opposed normalization with either Cambodia or Vietnam. Chatachai also moved to improve ties with Laos after decades of intermittent border skirmishes and diplomatic conflicts.

Chatichai's policies were supported by his coalition majority. However, oppositionists spoke against many of his initiatives, and a free press presented all sides of the controversies. Military leaders initially expressed support for Chatichai's administration and rejected intervention. In a move to mitigate potential military opposition, Chatichai invited General Chavalit to enter the cabinet as defense minister and deputy prime minister. Chavalit quickly tired of criticism directed toward him and resigned his position to form the New Aspirations Party (NAP). He then campaigned throughout the country in preparation for a bid to become the new prime minister.

Despite Chatichai's widespread support, several issues raised concern about the government's stability and effectiveness. Democratization had not completely ended the personalism and factionalism that have long been a part of Thai politics. Even among the coalition partners, factional infighting remained the norm as party leaders vied for the most influential cabinet positions. The fact that much of the popularity of the administration has been focused on Chatichai personally has become a source of discontent among leaders of coalition parties. Although votes of no confidence did not succeed, a minority of coalition members have on occasion defected, raising the possibility that Chatichai would dissolve the government. Indeed, in December 1990 Chatichai did dissolve his cabinet as a maneuver to offset criticism of his administration. The king immediately reinstated Chatichai as prime minister, thus providing him with an opportunity to bring in new faces and to mitigate military disapproval of certain members of his cabinet. Because he was seventy in 1990, Chatichai has stated on several occasions that he was "too old" to remain in his position of leadership for long. The uncertainty of his tenure exacerbated factional maneuvering and set the scene for the February coup.

Related to this problem of personalism, corruption continued to be an important part of the political process. The phenomenal economic growth rates of the 1980s brought large amounts of capital into the system, and these new resources were the financial target of public officials for private gain. Thai citizens were skeptical about the administration's professed concern for the majority, which has not gained from the economy's high growth rates. Many Thais viewed the administration as primarily concerned with big business interests. Indeed, the military claimed that the primary motivation for carrying out the coup in 1991 was the pervasive corruption of the kingdom's politicians.

Institutions and Social Groups

Patron-Client Ties

Historically, the key to understanding Thai society has been the patron-client relationship. Patron-client ties are hierarchical, face-to-face relationships of reciprocity. However, the relationship is not one of balance, as the superior has power over the subordinate. When individuals have few resources at their command but have various needs, persons who can supply the resources and meet the needs attain power over them.

At every level, from the village to the central government in Bangkok, patron-client groups have disseminated information, allocated resources, and organized people. These groups have formed a network of personal relations that extends throughout Thai society and that traditionally has formed the heart of Thai politics. Although both personalism and patron-client relationships remain important, in the past several decades Thai politics has evolved in the direction of decreased personalism and more formalized participation in the political structures.

Constitutions

The Thai propensity for changing constitutions has been referred to as *faction constitutionalism*, whereby each successive draft reflects, legitimates, and strengthens major shifts in factional dominance. Thai constitutions have not been considered the fundamental laws of the land; rather, they have functioned to facilitate the rule of the regime in power.

Since 1932, Thailand has been governed under thirteen constitutions, three of which were democratic and based on the British parliamentary model with the executive accountable to the parliament. Military leaders were not allowed a dominant role in this model. In the six of the constitutions that were semidemocratic, the prime minister did not have to be an elected member of parliament, and the upper house was controlled mostly by military and civilian bureaucrats who were appointed. Four constitutions were undemocratic, providing for neither an elected parliament nor political parties.[2]

The most recent constitution, promulgated in 1978 (and abrogated by the 1991 coup), struck a balance between democracy and military dominance. It called for a bicameral parliament with an appointed upper body, the senate, and an elected lower body, known as the assembly. This constitution had more longevity and stability than previous documents and was the underpinning for the semidemocracy that emerged. Semi-democracy refers to the balance between Western-style democracy and continuing authoritarian values that favor and buttress military involvement in governmental affairs. The balance is uniquely Thai: a blend that was legitimated in the minds of the rulers and the ruled until the February 1991 coup.

Military

Since the overthrow of the absolute monarchy, the Thai military has played the dominant role in Thai politics. Of the forty-six cabinets during the period 1932 to 1990, twenty-three must be classified as military governments, eight as military dominated, and fifteen as civilian. The civilian governments, which were the most unstable, were often replaced by military regimes following army coups.

The reasons for military dominance include the weakness of civilian governments and the fact that the military is the most highly organized institution in the kingdom. Because of perceived external and internal threats to Thai security, the military has proclaimed itself the only institution capable of protecting Thai sovereignty. Moreover, the hierarchical nature of the military is congruent with the nation's highly centralized political culture. Because Bangkok, as Thailand's primary city, dominates every aspect of the country's political and economic life, the military has needed to control only this one city in order to control the entire kingdom. Military, police, communications, and governmental agencies all emanate from Bangkok. Bangkok is to Thailand what Washington, D.C., New York, Los Angeles, Chicago, Philadelphia, and Dallas together are to the United States. Army divisions that have jurisdiction over Bangkok can control those ministries that are necessary for dominating the society: defense, interior, and communications.

Reacting to the view that neither internal nor external threats are menacing the Thai national slogan, "nation, king, religion" and that the regional situation has changed from confrontation to peaceful coexistence, General Chavalit initiated a comprehensive modernization program to streamline the army. Following the Indonesian model of dual function (*dwi fungsi*) with the army playing a national developmental as well as security role, he launched civil development projects manned by army units in all four regions of the country. The most prominent project, Green Northeast (*Isaan Khiaw*) is designed to improve irrigation and reforest denuded hillsides in Thailand's most impoverished region. Likewise, the army's New Hope (*Harapan Baru*) projects in the southern provinces have also been planned to legitimize the military's new role as chief developer of the kingdom. Neither program had achieved its stated goals by 1990.

The military's role in development stems from a government order in 1980 placing responsibility for defeating Communist insurgency on the army. Order 66/2523 suggested that stable government and higher levels of economic development were necessary before the Communist party of Thailand could be destroyed. The military was believed to be the most effective instrument for bringing about these conditions.

The fact that there has been no successful coup d'etat from 1977 to February 1991 is testimony to the professionalization of the army compared to the first four decades after 1932. The facts that Communist insurgency, which plagued Thailand in the 1960s and 1970s, has been quelled and that there is no external threat to Thai security had also undermined the major rationale for military intervention into governmental affairs.

The strengthened role of political parties and the parliament as well as a general attitudinal change more favorable to democratic civilian rule, especially among the politically aware, also reduced the military's influence. The fact that Prime Minister Chatichai gave the armed forces a free hand in personnel matters, provided generous budgets to all branches of the military, and supported the army's development projects mollified the military. Perhaps most important, the Thai king's determination to oppose a military coup greatly reduced the chance that such a coup would succeed. Nevertheless, two unsuccessful coup attempts in 1981 and 1985, respectively, and the successful coup of 1991 are reminders that military factionalism and personalism are still a part of Thai politics.

The military's projects in the southern region have stirred up the most controversy because the army has criticized local administration officials there for ineffectively governing areas in which Muslims are a prominent minority or even a majority. Civilian officials, on the other hand, see the army program as interference in their affairs. Prime Minister Chatichai chose not to intrude into the controversy except to provide economic support to these programs.

Military leaders continue to be involved in foreign policy matters. Indeed, the Thai military set forth the notion of Golden Peninsula (*Suwanabhum*), a geostrategic concept designed to make Thailand the economic and military leader of mainland Southeast Asia. *Suwanabhum* had been trumpeted by the prime minister's academic advisors as well, but more as an economic than a military notion.

The longest period of rule by a civilian prime minister since 1932 followed the July 1988 election, when Chatichai Choonhavan became prime minister after being elected to the parliament from Khorat Province. Although Chatichai had been a military general, he retired from the army thirty years previously and had been active in both governmental and business affairs. He appointed a civilian cabinet that consisted of elected members of parliament who were party leaders in his coalition administration.

Conventional wisdom suggested that as Thailand moved toward the status of a newly industrialized country (NIC), military coups became anachronistic, no longer a suitable means to change administrations. The Kingdom's remarkable economic growth rates of 11 percent (highest in the world for three years), its more politically aware and highly educated middle class, and its strengthened political institutions (political parties, interest groups, and parliament) were factors thought to provide a buffer against intervention by the military. Moreover, the lack of foreign or domestic threats to Thai security and the disapproval of venerated King Phumipol Adunyadej toward the failed 1981 and 1985 coup attempts seemed to insulate Chatichai's regime from a military takeover. Finally, the Thai military was thought to accept Chatichai, himself a former army general, because of the generous budgetary allotments he provided to them. Military leaders were thought to have a stake in the status quo because they benefitted from the enormous profits available from the rapid transformation of the Thai economy.

Countering this analysis, in 1991 Supreme Commander Sundhara Kongsompong and Army Commander-in-Chief Suchinda Kraprayoon abrogated the constitution, dismissed the elected government, and set up a temporary National Peace Keeping Council (NPKC) with powers of martial law and themselves as the ultimate arbiters of public policy.

The conventional wisdom, however, was not completely wrong. Realizing that times had indeed changed, the NPKC moved quickly to establish an interim constitution and to choose Anand Panyarachun, a distinguished civilian, as prime minister. Anand's appointment, announced on March 2, was universally praised, reflecting his impeccable reputation as a diplomat, administrator, and businessman. Prime Minister Anand, in turn, appointed an interim cabinet consisting of outstanding technocrats, notable scholars, and senior military officials in the Defence and Interior Ministries. Once the interim government was in place, former Prime Minister Chatichai was released from custody.

The coup leaders also emphasized their commitment to policy continuity in economic matters, calling in leading Thai bankers and business executives to assure them that Thailand's market- and export-oriented economy would remain intact. Political parties were retained and a National Legislative Assembly was planned to approve a permanent constitution and arrange for future elections. Indeed, for the overwhelming majority of Thais, the coup changed nothing except the names of the Kingdom's top government leaders.

One reason the coup was greeted passively can be traced to the increasing discontent and disgust Thais had been feeling toward the

Chatichai administration. Thai newspapers, unencumbered by censorship, reported daily on the rampant corruption among top-level cabinet members. Many ministries were led by political lightweights who were appointed solely to keep Chatichai's coalition together.

Although Thailand's politics has always featured massive corruption, especially during former military regimes, the degree of graft under Chatichai went beyond public tolerance. Huge telecommunications projects, massive road and elevated commuter railway ventures, cable television contracts, and new oil refineries are examples of multibillion dollar deals arranged and managed (or more accurately, mismanaged) by politicians whose main aim was to perpetuate their power base and personal wealth.

While this substantial corruption was an important legitimizing rationale for the coup, the more direct cause was a pattern of slights carried out by Chatichai and perceived by the military as threats to their traditional prerogatives. The most important slight was Chatichai's choice of General Athit Kamlangek for the post of deputy defense minister. Because Athit was an adversary of Generals Sundhara and Suchinda, his appointment was interpreted as a frontal attack on the autonomy of the army. Second, rumors were circulating that Chatichai and Athit were about to request that the king ask for the resignations of Sundhara as Supreme Commander and Suchinda as Army Commander-in-Chief. The coup leaders believed it was necessary to stage the coup before Chatichai made this request so as not to dishonor the monarchy.

The third piece of the pattern was a complex and confusing story about an alleged assassination plot in 1982 against then-Prime Minister Prem Tinsulanond, General Athit, and Queen Sirikit. Chatichai was said by the military to be harboring persons involved in the plot, including General Manoon Rupkachorn and Chatichai's son, Kraisak Choonhavan. Despite the fact that General Manoon was the major power behind the 1981 and 1985 coups, Chatichai had promoted him and made him an important adviser in the Defense Ministry. Manoon was detested by Generals Sundhara and Suchinda, both of whom viewed his high position as a menace to their own positions.

The assassination case again came into the limelight in the week prior to the coup, when Chatichai replaced the chief investigator of the case, a friend of the military, with his own colleague. The junta leaders believed the appointment would undermine their case and saw it as a further piece of the anti-military pattern Chatichai was fashioning.

For most Thais, the coup will matter little. The major political parties, however, will be hurt because their leaders are among those being investigated for corruption. Chatichai, leader of the *Chat Thai* Party, the nation's largest, announced he was abandoning politics. Coming out of the crisis stronger than ever is General Chavalit Yongchaiyut, the former army commander-in-chief, mentor of the coup leaders, and founder of the popular New Aspirations Party. Chavalit's apparent lack of complicity in the coup enhanced his reputation and strengthened his chances for the prime ministership in the post-coup period.

Moreover, economic policy has changed little except to take some of the more important fiscal decisions out of the hands of the politicians and put them into the hands of technocrats. Indeed, the American Chamber of Commerce in Bangkok endorsed the coup as a positive step toward decreasing the role of corruption. Infrastructure projects that were delayed because of political infighting under Chatichai can now be carried out more efficiently.

Although the junta leaders were given near-absolute powers to replace the prime minister and to stop activities threatening "peace and security," Thais expect that their experience of almost two decades of movement toward democracy will mitigate military suppression of their rights. The military had already been influential in past "civilian" administrations, including that of Chatichai. Under the new interim administration, its role is simply more overt.

Bureaucracy

For most of the contemporary era, Thailand has pursued a bureaucratic polity with the arena of politics within the bureaucracy itself. The bureaucracy has been the bedrock of stability in a political system in which top leadership positions have changed unpredictably. While coups may bring new factions into power, the bureaucracy continues its conservative policy role with little change in direction.

The formerly exclusive role of the bureaucracy has been widened in recent years by the new role of technocrats who have attained important positions and brought a more rational mode to policymaking. These highly trained and educated officials have public-regarding values rather than the traditional values of hierarchy, personalism, and security.

Moreover, the bureaucracy is no longer the only arena of politics. Extra-bureaucratic groups, such as parliament, political parties, and pressure groups, and, of course, the military now play a significant role in determining public policy. Still, the bureaucracy is powerful in determining the direction and implementation of policies.

Parliament

At one time, elections in Thailand were held only when the ruling groups became convinced that they could control the process so that elections would merely enhance their power. Today, elections provide more meaningful choices among candidates who represent alternative ideas. The bicameral parliament, no longer just a rubber stamp of the prime minister, engages in public debate about important issues.

In the present form of semidemocracy, the upper house—that is, the appointed senate—is still dominated by the military. However, the senate has lost much of its influence. For example, a constitutional amendment has been passed making the elected lower house speaker, rather than the appointed senate speaker, the president of parliament. Another sign of parliament's higher standing has been the diminished criticism of members of parliament by military leaders. For example, General Chavalit had been scathing in his criticisms of "self-interested" members of parliament, but, since Prime Minister Chatichai's rise to prominence, he has softened his rebukes.

After the 1988 parliamentary election in which eleven parties won seats, Prime Minister Chatichai brought five of these into his coalition, whereupon the others formed the opposition. Chatichai's coalition included: Thai Nation (*Chat Thai*), Social Action (*Kit Sangkhom*), Democrat (*Prachatipat*), People's (*Rasadorn*), and Mass (*Muanchon*). Cabinet positions were distributed to the coalition partners in accordance with their numbers in parliament.

Parliament includes an unprecedented number of Sino-Thai business executives. In the past, Thailand's Chinese minority had stayed mostly in the economic sphere, and its greater involvement in political affairs has raised concerns that an emerging "bourgeois polity" will be dominated by Chinese Thai.

The new politics of contemporary Thailand is characterized by the strengthening of parliament and the political parties. The elites who dominate policymaking have come increasingly from both institutions. For example, Chatichai's cabinet consists of party leaders who are elected members of parliament. The parliament is no longer peripheral to authoritative decisions thanks to a greater role granted it by Prime Minister Prem, under whose leadership the parliament began to act independently, particularly on economic matters.

Political Parties

In the past, political parties centered around individual personalities. The parties had only rudimentary organization and were almost devoid of disinterested programs or issues. Elections often involved more than twenty parties, most of which were established for a particular candidate in a specific election.

Since the short-lived democratic period of 1973 to 1976, there has been a movement toward party institutionalization and longevity. The organizational apparatus for the major parties remains intact after an election and plays an important role in the strategies of both the ruling coalition and the opposition. The parties are beginning to build long-term links with the citizenry along with party discipline, so that they can exert greater influence on policymaking and assure themselves of an important role in coalition governments.

Thai political parties can be visualized as a spectrum that runs from liberal to conservative, but most parties fall into the moderate and non-ideological category. Ideological positions are not paramount in campaigns because only a minority of voters make choices based on issues. In the last several elections, parties have been fewer in number, more coherent in structure, and better able to represent citizens' demands. Prime Minister Chatichai was leader of the conservative and pro-business *Chat Thai* party.

In the 1988 election, the *Chat Thai* party won the largest plurality of votes, increasing its number of seats in parliament from sixty-three in the 1986 elections to eighty-seven. *Chat Thai* had excellent organization and access to unlimited funds because of its support for business and military interests. The longest serving party, the Democrats, obtained only fifty-seven seats, a loss of forty-three from the previous election. Prior to the election, the party had split into factions, thus explaining its poor electoral performance. Altogether, seventeen parties won seats to the lower house in the 1988 election.

In general, voters in rural areas do not affiliate with political parties but do identify with candidates who are famous in their electoral districts. In Bangkok, however, party voting is the norm. For example, in the January 1990 election for governor of Bangkok, the *Palang Dharma* party, led by Governor Chamlong Srimuang, swept fifty of fifty-seven seats in the city assembly.

Campaign spending continues to be an important part of the electoral process. Candidates with solid financial support and with patron-client ties to wealthy Thais have a significant advantage, which helps to explain why one-third of the total number of elected MPs were in business.

Monarchy

Theoretically and legally above politics, the Thai monarch is the national symbol, the supreme patron who reigns over all, and the leader of the Buddhist religion. The prestige and veneration of the monarchy have grown since the 1950 coronation of King Phumiphol Adunyadej, who recently became the kingdom's longest reigning monarch.

In the 1980s the king became more involved in Thai politics. He supported the government of Prime Minister Prem Tinsulanond in both 1981 and 1985 when military coups attempted to overthrow Prem's administration but chose not to intervene in the 1991 coup. The king's strong resistance to the earlier coups helped to defuse the crises and to heighten his prestige and influence.

The Thais' universal veneration for their monarch has raised concerns about a potential succession crisis. The king promoted his daughter, Princess Sirindhorn, to the rank of *Maha Chakri* (crown princess), thereby placing her in the line of succession along with her brother, Crown Prince Vachiralongkorn. The crown prince has often been criticized for his lack of commitment and discipline, whereas the princess has been universally admired for her brilliance and dedication. At present, however, the crown prince has become involved in ceremonial duties and is being trained to succeed his father. Because the king is the symbol of all that is great in Thailand, a contentious succession could undo the present high level of stability by unleashing forces now held in check by the knowledge that the king would object to them.

Peasantry

About 70 percent of the Thai people live in rural areas as farmers. However, they are not the passive peasantry once depicted in textbooks. As modernization arrived, Thai farmers became sophisticated economic actors, moving from subsistence to surplus agriculture. Increasing numbers of rural Thais engage in political activity, contact officials, join special interest groups, participate in village projects, and have knowledge of governmental processes.

Changes in the countryside in the past several decades have significantly affected the lives of the vast majority of Thais. Roads now penetrate into formerly isolated areas. Electricity is almost universally available. Transistor radios, motorcycles, televisions, and daily newspapers are integral parts of village life. Agricultural diversification has introduced cash crops into the Thai economy. Whereas rice constituted more than 90 percent of agricultural output twenty years ago, today the percentage is less than 50.

Sino-Thai Business Community

Traditionally, the Chinese minority (about 10 percent of the population) has dominated the Thai economy while the Thai majority has prevailed in politics. Since 1980, however, a fundamental change has occurred in Thai politics, with the Sino-Thai becoming more involved.

Because of the high degree of Sino-Thai assimilation (compared to all other Southeast Asian nations), the expansion of the middle class, the new importance of technocrats in the running of ministries, and the realization that government policies affect the economy, business interests have become increasingly involved in politics.

The importance of the middle class (in a nation that had no such class until recently) suggests that Thailand has become a bourgeois rather than a bureaucratic polity. This new class of entrepreneurs, technocrats, and government officials has viewed military rule as an anachronism, unsuited to the nation's well-being. It supports the move away from the personalistic politics of the past to the more stable, pluralistic, and institutionalized politics of the period of semidemocracy.

Intellectuals

Thai students and intellectuals were leaders of the 1973 revolt against the military that ousted the ruling generals and placed civilians in power. Although the period of civilian democratic rule lasted only three years before the army returned to regain its dominant role, Thai politics has never been the same. The interim democratic period brought new groups and attitudes to Thai politics and showed that the military is not an invincible force.

During the regime of Chatichai, leading Thai academicians played an important role in fashioning domestic and foreign policies. Chatichai's "new nationalism" and opening of relations with Indochina were examples of policies formulated by his academic advisory council, consisting of a group of prominent university scholars. The advisors were criticized by officials of the Ministry of Foreign Affairs as well as by the military for allegedly overstepping their legitimate sphere of influence.

In the clearest instance of conflict between the military and the academic advisors, top military officers showed their strength in a controversy set off by a speech by Professor Sukhumbhand Paribatra, a famous scholar of international relations and advisor to Chatichai. In response to a charge by then-army Commander-in-Chief Chavalit that government officials were steeped in corruption, Professor Sukhumbhand noted that "anyone who says the government is 90 percent corrupt should clean up his own act first." He also suggested that the army's most prestigious academy overhaul its curriculum to make it more appropriate for the new era of democracy in Thailand.

Sukhumbhand's challenge and "interference" were attacked by a group of some one thousand high-level military officers who assembled to demand the ouster of Sukhumbhand from the prime minister's official advisory council. Sukhumbhand's remarks calling for the depoliticization of the military were said to be offensive and damaging to the reputations of General Chavalit and the Thai military. Prime Minister Chatichai accepted Sukhumbhand's resignation, thereby affirming the army's continued power and raising questions about the government's commitment to freedom of speech and the military's subordination to civilian authority.

Women

Women have never been serious contenders for positions of power in Thai politics. The percentage of women in the national assembly is minuscule, women have never been appointed as governors of provinces, and except for the "appropriate" positions in health or human services, they have not served in cabinets. There are no women generals in the military.

Nevertheless, women play an important role in Thai society, especially in the professions. The percentage of women doctors, lawyers, accountants, and professors is higher than that in the United States. The same number of women as men vote in elections for the national assembly. A more important point, however, is that a societal double standard exists whereby men are allowed far more leeway of behavior and participation than are women. The socialization patterns in Thailand continue to reflect the traditional view that women defer to men in the public sector.

Democratization

The history of politics in Thailand is a history of authoritarian rule. Thailand's political culture, with its emphasis on deference to authority and hierarchical social relations, is not conducive to democratic rule. Democracy entails citizen involvement and a tolerance for different points of view. For involvement to occur, an individual must feel competent to exert influence and to cooperate with fellow citizens in common cause. Thus, perceptions of self-competence, willingness to work in concert, and tolerance for different points of view make the prospect for democracy in Thailand problematic.

The strength of Thailand's semidemocracy was partially a function of the economic boom and the government's resulting capacity to meet the needs of the citizenry. When basic needs are met, other nondemocratic values become secondary. However, when a government is perceived as unable to meet citizens' needs, the values of security and stability, for example, take precedence. Hence, a severe downturn in the economy or an unexpected external threat to Thai sovereignty could undermine the prospects for the evolution toward democracy.

This move was put to the test by army Commander-in-Chief Chavalit's cabinet positions as defense and deputy prime minister, positions that lasted only a few weeks before he resigned. The positions initially assured Prime Minister Chatichai of continued military support but undermined the prevailing view that cabinet members should be party members and elected members of parliament. The fact that Chavalit could move into two important cabinet posts without a popular mandate reminded Thais that military leaders continue to seek political office. Those ambitions were formally achieved by force when the 1991 coup succeeded.

Another potentially serious threat to Thai democratization relates to monarchical succession. The Thais' veneration for their king is also directed to his daughter, the crown princess, rather than to the crown prince. Although it appears that the crown prince is being groomed to succeed his father (there has never been a reigning queen in Thai history), the role of the monarchy as the symbol of all that is great in Thailand could change fundamentally with his succession. The Thai king has consistently moderated governmental policies and on recent occasions has acted to prevent the military from undermining democratic rule.

Democracy requires a political culture supportive of democratic values. Modernization has brought high levels of education, literacy, access to the media, and travel—all of which has heightened Thais' awareness of democratic values and expanded their horizons. Democracy also requires an example of a time when democratic government was successful; however, the 1973–1976 period of democracy was viewed by most Thais as a time of chaos, disorder, and economic travail. In the Chatichai period, semidemocracy was sanctioned by the people because of the high level of societal order and economic growth. In the past, the democratic orientations of the Thais have been formalistic in the sense that these orientations have had little depth. Other values—such as security, development, deference, personalism, and economic stability—have taken precedence over values more directly related to citizen participation in governmental affairs. Thus, the status of democratization in Thailand has been tenuous.

Economic Development

For several decades Thailand has sustained a 7 percent economic growth, a rate equaled by only a few other developing nations. More remarkably, the kingdom's economic growth in 1987, 1988, and 1989 averaged over 10 percent, higher than any other country. During these boom years, inflation was under 4 percent.

Coincident with these high growth rates was the increase in the export sector, which in the late 1980s grew about 24 percent each year. Foreign investment has also grown at a rapid rate, with Japan, Taiwan, the United States, Hong Kong, and South Korea the leading investors. Manufacturing is now responsible for a larger share of the gross domestic product than is agriculture.

While 70 percent of the Thai people are in the agricultural sphere of the economy, the number of those in rice farming is decreasing. Thai farmers have diversified into crops such as vegetables, fruits, maize, tapioca, coffee, flowers, sugar, rubber, and livestock. Although the farming areas have not developed as rapidly as urban areas, the standard of living in the countryside has improved noticeably since the 1970s. Nevertheless, the urban bias of Thai economic development is clear from both the emphasis on manufacturing and the higher percentage of budget allocations centered on Bangkok.

The factors responsible for the kingdom's economic successes include a commitment to free-market, export-driven policies carried out by highly trained and generally conservative technocrats. These new officials are not as steeped in personalistic, clientelist politics as are their predecessors or their peers in neighboring countries. Those in charge of economic policy have carefully screened pending development projects to ensure that they will contribute to overall economic growth.

An important component of sustained economic development is political stability. Although coups have been the standard mechanism for changing governments, they have rarely undermined the continuity of the policy process. Following the 1991 coup, Thai politics has adhered to a consistent set of policies, with incremental (rather than fundamental) changes the norm.

The vital involvement of Thailand's Chinese minority cannot be overestimated as a factor explaining the vibrancy of the economy. This dynamic minority has provided leadership in banking, export-import manufacturing, industrialization, monetary policy, foreign investment, and diversification. The autonomy granted the Chinese has resulted in an entrepreneurial minority's reinvesting its profits into the kingdom, with comparatively little capital leaving the country.

Liberal regulations on foreign investment have made possible a capital influx from industrial nations. Thailand, now further integrated into the world capitalist system, has access to foreign credit and technical assistance in addition to enjoying flourishing trade relations throughout the world. Thailand is a favorite site for production plants owned by

Japan, South Korea, and Taiwan. The Thai government's decisions to move toward an export-oriented industrialization strategy emerged from high-level technocrats in the development agencies, most of whom are insulated from political pressures by other bureaucratic and societal forces.

In just one generation, Thailand has managed to lower its population growth rate from 3.0 percent to 1.5 percent. The decrease resulted from a massive government-sponsored education program that has changed attitudes about the optimum family size and made birth control devices available throughout the kingdom. This has resulted in a higher standard of living for families, higher educational attainment and literacy, and lower poverty rates.

The greatest obstacle to continued economic growth is the poor state of infrastructural facilities. Car traffic in Bangkok is gridlocked, and port facilities cannot handle the growing ship traffic. Electricity and tele-communications are unreliable.

A second problem is the depletion of Thailand's natural resources, especially its forests. Despite recent legislation banning logging, floods, soil erosion, and droughts have resulted from the government's almost total lack of control over the implementation of the legislation. In 1987 and 1989, Thailand suffered its worst natural disasters in many years. Flooding and landslides, directly attributable to deforestation, killed hundreds of people.

The number of college graduates in the "hard" sciences and technology is not sufficient to meet developmental needs. Thai universities graduate only one third of those needed in engineering. Many graduates move into the private rather than the public sphere because of the former's higher salaries.

One further difficulty of the Thai economy stems, ironically, from its success. Foreign investment and trade have made the economy vulnerable to the vagaries of the world's capitalist system. Thus far, the economic policymakers have diversified imports and exports sufficiently to ensure that a downturn in one sector will not cripple the overall economy.

The Thai State

Thailand is an interesting case study of the role of the state because its economy is growing rapidly and there is considerable controversy over the role the state has played in the kingdom's economic and political development.[3] The state refers to public officials, elective and appointive, who decide public policy that is binding upon all members of the society. The state represents the totality of authoritative, decision-making authorities and institutions as they promote the public good, independent of societal forces.

Until the 1980s, scholars referred to Thai politics as a *bureaucratic polity* in which politics took place within the bureaucracy and extra-bureaucratic institutions were negligible. External institutions, such as the parliament and political parties, were deemed to have little influence over the state's policy decisions. The bureaucratic polity included the military, as many of the generals held important government posts (including the position of prime minister). The state, then, was considered to be strong and autonomous, independent of such societal organizations as political parties, business associations, farmers' groups, and labor unions. When these groups began to emerge, they were co-opted, manipulated, or oppressed by the bureaucracy, using the military as its control. By integrating the military into the political process, the government established a broad-based regime. Emphasizing both collaborative and coercive forces, the state increased its stability and capacity.

Since the student-led revolt against the military in 1973, however, Thai political institutions have increased in number and have broadened their bases considerably, strengthening the role of the legislature, political parties, and business associations while reducing direct military domination. As societal groups have come to play a more important role in Thai politics, the state has lost some of its autonomy and consequently become weaker. On the other hand, Thai authorities enjoy autonomy from societal actors, especially rural citizens who are politically passive. Because rural citizens constitute about 70 percent of the population and make few demands on the central authorities, this notion of passivity is central to the argument that the Thai state can act autonomously.

Similarly, state autonomy has derived from the fact that Thai authorities have successfully co-opted nonbureaucratic but nevertheless elite groups. The state has managed the political-economic affairs of the kingdom effectively and in the best interests of potential countervailing groups, such as business elites; thus there is little need for these groups to challenge the authorities.

This view of state autonomy stems at least partially from the success of Thai authorities in preserving the state's independence and sovereignty. The government is legitimate precisely because of this success, and the related outcome of political continuity and stability as well. Having escaped colonial rule, established a stable political system, and met the basic needs of the majority of the citizenry, the Thai state has proved its effectiveness.

In the last two decades, Thailand has achieved one of the highest economic growth rates in the world, which since 1987 has averaged over 10 percent. That record comes partly from the state authorities knowing when to get out of the way of the society's entrepreneurs, including the ethnic Chinese who have been the engine of the Thai economy for generations. Moreover, Thai state authorities have promoted the kingdom's economic strength through generally conservative policies (such as supporting technocrats, forming economic development agencies and devising five-year plans, and the necessary but unpopular devaluing of the currency in the face of intense opposition from business and military leaders).

The strength of the state is also shown by the progression from authoritarian to democratic rule between 1970 and 1990. From the 1973 student-led revolt against the military dictatorship to the 1991 coup, Thai politics had steadily become (albeit with fits and starts) a more open and responsive system. The most recent manifestation of this nascent democracy occurred when Prime Minister Chatichai Choonhavan, the leader of the largest political party, was elected to parliament and then chosen as leader of the governing coalition. Ironically, as the Thai state has shown the capacity for effective adaptability, formerly nonstate institutions such as the parliament and political parties have become focal points for public policy discussions. Indeed, these significant changes in Thai politics attest to a system that has effectively coped with changing internal and external demands. However, these changes also reflect a political system in which the number of authoritative decision makers has expanded.

From the standpoint of criteria for a strong state—compliance with state demands by the citizenry, citizen participation in state-run institutions, and legitimation (acceptance) of the state authority—the Thai state's progress toward democratization demonstrates strength.[4] From the standpoint of state strength, defined in terms of autonomy from societal actors and institutions, democratization has moved the kingdom's state toward weakness.

The Thai state has gained citizen conformance to its demands through a highly centralized administrative system with control over the police, and other essential institutions. The fact that these policies have not been considered intolerable has made the state's efforts easier to carry out compared to states in which the authorities have thrust unwanted burdens on the populace.

Legitimation is a potent factor accounting for the strength of the state. Here again, the Thai state has managed to receive acceptance, even approbation, of its rules of the game. The primary reason for this is that contemporary Thai authorities have basked in the aura of the king, the symbol of unity of the Thai state. Thais have accepted the state's symbolic configuration within an ideology of king, state, and religion. Through socialization and the deliberate exploitation of the king's popularity by regimes in power, the Thai state has become identified with the king and Buddhism, resulting in an extraordinarily high level of acceptance.[5]

Even scholars who view the state as weak agree that Thailand has had remarkable achievements. However, they do not believe that the state is responsible for these achievements. Instead, they argue, various organizations—such as the National Economic and Social Development Board, the Bureau of the Budget, and the Bank of Thailand—have, as individual agencies, produced the economic growth that has in turn provided political stability.[6] These agencies, all crucial to the kingdom's economic development, have been able to act autonomously, apart from the patron-client relations that pervade Thai officialdom and society.

Despite these achievements, the Thai state has failed to carry out public policies in many areas. Its failure to collect personal and corporate taxes in a fair and efficient manner, for example, has resulted in meager state resources and the inability to build an infrastructure and establish adequate health, environmental, and educational services. As a proportion of gross domestic product, Thailand's public investment is one of the lowest among the developing world economies.[7]

Public policies approved by institutions with newly expanded authoritative powers, such as the national parliament, are often ignored due to the inability of the government to implement and monitor these policies. For example, the law to ban logging operations, promulgated in 1988, has done little to end the practice. Nor has the government realized its goals of adopting the value-added tax, privatizing state enterprises, or improving revenue collection. In these cases, the state has not been able to enforce its policies.

The Thai state does not always implement its policies consistently, effectively, and reliably. Thai policymaking has at times been characterized by a lack of coordination among governmental ministries, a muddling-through approach to economic policy—in contrast to South Korea and Taiwan where policy is more coherently and strategically dictated by the state.

The Thai state, for example, has not played an active developmental role in the country's economy.[8] Instead, the state has refrained from intervention in the economy in terms of regulation and investment, allowing the private sector to take the lead. The low level of state activity in industrial development as well as the initiatives of the private sector in what amounts to a laissez-faire economy suggests that Thailand's growth has been achieved in spite of the state, not because of it.

If autonomy is a key variable for assessing strength, the Thai state is weak, for the officials who make authoritative decisions are not insulated from patronage networks. In fact, Thai officials are integrated into a network of patron-client exchange relationships that are at the very heart of the political process. These relationships act as links between state officials and societal groups in business, agriculture, labor, the aristocracy, and the intelligentsia.

Prior to the 1973 revolt, the bureaucratic polity insulated state officials from these societal forces. As a result, virtually all political decisions were made within the bureaucracy where intrabureaucratic patron-client ties prevailed. In the post-1973 period, the patron-client network widened as new groups formed alliances with state officials. Whereas the centralized state had formerly precluded the development of societal interest groups and political parties, the recent Thai polity has nurtured, co-opted, manipulated, and controlled new groups. The present government is seeking a balance between centralization of authority and an open polity with a strong legislature and political parties. Such a balance is difficult to attain because both civilian and military authorities feel threatened by societal groups while simultaneously the new technocrats and westernized officials are committed to a more democratic polity. At present, these societal groups have shown only a limited capacity to perform their functions.

Political parties remain largely self-interested patronage groups, revolving around particular personalities. The parliament as well has had difficulty developing public-regarding policies and asserting alternative sets of policies for state officials to implement. The state, led by the military and the bureaucracy, has dominated policymaking, at least in the areas deemed important to these institutions.[9] However, as democratization has taken hold, societal groups enjoy more autonomy and clout in policymaking as long as they do not unduly press upon the prerogatives of the more dominant bureaucratic and military interests.

Thailand's remarkable economic growth can be explained in many ways. Certainly, the generally prudent state policies since 1977 have been crucial for providing the necessary stability and environment. In some respects, the Thai state has been "strong" enough to get out of the way of the dynamic Sino-Thai entrepreneurial class, while in other respects the government has supported the demands of these entrepreneurs for an open, market-oriented economy. Conversely, since the 1970s, business organizations have initiated, transformed, or even blocked important economic policies and legislation they have deemed antithetical to their interests.[10]

Thai success in economic development does not require a strong state explanation. Examples abound of strong states that have produced disastrous economic policies because they were insulated from societal groupings. Nor does Thai success require a weak state explanation, which could lead as well to economic stagnation stemming from the state's attempts to meet demands made by numerous forces. A weak state may not be able to maintain order in an environment of conflicting, multiple demands.

A better explanation is that the Thai state has achieved a proper balance between the state and civil society.[11] In a period of great development, this state is coping with the changing demands of its citizenry as well as those of the international arena. The adaptive ability of the state partially explains why societal forces have not taken over the traditional roles of the bureaucracy and the military.[12] At the same time, the Thai state has opened its policymaking process to new institutions such as political parties, business associations, and the parliament. The result has been that new ideas have been assimilated and occasionally acted on for the best interests of the public. All of this is happening while traditional, informal personalism, mostly in the form of patron-client relations, remains central to modern Thai politics. In some respects, therefore, the Thai state has been flexible and responsive to changing political-economic circumstances.

Thus, the Thai state can be viewed as either strong or weak, depending on the issues and state components one chooses to emphasize. These characterizations can also change over time.

Scholars who have chosen to analyze Thailand from a state-centered context uniformly view the Thai state as weak.[13] On the other hand, scholars who focus on the continuing capacity of the Thai government to cope with changing demands do not generally deal with state-centered issues and their vocabulary.[14] Instead, they focus on the institutional strength of the bureaucracy (including the military). Although these scholars do not ignore problems of factionalism, lack of coordination among government agencies, corruption, and the ubiquitous patron-client networks, they emphasize political stability, policy continuity, economic growth, and legitimacy. From this vantage point, the strength of the state has been measured by governmental outcomes rather than the issue of autonomy.

A factor encouraging state strength is massive societal dislocation, which has severely weakened the capacity of a society to inhibit the growth of a strong state.[15] The most common forms of dislocation are wars, revolutions, mass migrations, and great economic depressions. The "strong states" of China, Korea, Vietnam, Taiwan, Cuba, Japan, and Israel have undergone such dislocation in varying degrees.

Inasmuch as Thailand is the only Southeast Asian nation that did not experience formal colonialism by Western imperialists (Thailand also did not suffer grievously from the Japanese invasion in World War II), its experience is in sharp contrast with the ordeal of Indonesia, which suffered severe dislocation from the Japanese occupation and the independence war against the Dutch at the end of World War II. Moreover,

Thailand has not lost large areas of land or experienced mass migrations, wars, or revolutions comparable to those of states deemed strong. Even the overthrow of the absolute monarchy in 1932 did not appreciably change conditions in the kingdom. Thailand did not face the horrors of mass executions, as did the Indonesians in the mid-1960s following the rise of the military government.

Indeed, relative to its neighbors, Thai society has been characterized more by continuity and stability than by dislocation. And whereas Indonesia was faced with the potential for Communist rule (the Communist party of Indonesia included some nineteen million persons in the early 1960s), the Communist threat to Thailand was negligible. At its height, the Communist party of Thailand had only sixty thousand members. From these perspectives, then, Thailand does not meet the necessary conditions for the emergence of a strong state.

Dislocation is more likely to lead to a strong state if it occurs at a historical moment in which external political forces favor concentrated social control.[16] When a threat of foreign invasion exists, the impetus toward a strong state is even greater. For Thailand, U.S. economic and security dominance in the postwar period supported the Thai state as the best bulwark against the perceived Communist threat. As both the internal and external Communist threats were minor compared to those against China, Taiwan, Korea, and Vietnam, the impact on the Thai state was correspondingly small. Most important for strengthening the state was the Thai military's claim that the Communist threat necessitated its primary role in state control over the society. Indeed, in the postwar period, Prime Ministers Phibun Songkran, Sarit Thanarat, and Thanom Kittikachorn were able to parlay the threat into temporary strongman rule. Since 1975, the internal insurgency threat has receded. Moreover, no serious analyst of Southeast Asia believes there is an external threat to the security of Thailand. In contrast, Cuba, Israel, North and South Korea, and Vietnam have all been invaded at least once since World War II. Both China and Taiwan have had reason to expect such an invasion. Thus, on this condition as well, Thailand does not fit the conditions necessary for a strong state.

The next condition important for creating a strong state is the "existence of a social grouping with people sufficiently independent of existing bases of social control and skillful enough to execute the grand designs of state leaders."[17] The issue is whether a state has bureaucrats, technocrats, and socioeconomic leaders who identify their ultimate interests with those of the state. Although the military-dominated bureaucratic polity in Thailand brought technocrats into leading policy-making positions, these technocrats had no autonomous political base or constituency. While aristocrats and intellectuals have had strong constituencies outside of the bureaucracy, they have not constituted a separate power base opposing the interests of the authorities in power.

The economically powerful Chinese minority was similarly co-opted by Thai authorities through the system of "pariah entrepreneurship," wherein Chinese business executives and the Thai political authorities agreed to respect and support each other's spheres of influence. The Chinese provided much of the financing for political leaders, who used the funds for concentrating their political power. Until the 1980s, the Chinese only rarely participated in political affairs. With increased intermarriage and assimilation of the Chinese into Thai society, it became increasingly difficult to keep these spheres of influence separate. The important point is that the business class has rarely acted as an autonomous force, separate from the interests of the ruling authorities.

Thailand does not have strong autonomous societal groups whose primary loyalties are with religious, regional, economic, or ethnic sects. The principal extra-bureaucratic groups have interests that coincide with those of the state. In this respect, Thailand meets the condition of a strong state, requiring independent groups skillful enough to execute the grand designs of state leaders.

The last condition concerns skillful leadership, which must be present to take advantage of the conditions to build a strong state. Among Thailand's dozen prime ministers in the past twenty-five years, quality and strength have varied, but none has been so incompetent as to jeopardize the fabric of the kingdom. On the contrary, most have been carefully selected bureaucrats who have set forth generally conservative policies, adapting those aspects of modernization and development that were appropriate to traditional Thai ways. In addition, the fact that there has been only one successful coup d'etat since 1977 is testimony to the growing professionalization of the army. Thai leaders have both enhanced and undermined the conditions necessary for a strong state.

Foreign Policy

Thailand's foreign relations must be seen in the context of the new international era that has seen the end of the cold war. The most obvious manifestations of this new world order include the perception that there are no regional or great-power threats to Thai security and that the U.S. security role in Southeast Asia has declined.

Internal considerations have also brought changes in Thai foreign policymaking. Thailand's sustained economic development and the rise of business and other nonbureaucratic interests in the political sphere are partially responsible for the new directions. Prime Minister Chatichai surrounded himself with a Council of Academic Advisors that viewed these international and domestic changes as an opportunity for Thailand to reassess its foreign policy and to initiate new policies more appropriate to the new international order. The thrust of these initiatives was in the direction of a "new nationalism," toward normalization of relations with the Indochinese nations and toward economic rather than security relations. Chatichai emerged as the leader for these new priorities, and the Ministry of Foreign Affairs had to subordinate its views to those of the academic advisors.

Chatichai's academic advisors set forth the notion of *Suwanabhum*, envisioning Thailand as the core of continental Southeast Asia, including Burma as well as Indochina. Thailand was to become the "economic engine" of the area, with economics instead of security considerations in command. This view was consistent with that of Thai businessmen who have longed for the opening of the Indochinese marketplace for investment and trade. Thailand was to be the hub of this new economic grouping, supplying technology and capital in exchange for the natural resources of its more impoverished neighbors. As the Cambodian crisis was not resolved when the concept of *Suwanabhum* was set forth, the move toward a closer economic union had not borne fruit by 1990.

The new nationalism took the form of relating to the United States as an equal rather than as a client. Under Chatichai, Thai foreign policy lessened security dependence on the United States, asserted a policy of equidistance in its relations with allies and adversaries, and launched a dramatically new Indochina policy without seeking U.S. support.

The clearest example of the new era of Thai-U.S. relations concerned the intellectual property rights (IPR) controversy. From the perspective of the United States, the issue concerned the lack of Thai protection of the copying of U.S. products, such as computer software copyrights and pharmaceutical patents, as well as fairness in trade relations. From the Thai perspective, the issue was defined in terms of U.S. protectionism, U.S. bullying of a long-term ally, nationalism, and economic development.

The IPR issue symbolized the new importance of economic concerns and the decline of security considerations in relations between the two nations. Moreover, the issue showed the new importance of various forces in determining Thai foreign policy. Until the period of semidemocracy, the military dominated foreign policy in Thailand, with leading bureaucrats in the Ministry of Foreign Affairs, cabinet ministers, and political party leaders playing secondary roles. Regarding the IPR issue, the United States had to consider the reactions of the military, the Ministry of Foreign Affairs, advisory councils of the prime minister, the prime minister himself, the parliament, mass media, and activist students, all of which played a role in resolving the IPR dispute. The IPR negotiations were far more complex than those of the past, when U.S. officials could deal directly and solely with military leaders.

For the Thai government, the IPR controversy was another in a series of issues that brought about a crisis in U.S.-Thai relations. Foreign Minister Siddhi Savetsila spoke about the "cracks developing in the reservoir of goodwill" that had been built during a century and a half of friendship. The first crack came with the U.S. Farm Act and the textile quota bill, both viewed by Thais as protectionist acts, and the second with demands that economic sanctions would be applied to Thailand if the government did not amend its copyright laws in keeping with U.S. wishes.

Domestic politics played a role in Thailand's response to U.S. demands. Chatichai's desire to be active in foreign policy caused tension between the prime minister and the Ministry of Foreign Affairs, especially as Foreign Minister Siddhi is leader of a coalition—but nevertheless rival— political party. Controversy over the parliament's copyright bill caused defections from the coalition, dissolution of the parliament, and new elections. The academic advisors convinced Chatichai that a strong stand against U.S. demands would be popular, a view that turned out to be accurate.

IPR became a rallying point for Thai sovereignty and its break from traditional patron-client ties with the United States. The response to U.S. cuts of about $165 million in Thai benefits under the Generalized System of Preferences (GSP) did not appreciably affect Thai exports. From the Thai perspective, the political gains of resisting U.S. pressure more than compensated for the loss.

Economic relations have replaced security ties as the kingdom's major foreign policy concern. The Thai economy is now integrated into the world capitalist system; therefore, the nation's stability is increasingly vulnerable to external pressures and fluctuations, which explains why the perceived protectionism of U.S. trade policy has been regarded with alarm. Although Thailand has enjoyed a billion-dollar-per-year surplus in trade with the United States, the importance of the trade relations is asymmetrical. With Thai exports to the United States accounting for only 1.2 percent of U.S. imports, and U.S. exports constituting almost 20 percent of Thai imports, the U.S. market is more vital to the Thai economy than the Thai market is to the United States.

As cold war considerations continued to ebb, the importance of the United States to Thai security concerns correspondingly decreased. Cuts in U.S. security assistance to Thailand, the reluctance of the United States to play a major role in resolving the Indochina crisis, and Thailand's new nationalism have diminished the importance of U.S. security and contributed to the intensification of Thai efforts to forge closer ties with China, Indochina, Japan, the Soviet Union, and its ASEAN neighbors.

The new tone of U.S.-Thai relations reflects Thailand's growing importance in the world economy. Major aspects of U.S.-Thai relations continue to include financial aid, joint military exercises, collaboration on Thai-Cambodian relations, common efforts to save Indochinese refugees, cooperation to wage war on narcotics, and support for the Peace Corps. The larger point, however, is that the relationship has irrevocably changed as both nations find their way in the new era of international relations and domestic political and economic forces.

A centerpiece of Chatichai's new foreign policy initiatives was the movement toward normalization of relations with Vietnam, Laos, and Cambodia. This abrupt change in policy resulted from, first, the view of the prime minister's advisors that Vietnam no longer constitutes a direct threat to Thai security; second, the fact that Vietnam itself desired normalization; third, the feeling that closer economic ties would do more to lessen tensions between the two nations than would confrontation; and finally, the fact that Thailand could be master of its own destiny. The last point refers to the Thai government's willingness unilaterally to forge new relations with its neighbors without consultation with the United States or ASEAN allies.

Chatichai's invitation to Hun Sen, prime minister of the Phnom Penh government, to visit Bangkok was a striking example of the government's willingness to move from entrenched policies and take a leadership position in resolving regional problems. The Thai prime minister enmeshed himself in the complex negotiations designed to secure a ceasefire in Cambodia and head off a civil war. Simultaneously, however, the Thai government allowed the Chinese to use Thailand as a route to deliver lethal aid to the Khmer Rouge forces ensconced in the western Cambodian mountains. The Thai military also provided support to the rebel forces fighting against Hun Sen's Phnom Penh administration. To critics of Thai foreign policy, this dual policy appeared to be a contradiction.

In 1989 Thailand and Laos began cooperating in securing their common border. High-level meetings reduced the tensions between the two countries that began after the Communist takeover in 1975. The resolution of border fighting over disputed territory in 1987–1988 facilitated the warming of relations. The major element of the new ties is a flourishing trade, to be capped with an Australian-built bridge across the Mekong River to facilitate the transport of trade items.

Conclusion

Thailand evolved into a semidemocracy, with new institutions available for more effective political participation. These new institutions have been assimilated into existing patterns in ways that fit traditional patterns of political activity. Thai leadership has been able to cope with the tensions that have arisen from the process of democratization. The Thai political system, with its modified, open form, meshes with the personalism and hierarchy that have been important parts of Thai culture.

At a formal level until the 1991 coup, there has been open participation, a free press, and free elections. At an informal level, Thai society is still dominated by a small proportion of the society that controls the military, economic, and political spheres. During the Chatichai period, the Thai people deemed that their government is legitimate because of both democratization and steady economic growth. The prospects for parliamentary democracy depended on the capacity of the government to meet the needs of the people, the continued vibrancy of the economy, the restraint of military leaders, and a smooth monarchical succession. The prospects also depended on the continued strengthening of such institutions as the parliament and political parties and a concomitant decrease in personalism and self-interested, corrupt policymaking.

Thailand today is fundamentally different from Thailand of just a decade or two ago, when the military-dominated bureaucracy controlled society. As democratization and economic development flourished simultaneously and new groups emerged to challenge the traditional power elites, Thai society evolved into one more independent, confident, stable, and thriving. Thai history is replete with examples of successful management of problems to ensure the independence and stability of the kingdom.

Semidemocracy involves the participation of most groups within the society; thus the political system has been accepted as legitimate by rulers and the ruled. Until the 1991 coup, Thais have not felt oppressed by their government leaders, and (with rare exceptions) civil liberties have been protected. Thailand's continuing capacity to cope with changing demands and to assert its own destiny has strengthened despite the interlude of martial law in 1991.

Notes

1. A portion of the following chapter has been updated from the author's previous writings on Thailand. See "Change in Thailand," *Current History,* vol. 89, no. 545, March 1990, pp. 101–104, 127–130; and "Changing Perceptions of U.S.-Thai Relations: American Perspective," in *U.S.-Thailand Relations in a New International Era,* ed. Clark D. Neher and Wiwat Mungkandi (Berkeley: Institute of East Asian Studies, University of California, 1990).

2. Chai-Anan Samudavanija has suggested these three patterns in his article "Democracy in Thailand: A Case of a Stable Semi-Democratic Regime," *World Affairs,* vol. 150, no. 1, Summer 1987, pp. 31–41.

3. For the fullest treatment of Thailand from a state-centered perspective, see Daniel H. Unger, "Industrialization in Thailand: Soft State in a Strong Regional Economy," unpublished Ph.D. dissertation (Berkeley: University of California, 1989).

4. Joel S. Migdal, *Strong Societies and Weak States: State-Society Relations and State Capabilities in the Third World* (Princeton: Princeton University Press, 1988).

5. See ibid., pp. 32–33, for elaboration of these points.

6. Daniel Unger has written most persuasively on Thailand as a weak state. Many of his insights are incorporated into the next section of the chapter.

7. For a detailed discussion of the state's role in the economy, see Anek Laothamatas, *From Bureaucratic Polity to Liberal Corporatism: Business Associations and the New Political Economy of Thailand* (Boulder, Colo.: Westview Press, 1991)

8. These points are made in Scott Christensen, Clark D. Neher, and Wiwat Mungkandi, "U.S.-Thailand Relations in a New International Era," in *U.S.-Thailand Relations in a New International Era,* ed. Clark D. Neher and Wiwat Mungkandi (Berkeley: University of California, Institute of East Asian Studies, 1990).

9. The best analysis of the Thai state is in Chai-Anan Samudavanija, "Thailand: A Stable Semi-Democracy," in *Democracy in Developing Countries: Asia,* ed. Larry Diamond, Juan J. Linz, and Seymour Martin Lipset, eds. (Boulder: Lynne Rienner Publishers, 1989).

10. See Laothamatas, *From Bureaucratic Polity,* for a lengthy discussion of the increased role of businessmen and business associations countrywide in determining Thai economic policy.

11. This point is found in Diamond, Linz, and Lipset, eds., *Democracy in Developing Countries,* p. 22.

12. Samudavanija, "Thailand: A Stable Semi-Democracy," p. 333.

13. See Anek Laothamatas, *From Bureaucratic Polity;* Samudavanija, "Thailand: A Stable Semi-Democracy"; Ansil Ramsay, "Contemporary Thai Political Evolution," in *Thailand-U.S. Relations: Changing Political, Strategic, and Economic Factors,* ed. Ansil Ramsay and Wiwat Mungkandi (Berkeley: Institute of East Asian Studies, University of California, 1988); Unger, "Industrialization in Thailand"; and Richard

Doner, "Weak State–Strong Country? The Thai Automobile Case," *Third World Quarterly*, vol. 10, October 1988, pp. 1542–1564.

14. See the readings by David Wilson, Clark Neher, Fred Riggs, and William Siffin in *Modern Thai Politics*, ed. Clark D. Neher (Cambridge: Schenkman Publishing Co., 1979).

15. Migdal, *Strong Societies and Weak States*, p. 269. The following section is based on the framework developed by Joel S. Migdal. Donald Emmerson in his unpublished essay, "Beyond Zanzibar: Area Studies, Comparative Politics, and the 'Strength' of the State in Indonesia" (paper presented to the Association for Asian Studies, Chicago, April 1990), has adapted Migdal's framework in his evaluation of the Indonesian state. The following section follows Emmerson's adaptation.

16. Migdal, *Strong Societies and Weak States*, pp. 271–272.

17. Ibid., p. 274.

4

THE PHILIPPINES

In the quest for political and economic development, the experience of the Philippines has been different from that of Thailand. Whereas the Thais have shown an ability to meld traditional cultural values with selected modern values in order to achieve development, the Filipinos have had considerably less success finding the appropriate blend. In contrast to the Thais, who have never had a foreign culture thrust upon them through colonialism, the Filipinos, colonized for four hundred years by the Spanish and then for forty-eight years by the Americans, were not as free to choose those aspects of westernization most conducive to development. Instead, the nation is beset even today by the same difficulties that arose during colonialism: oligarchical politics, personalism, economic inequality, and decay. Political development in Thailand was viewed from the perspective of the Thai political system's large capacity to cope with the changing needs and demands of the people through the strengthening and expanding of political institutions and the reduced importance of personalism in determining public policy. In the Philippines, this process toward development and democratization has been stymied and in some cases reversed, diminishing the system's capacity to cope with the people's demands. The result is more often institutional decay rather than development and authoritarianism rather than accountability.[1]

The long Spanish and shorter (but profound) U.S. domination of the Philippines left a mixed legacy. From the Spanish, the Filipinos inherited a highly unequal system of land tenure dominated by a powerful land-owning class. The landed families and the hierarchical society, still powerful in Filipino politics, were rooted in clan warfare and Spanish feudalism. The U.S. presence from 1898 to 1946 integrated the Philippine economy into the U.S. economy, nudged the country's political structures toward competitive democracy, introduced a system of public education that vastly improved literacy rates (along with incorporating English as the national language), and fostered the rise of highly trained technocrats, bureaucrats, and entrepreneurs. The economic relationship of the Philippines with the United States was built on the primary products produced by Filipinos for the U.S. market. Sugar, under the control of a few landholding "barons," was the forerunner of crops grown for the foreign market.

Philippine independence, proclaimed July 4, 1946, followed World War II and the Japanese occupation and began a period of semidemocratic rule within the context of a continuing oligarchy. A series of democratically elected presidents ruled over a society still pervaded by personalism in the form of patron-client ties. Civil liberties flourished, as did violence by the private armies that surrounded the nation's elite families.

When Ferdinand Marcos was first elected president in 1965, the Philippines was experiencing economic growth and political stability. The vital Liberal and *Nacionalista* parties, despite their fluid, nonideological nature, assured the nation of lively competition for public office. At the same time, Philippine society suffered from problems that originated during the colonial era, the most salient of which were social and economic inequality, corruption, food shortages, and widespread violence.

In 1969 President Marcos became the first president in the postindependence Philippines to be reelected. His reelection was "bought" in the sense that he gave government funds to local officials who manipulated the vote in his favor. A constitutional provision precluded a third term, so Marcos planned to stay in power by abrogating the constitution and asserting that national crises demanded extraordinary measures. His proclamation of martial law in September 1972 ended formal democratic rule and began a fourteen-year period of authoritarian rule.

A majority of Filipino citizens supported Marcos's initial steps to end the breakdown of law and order, his promise of land reform, and his strengthening of the army against insurrection by Communists throughout the nation and by Muslim dissidents in the southern islands. This support dissipated as it became clear that his achievements did not match his rhetoric and that the "temporary" period of martial law was merely a pretext to perpetuate his personal power.

Acting with the wholehearted support of the United States and using his martial law powers, Marcos was both executive and legislator. To give legitimacy to his regime, he instituted referenda, all of which turned out a 90 percent vote in favor of his continued tenure, and elections, all of which were fraudulent. Press censorship of criticism of the government, jailing of dissidents, lack of basic civil liberties, absence of a secret ballot, and control of ballot counting were the means Marcos used to win approval of his rule.

By the mid-1970s, Marcos's "New Society" began to disintegrate with the rise of lawlessness in the countryside, the realization that the "constitutional authoritarian" government was more authoritarian than constitutional, the imprisonment of respected political leaders such as Marcos's rival, Senator Benigno Aquino, Jr., and the awareness of a mismanaged economy. This last problem was perhaps the most crucial in generating citizen antagonism toward martial law. Unemployment rose to over 20 percent and underemployment to 40 percent, real income shrank as inflation increased, and corruption reached an intolerable state under "crony capitalism" whereby Marcos's friends were placed in charge of business conglomerates despite their lack of business acumen.

The "lifting" of martial law in 1981 temporarily improved the image of the New Society but did not significantly change the authoritarian political order. The government continued to be based on personalism with no legitimacy granted to governmental institutions. Compared to the period before martial law and to its Southeast Asian neighbors, Philippine politics during the Marcos era was increasingly characterized by decay rather than by development. As the regime lost its legitimacy, the Armed Forces of the Philippines (AFP) became less professional, the economy worsened, and the Communist party of the Philippines (CPP) and its military arm, the New People's Army (NPA), strengthened, thereby undermining the original rationale for martial law.

By 1983, after the hierarchy of the Philippine Catholic church and business leaders had turned against Marcos and when Marcos's health was known to be precarious, Senator Aquino returned to the Philippines after several years of exile in the United States. Senator Aquino, the single greatest challenger to President Marcos, was assassinated in August 1983 at the moment he stepped out of the airplane in which he returned to the Philippines, and the almost universal belief of Filipinos in the government's complicity in this assassination brought forth long suppressed grievances.

The Marcos regime would no doubt have fallen even without Aquino's martyrdom, for Filipinos already knew that Marcos and his associates were responsible for the country's low vitality, whereas other non-Communist Southeast Asian nations were flourishing.[2] After Aquino was assassinated, the Philippines faced disastrous declines in industrial and agricultural production and in wages and employment as well as a flight of capital, high inflation, severe undernourishment for children in the rural areas, a rich-poor gap greater than any other nation's in the region, and a negative economic growth while the other non-Communist Southeast Asian nations were boasting of the world's highest growth rates.[3]

A momentous event in contemporary Philippine politics took place during three remarkable months, from December 1985 through February 1986. Bowing to intense pressure from the United States, wishing to take advantage of better health during a remission of his illness, desiring to end the attacks on him by the opposition, sensing the disarray of potential opposition candidates, and confident about his capacity to engineer a mandate, Marcos called for snap elections to be held on February 7, 1986.

From the moment Marcos announced the elections, the key question was whether the opposition could unite around a single candidate, and the answer was unclear until the final filing day. Previously, the opposition had been able to unite only in its disdain for Marcos. Because of the highly personal nature of Philippine politics, the competing ambitions of potential leaders, and Marcos's ability to manipulate and co-opt rival forces, the opposition had a difficult time presenting a serious alternative.

Structurally, the opposition suffered from the disintegration of the two-party system during martial law. Instead, there were many parties and organizations, each with an ambitious leader who wanted to be the candidate to run against Marcos. Corazon "Cory" Aquino, the widow of the martyred Senator Benigno Aquino, Jr., emerged as the person around whom all the oppositionists could coalesce. Her genuine reluctance to lead added to her attraction as a sincere, honest, and incorruptible candidate, precisely the antithesis of the president. A grassroots groundswell of support culminated in a petition with over one million signatures from Filipinos urging her to run for the presidency. Mrs. Aquino met with Senator Salvador Laurel, himself a major contender for the presidency, and fashioned an eleventh-hour agreement whereby she and Laurel would be the presidential and vice presidential candidates, respectively, under the banner of Laurel's United Nationalist Democratic Organization (UNIDO). For the first time since 1972 when martial law was declared, the opposition achieved unity.

Candidate Aquino, realizing that she could not match the president in financial or organizational strength, proclaimed a "people's campaign." Marcos, her opponent, had easy access to government money during the campaign, which allowed him to raise officials' salaries, decrease taxes, and lower fuel and utility rates. By the end of the campaign, some $500 million from the government treasury had been spent to reelect the president. In contrast, the opposition spent $10 million, all of it raised from donations.

Whereas Aquino's first campaign speeches stressed her sincerity and honesty and her empathetic qualities as a sufferer under Marcos, her later speeches focused on issues and her program to reform the government. She vilified the president for his corruption and immorality as she cited evidence that the president had lied both about his role as a hero in World War II and about his fortune of several billion dollars in real estate around the world. The former issue arose after investigations of U.S. Army documents disclosed that Marcos's claim that he headed a guerrilla resistance unit during the Japanese occupation of the Philippines was "fraudulent" and "absurd." U.S. congressional investigations also documented the president's wealth overseas. Aquino's major theme was that Marcos had brought economic ruin and political dictatorship to the nation and that she would restore integrity.

Marcos's campaign focused on his experience, including his wartime record, in contrast to his opponent's "naïveté." He stressed the need for strong male leadership rather than weak female leadership, suggesting that a woman's place was in the bedroom rather than in the political arena. Marcos claimed that Communists had taken over Aquino's campaign and that only he could handle the Communist insurgency. He accused Aquino of planning to cancel the Military Base Agreement with the United States and to dismember the republic by giving away Mindanao.

The voting was marred by fraud committed by Marcos supporters. When the "official" count gave Marcos 54 percent of the vote, the National Assembly—the final arbiter for voting controversies, proclaimed Marcos the winner, but the opposition launched a peaceful crusade of civil disobedience to bring down Marcos and allow the real winner, Aquino, to assume office. The U.S. government, official observers, journalists from dozens of nations, the Catholic church, and most Filipinos agreed that Aquino had actually won the election by a large margin.

As Aquino's civil disobedience campaign took hold, Defense Minister Juan Ponce Enrile and Lieutenant General Fidel Ramos, vice chief of the armed forces, defected from the Marcos camp and called for his resignation and for Aquino's ascension to the presidency. This rebellion by former Marcos supporters began a series of defections from the president, leaving him with only a small, hard-core group of backers.

When Marcos threatened to retaliate by bombing the headquarters of Enrile and Ramos, thousands of Filipinos—urged on by the archbishop of Manila, Cardinal Sin—surrounded the building, some even lying in the streets to keep the tanks from approaching. This display by students, farmers, nuns, and shop owners became known as *people's power*. The tank commanders eventually retreated and many defected to the opposition. The United States signaled its support of the rebellion, thereby undermining Marcos's claim that only he enjoyed the confidence of the superpowers. On February 25, 1986, Aquino and Laurel proclaimed the people's victory and were sworn in as president and vice president. The next day, Marcos fled the country with his family to live in exile in Hawaii, where he died on September 28, 1989, at the age of 72.

With little bloodshed, people's power triumphed over a regime that had dominated the political, social, and economic life of the Philippines for twenty-one years. The republic was awash with optimism that a new era in Philippine politics had arrived. Indeed, in the first months of the Aquino regime the executive, legislative, and judicial institutions were revitalized, the military curtailed, political parties refurbished, electoral processes made honest and effective, the media freed, the Marcos cronies undercut, and the citizens given back their rights. However, the monumental problems faced by Filipinos remained: oligarchical politics, personalism, economic and social inequalities, and weak institutions incapable of meeting the needs of the people.

In both the political and economic realms, President Aquino's administration has achieved notable gains. Filipinos have again expressed pride in their country's government after years of corrupt and demeaning leadership. Governmental institutions have been rejuvenated under a president whose commitment to democratic values and procedures is irrevocable. Even during Aquino's first year as president when she had virtually unlimited powers, she focused on restoring the democratic process. Civil liberties were reinstated, including the writ of habeas corpus, the release of political prisoners, and free and regularized elections. These gains came about through the promulgation of a new democratic constitution approved by over 75 percent of the Filipino people in a referendum in February 1987.

Contending with a desperately sick economy resulting from mismanagement by the previous regime, the Aquino administration achieved slow growth. The Philippine economic growth rate had been negative during the last years of Marcos, but the rate under Aquino was 6.7 percent in 1988 and 5.5 percent in 1989 while inflation decreased. Growth was highest in the industrial sector, as confidence in the economy grew and construction projects flourished. Philippine exports increased 25 percent in 1987, 1988, 1989, and 1990, and the flight of capital ended by 1989.

These achievements are even more remarkable when viewed in the perspective of a regime that inherited a legacy of cronyism and corruption, persecution and privilege. The fact that the Aquino administration, as of late 1990, was able to survive at all is in itself an achievement. The fall of Marcos meant the fall of his cronies as well, for many of them—as well as certain disgruntled elements in the armed forces—viewed the Aquino regime as a threat to their status. Within a four-year period after assuming the presidency, Aquino survived six coup attempts.

Aquino had raised the expectations of the people with promises of reform in all areas of life. She promised the end of the politics of personalism and the beginning of the politics of principle. Compared to the recent past in the Philippines, the Aquino administration receives high marks, but compared to ideal standards or those of its Asian neighbors, its record is weak. Although the level of corruption and privilege decreased significantly under her administration, she has failed to change the system in a fundamental way. As with all presidencies during the postindependence period, the Aquino administration has been characterized by oligarchical rule, economic and social inequalities, desperate poverty, and the politics of personalism.

Even the higher economic growth rates during Aquino's presidency are not clear economic achievements. The benefits of the recovery have been reaped almost entirely by the economic elites, with the rural population remaining poor. The rural poor were also hurt by 16 percent inflation in 1989 alone for such basic commodities as food and energy.

Aquino's initial and unsuccessful attempts to end Communist insurgency were based on reconciliation, a policy the armed forces vigorously fought against, claiming that the NPA insurgents were taking advantage of the military's soft line by strengthening their positions. To keep the military from rebelling, Aquino's counterinsurgency policy eventually moved toward more conservatism and a harder line, including support for community vigilante groups established to repulse the rebels. These anti-Communist, local self-defense organizations proliferated with the failure of peace negotiations between the Aquino government and the NPA. Aquino's endorsement of vigilantism was a sign that the Communist movement was still intense, despite her administration's reforms.

In January 1988, the Asian Human Rights Commission criticized the Philippine government for "serious and unjustifiable" violations of human rights, citing abuses committed by government-supported vigilante groups. These groups were viewed as having "turned the whole of the Philippines into a battlefield . . . pitting civilian against civilian."[4]

Aquino, in short, failed to institutionalize the overwhelming personal support she received from the populace. She did not develop a political party that could carry on her reform policies when she is no longer in office. Her followers expected that she would solve the nation's problems singlehandedly. The plethora of parties during her administration actually weakened administrative discipline, as the leaders of various organizations vied for power rather than cooperating for the common good. Personalism triumphed over institutional legitimacy.

Personalism also became an issue when Aquino ineffectively dealt with allegations of corruption among her own family members. As a member of one of the wealthiest families in the Philippines, Corazon Cojuangco Aquino was raised in the tradition of family loyalty, and these ties precluded her from ending the improprieties of some of her Cojuangco relatives, several of whom had been Marcos cronies.

The Cojuangco family has been split both politically and financially. Supporting the president is her brother, Jose "Peping" Cojuangco, the leader of a major political party, the *Laban ng Demokratikong Pilipino.* On the other side is her first cousin, Eduardo "Danding" Cojuangco, a close friend of former President Marcos whom he joined in exile. Eduardo amassed one of the country's largest fortunes as a result of favoritism shown him by Marcos in numerous business ventures. He is the ultimate patron in his home area of Tarlac Province, where he is known as a one-man social security system. He is said to have awarded twenty-five million pesos in loans and scholarships to more than twenty-five thousand people in the province.[5]

This familial problem was exacerbated by Aquino's reluctance to move more forcefully toward meaningful land reform. Because Aquino's family owned a six thousand-hectare hacienda, Luisita, in Tarlac Province on the island of Luzon, her detractors viewed her reluctance as self-interest. Aquino had the opportunity and power to put forth a comprehensive land reform program when she had revolutionary powers during her first year in office before the National Assembly was constituted. However, she waited to promulgate her Comprehensive Agrarian Reform Program until assembly members could gut those parts of the reform damaging to their own interests. Because 130 of the 200 elected congressmen were leaders of established landowning families and another 39 were relatives of these families, the final land reform program was characterized by compromise and loopholes that guaranteed continuation of the status quo. Even Luisita was not broken up and divided among its tenant farmers.

The Aquino administration was also reluctant to move forcefully on the equally important problem of population growth. At the present rate, the population of 60 million will increase to 100 million in just 30 years. There is no longer a frontier beyond which a "surplus" population can move and be productive, and over 750,000 new jobs are needed each year just to maintain the status quo. Despite studies that show that the economy and ecology cannot sustain the country's population growth, the Aquino administration has been reluctant to offend the Catholic hierarchy by advocating contraception.

The reasons for the high (2.6 percent) population growth are many. First, high levels of poverty correlate with high population growth rates. Moreover, the leaders of the Catholic church, in a country in which over 90 percent of the population practices Catholicism, have opposed governmental involvement in family planning. Parish priests, on the other hand, have long been sympathetic to their parishioners' use of contraception. The machismo culture has also kept birth rates high because male prowess is defined in part by the number of children fathered.

Public opinion surveys show that President Aquino's initial, almost universal support decreased steadily as her tenure in office lengthened. Nuisances frustrated Filipinos every day, especially those living in Manila. Electrical blackouts, for example, continued three to four hours each day without any hope for remedy. (Ironically, the blackouts were caused by the higher-than-projected growth in demand as a result of the improvement in the economy.) Traffic jams were endless, and crimes of all sorts beset the people. Water shortages caused comfort and health problems, and drainage systems were clogged by sewage that might be left for weeks. Streets in Manila were repeatedly repaired, an example of inadequate coordination among ministries. The Metropolitan Water-works and Sewerage Company would dig up the streets to lay water pipes; the telephone company would dig up the same streets again to install telephone lines; then the Ministry of Public Works and Highways would dig up the streets again for flood control.[6]

Beginning in December 1989 with a military coup attempt that temporarily destabilized the government, a series of dreadful events occurred that many Filipinos saw as ominous indications that the government's mandate was tenuous. A horrendous earthquake in July 1990, which devastated one-fourth of the Philippine territory, was followed by the Iraqi invasion of Kuwait, which raised the price of oil, undermining the fragile economy. This was followed by a typhoon that struck half of the Philippines in November, claiming nearly four hundred lives. Half a million persons were left homeless by the typhoon, and crops were ruined in a dozen provinces.

Most Filipinos believed that stability would not return to the country without a resolution of the tragedy of Senator Aquino's assassination. In September 1990, a special court found a former air force general and fifteen other servicemen guilty of the death and sentenced them to life imprisonment. But even this verdict did not still the widespread belief that the assassination would not have occurred without the approval of persons high in government, namely the Marcoses.

Institutions and Social Groups

Patron-Client Relations

The Philippine government can be described as clientelist, a form of societal organization in which political life centers on relationships that are largely person to person, informal, hierarchical, reciprocal, and based on an obligation of indebtedness (*utang na loob*). Because they were too weak, interest groups, political parties, the legislature, and other government institutions have been supplanted by clientelist relationships. Thus, political life in the Philippines has consisted of constantly changing coalitions of clientele groups that serve for both the articulation of mass interests and government control over the people.

The need for patrons to provide resources to their clients has been a major cause of corruption throughout Philippine society. Indeed, public office has been used both for private gain and for the support of clients. Clientelist systems rely neither on rational allocations of resources nor on market forces; their first priority is to perpetuate the power of those who already rule.

Under President Marcos, the clientelist nature of Philippine society was most obvious in the president's grant of monopoly privileges to selected followers. Marcos put control of numerous industries in the hands of his clients and assured them of immunity from loss; when the economy began to collapse and his authority lost legitimacy (after the assassination of Senator Aquino), Marcos lost control, first, over the resources he used to reward his clients and, eventually, over the entire society.

With the rise of President Aquino, Marcos's clientele lost its source of favors, and new patronage groups emerged in the same fashion as has occurred throughout Philippine history. President Aquino found it impossible to ignore these relationships and eventually relied on her own clientele, albeit in a less corrupt manner than Marcos. Her reliance on clientelism further undermined the importance and legitimacy of political institutions, resulting in the continued decay rather than development of Philippine politics.

Constitutions

The Philippine experience with constitutions is less than one hundred years old. The Malolos constitution of 1899, the first democratic constitution in Asia, was borrowed from South American and Spanish constitutions and embodied the ideas of liberal democracy, representative government, and separation of powers and checks and balances. This constitution endured only a short time before the United States ended the short-lived republic.

The U.S.-sponsored constitution of 1935 provided for a representative democracy based on the U.S. model. A bill of rights safeguarded the people's involvement in the polity through the electoral process. A bicameral legislature, an independent judiciary, and a chief executive (elected for a fixed term of four years) provided for a separation and balance of powers. The constitution remained in force until the 1973 constitution was adopted, although in reality it became irrelevant with the advent of martial law. In 1972, Marcos convened a constitutional convention to draft a new constitution based on a parliamentary rather than a presidential model. However, Marcos's declaration of martial law silenced debate on his proposed constitution; a few months later a constitutional convention approved the new constitution, which called for a parliamentary form of government led by a prime minister and allowed the interim president (Marcos) to decide when to convene the interim national assembly and to make and execute all laws until he convened the assembly. The constitution was then approved by people's assemblies (*Barangay*) and went into effect January 17, 1973.

President Aquino's victory led to a Freedom constitution, a provisional document issued by presidential proclamation. It provided for presidential appointment of a constitutional commission to draft a new, permanent constitution. Meanwhile, until the commission presented a new constitution that was similar to the one of 1935, President Aquino held executive and legislative powers. A plebiscite on February 2, 1987, supported the new document, with 75 percent of the voters approving.

Under the 1987 constitution, the powers of the president are more circumscribed than under previous Philippine constitutions. The presidential term is six years, with no reelection. To curb the familial patronage of the Marcos years, the president's spouse and all close relatives are barred from appointment as public officials. Martial law powers are also circumscribed, providing both the legislative and judicial branches the power to review legal bases for the imposition of martial law.

The Aquino constitution is the most democratic in all of Southeast Asia, providing for citizens' civil liberties, a meaningful separation of powers, and rights of participation in choosing government representatives.

The Legislature

In the postindependence period, the legislature has been both a bulwark for freedom and a tool for legitimizing presidential decrees. The Aquino constitution gives numerous prerogatives to the congress, including the sole power to declare war, to withdraw presidential emergency powers, and to determine revenue origination and appropriation. While the Marcos constitution of 1973 allowed President Marcos to exercise both legislative and executive powers, the 1987 constitution in contrast makes a clear separation between these powers.

The new constitution called for a bicameral congress, consisting of a twenty-four-member senate elected at large for six years and for not more than two consecutive terms. The house of representatives consists of not more than two hundred and fifty members elected from legislative districts apportioned on the basis of population. There are also members who are elected through a party-list system constituting 20 percent of the number of representatives. For the first three terms, half of the representatives are to include labor, the peasantry, the urban poor, women, youth, and other underrepresented groups.

Political Parties

The Philippines had a two-party system for most of its democratic period (1946 to 1972) when the Liberal and *Nacionalista* parties held power in alternation, with neither party able to get its presidential nominee reelected.[7] The ideological differences between the two parties were negligible, and neither party appeared to represent the interests of the vast majority of Filipinos. For the most part, the two parties functioned as mobilizers of votes for specific candidates.

Under Marcos, one party dominated the political scene. Marcos's New Society Movement (*Kilusang Bagong Lipunan*) (KBL) was a noncompetitive, authoritarian party devoted to keeping Marcos in power and to maintaining the support of the U.S. government. Through his magnetic personality, his dominance of the bureaucracy and the legislative and executive branches, his fraudulent plebiscites and referenda, and his manipulation of nationalist symbols, Marcos controlled every aspect of the party and its program.

When Marcos allowed other political parties to be established in 1978 in preparation for elections for an interim national assembly, some thirty parties emerged with regional constituencies. However, these parties were fragmented and unable to find financial backing. Thus, President Marcos thwarted every attempt at achieving a semblance of opposition activity.

In the postmartial law era after 1981, the KBL continued to dominate politics. However, as Marcos's support deteriorated, opposition parties began to emerge. The most important of these was UNIDO, formed in 1979 by Salvador Laurel who had broken from KBL. UNIDO, largely an alliance of establishment politicians who had lost out when Marcos took control, was united primarily in its opposition to his domination of the political scene. Thus, UNIDO became an umbrella organization encompassing a number of smaller parties under the leadership of prominent politicians such as Senator Benigno Aquino, Jr., who established *LABAN!* (Fight!) while still a political prisoner of Marcos. These parties formed the core of support for Corazon Aquino when she became a candidate for the presidency.

After Marcos fell from power, KBL members scattered to different parties, including the once moribund *Nacionalista* party now led by Juan Ponce Enrile, defense minister under Aquino (and later implicated in coups against her). Vice President Laurel joined Enrile in the *Nacionalista* party when he, too, broke with Aquino. At the other end of the ideological spectrum, former Communist and labor leaders formed the *Partido ng Bayan* to contest elections for the National Assembly.

No one party emerged around Aquino's centrist-reform administration. Instead, a series of parties under the leadership of prominent politicians was established to enhance the politicians' political ambitions. However, in contrast to the two parties during the premartial law era, these new parties had ideological as well as personal causes. The centrist and left-of-center parties have given support to Aquino, although among themselves they have disagreed over power sharing. The right-of-center parties, which have opposed her leadership, have also squabbled over a sufficient number of issues to prevent them from uniting. Thus, party politics has remained largely an elite-establishment activity, based on patronage and personalism and now revolving around Corazon Aquino.

The Military

Although long involved with supporting particular candidates for office, the military has never played the dominant role in Filipino politics. In contrast to Thailand, the Filipino military has been subordinated to civilian leaders and given the orthodox task of providing external defense and security against domestic subversion. (This second task was exploited by Marcos to protect his personal interests.)

The AFP consisted of 37,000 personnel in the 1940s. In the 1960s the figure was 62,000; between 1975 and 1976 the number jumped from 90,000 to 142,000; and today the total is about 154,000. Marcos expanded the army three-and-a-half times its former strength during his tenure, which increased military involvement in civilian life, including the militarization of internal security forces.[8] Under Marcos, the military was deprofessionalized through his appointments of cronies and fellow Ilocanos (from Northern Luzon) to the commanding positions. The clearest such example was Marcos's appointment of his cousin and fellow Ilocano, Fabian Ver, as armed forces chief of staff. Ver, who was subsequently determined by a government-appointed investigatory commission to have been a planner in the assassination of Senator Aquino, politicized the military, turning it into a security force for Marcos and the enforcer of his martial law. In return, Marcos provided military leaders with access to financial benefits.

A group of reform-minded soldiers who reacted against the politicization of the military and its diminished professionalism organized into the Reform the Armed Forces Movement (RAM) and led the army rebellion against Marcos after the elections of 1986. A RAM leader, Juan Ponce Enrile, was awarded the position of minister of defense for his role in ousting Marcos and supporting Corazon Aquino. He along with other RAM officers eventually turned against Aquino and led coups against her government.

In response to RAM demands, Aquino changed her policies by replacing cabinet ministers who were anti-military, taking a harder line against Communist insurgents, and increasing the defense budget. She moved to professionalize the military by dismissing "overstaying" generals, who had kept their positions out of loyalty to Marcos, and by regularizing the promotion system.

Despite these reforms, members of the elite Scout Rangers and Marines led the most violent and threatening coup attempt on December 1, 1989. They captured airbases, the Fort Bonifacio army camp, and two television stations and attacked the presidential Malacanang palace. To repulse the attack, Aquino asked the United States to provide air support to forces loyal to the government. U.S. F-4 Phantom jets, flying from Clark Air Force Base, immobilized the rebel forces who had occupied hotels and office buildings in Manila before agreeing to a negotiated settlement. Gregorio Honasan, the escaped leader of previous coups and a founder of RAM, once again escaped capture.

The coup, thus far the best funded and organized of all such attempts, was a surprise, as the military seemed to have grudgingly acquiesced to Aquino because she had moved closer to the military's viewpoint on countering Communist insurgency. The leadership of the coup was traced to RAM, which had also led previous mutinies. Except for a call for President Aquino's resignation, no specific demands were made by the rebel forces. An eight-member provisional junta was to have been set up, consisting of military leaders (including Honasan) and former Defense Minister Enrile and Vice President Laurel. Following the coup, however, both Enrile and Laurel were charged with involvement, but the charges were dropped when no concrete evidence was found to substantiate them.

During the coup, which was devastating to the Aquino regime, seventy-nine people were killed and six hundred wounded. Moreover, the image of stability, so important for the country's continued economic growth, was shattered. Also, Aquino lost face because of her decision to request U.S. support. Finally, the role of the U.S. military in a domestic issue complicated later negotiations on the bases used by the United States and exacerbated nationalist and anti-U.S. sentiments that were already near the surface.

The Bureaucracy

In Thailand the bureaucracy along with the military has been the dominant institution of government. In the Philippines, on the other hand, the bureaucracy has been subordinate to the politicians, in particular to the president. The original bureaucracy in the pre-Spanish period was called the *Barangay*, and it was responsible for law and order and for the collection of tribute. The Spanish centralized the bureaucracy and turned it into a patronage-oriented institution designed to keep the rulers in power.[9]

When the Americans came, they took over the top positions in the bureaucracy for themselves and attempted to make the institution more accountable to the public. Nevertheless, the bureaucracy remained highly personalistic, centralized, and administratively inefficient. Under Marcos, the bureaucracy was mobilized for his personal benefit. Graft and corruption in the bureaucracy have accounted for the country's annual loss of some 10 percent of its GNP.[10]

Despite personalism, the Philippine bureaucracy has also contained highly educated and technologically proficient civil servants. Even under Marcos, technocrats were placed in key positions, lured by other bureaucrats from the better-paying private sector. Often, however, the technocrats have had difficulty putting their policies into effect because they do not have the requisite political skill or clout.

Women

Traditionally, women have played only minor roles in Philippine politics. Women have never held key positions of power in the parliament, cabinet, military, or bureaucracy. The rise of Imelda Marcos and Corazon Aquino to positions of immense power is anomalous rather than a pattern, as both were the wives of famous and powerful politicians. Marcos, who was governor of Metro Manila and minister of human settlements until her husband was overthrown in 1986, owed her claim to leadership to the authoritarian rule of President Ferdinand Marcos. Aquino was the saintly widow of Senator Benigno Aquino. These women's power is more a function of their familial ties to prominent male politicians than the successful surmounting of the formidable barriers that have traditionally kept women out of political positions of power.[11]

Filipinas are socialized to play subordinate roles to men in most areas of life, although many women are prominent in the professions and in the business world. In rural areas, women are responsible for the traditional family responsibilities as well as farming chores. Women work many more hours each day than do men. Among the wealthy Filipinas, however, women are more active in societal affairs because they can afford to hire helpers who take care of the children and household tasks. Even among the wealthy, however, women are socialized to let the men lead and to do so demurely. Imelda Marcos's flouting of such conventions caused her to be ridiculed by both Philippine men and women.

Aquino's rise to power was facilitated by the perception of her male counterparts that she would be a pliable and temporary leader, easily manipulated by the traditional male leaders. However, her refusal to step aside and allow her vice president, Salvador Laurel, to control her cabinet choices and policy decisions surprised Laurel, the military, and other influential leaders. Ironically, however, her unexpected strength and popularity and her commitment to democratic procedures have been major causes of six coup attempts against her by forces who believed she was only a temporary leader.

Insurgents

The revolutionary opposition in the Philippines gained strength during the 1950s and 1960s but became a meaningful threat to the nation's security during Marcos's rule. The CPP, the central organizational unit of the revolutionary opposition, is the largest Communist party in ASEAN and the only such group to remain a viable threat. Serving as the military arm of the CPP and consisting of some 16,000 to 20,000 armed personnel, the NPA has actively engaged in insurgency activities, building strength throughout the archipelago's 73 provinces. The NPA controls about 20 percent of the country's territory.

NPA strength has come from disillusioned peasants, especially tenant farmers and day laborers, whose hopes for a better life were lifted by Marcos's announcement of a New Society and then dashed by unfulfilled promises and expectations. Similarly, the rise of Corazon Aquino initially weakened the NPA until promises of meaningful land reform and improvement in the standard of living went unmet. Students and intellectuals were persuaded to join the NPA by the movement's claim to reflect the nationalist struggle against imperialism and the peasant-worker struggle against feudalism and dynastic politics. Other citizens supported the NPA as the only viable force against the corruption and abuses of rights perpetrated by local dynastic politicians and by military units.

President Aquino began her administration with a conciliatory policy toward the NPA, inviting its members to join her government and to become contributing citizens. However, the military balked and the NPA rejected her ceasefire proposals, forcing her to return to a harder line. During the first four years of her term of office, the NPA continued to engage in violent actions designed to undermine the legitimacy of the administration and to steer the populace toward support for the insurgents.

The Thai success in countering insurgency stemmed from combined policies of reconciliation and amnesty with economic development. In the Philippines, however, Aquino's reconciliation policy was not matched with a concomitant improvement in the standard of living. Although very little outside support is provided the NPA, it has been able to capitalize on the extreme poverty and negative economic growth rates suffered by nearly half of the Filipinos. The nation's interminable economic plight bodes ill for a resolution to the protracted guerrilla war.

The Church

As citizens of the only Christian country in Asia, Filipinos have felt themselves to be different from and even superior to their Asian neighbors. With 84 percent of the population Roman Catholic, over 12,000 priests and nuns throughout the archipelago, the largest land holdings in the nation, and control over thousands of parishes, schools, and hospitals, the Catholic church is a significant political, economic, and social institution. Factionalized among conservative, centrist, and progressive forces, the church has played a crucial role in all areas of Philippine life.

The current leader of the church is Jaime Cardinal Sin, archbishop of Manila and head of the centrist faction. Cardinal Sin, in conjunction with church bishops and clergy, played an important role in undermining President Marcos's administration and in fashioning the compromise that unified the opposition under Corazon Aquino.

The church's role in bringing down Marcos and Cardinal Sin's close relationship to President Aquino have provided the church with an important say in policy matters. Church leaders have been outspoken in their condemnation of corruption and other dishonest practices and in their support for programs that favor the poor and greater social justice.

Because of her devout religious beliefs, President Aquino has acquiesced to the pronouncements of the church on most issues. The most contentious controversy concerns the desire of government officials to launch a family planning program to slow the highest birth rate in Asia. The nation's population will double in just twenty-five years at the current birth rate. The church's condemnation of family planning, specifically regarding the use of contraceptives, has kept the government from achieving a plan designed to improve health standards and reduce poverty. With 49 percent of the population living below the poverty line and the population growth rate at 2.8 percent a year, the chances of solving the poverty crisis are limited. A decline in the growth rate by just .1 percent per year would decrease the number of Filipinos in the year 2020 by forty million.

The other church-government controversy concerns the rapid rise of AIDS cases. By the end of 1990, government health officials expressed alarm that AIDS may be a far greater crisis than previously believed. The church's stand against homosexuality and artificial contraception makes it difficult for condoms and sex education to be distributed to those most in need. Thus far, President Aquino has chosen not to disagree with the church on these issues. Notwithstanding these controversies, the church has emerged as the primary symbol of peaceful change, warning against political excesses by government and opposition groups.

Democratization

The Philippines used to be known as Southeast Asia's "showcase of democracy," and in terms of the formal institutions of government, that description is accurate. In the postindependence period up to the time of martial law, the Philippine government has carried out its functions on the basis of constitutional guidelines, through the separation of powers, and by adherence to a bill of rights.

Behaviorally, however, the picture is much different. Since the Spanish colonized the Philippines almost five hundred years ago, the nation has been ruled by a small number of family dynasties that have controlled both the economic and political spheres through decidedly undemocratic means. From the great haciendas of the Spaniards to the patronage politics during the U.S. period, these dynasties have ruled in a baronial, feudal manner, each controlling a particular area of the archipelago.

Even today, following the people's power revolt, a group of provincial barons commands the rural areas. In Cebu Province, for example, the governor, the mayor of Cebu City, and the congressman are all named Osmeña and are from the politically powerful clan once led by a former president. That example, which is multiplied throughout the republic, is indicative of a system that has remained essentially undemocratic throughout Filipino history.

The country's archipelagic nature is partially responsible for the decentralized, dynastic systems. Pervasive poverty also helps explain why the poor learn to rely on their wealthy patrons. Dynastic families sponsor the weddings of their laborers and tenants, pay for children's educations, and care for the sick, thereby forming a dependent tie that keeps the poor deferential and loyal. Without strong government institutions, patron-client relations develop to meet the needs of the majority poor.

The explanation for the dynastic nature of Philippine politics is also cultural. A Filipino's loyalty is directed first to family, then to close friends, then to the local community, then to personally known political leaders, and finally to distant, impersonal governmental agencies. Although all of these concentric circles of allegiance place emphasis on the personal nature of loyalty, an individual's family and patron family demand the deepest loyalties.[12]

These feelings of loyalty and deference have been strengthened by a ritual kinship (*compadrazgo*) in the form of godparents (*compadre*). This means of formalizing a friendship is employed between persons of higher status and lower status. In the *compadre* system, a reciprocity is formed in which the higher-status *compadre* renders material benefits and prestige and the lower-status family provides loyalty, deference, and support. Thus, a candidate for office may be asked to sponsor a marriage or a newborn baby in return for a family's electoral support, and the family then has the right to seek political patronage from its new *compadre*.[13] Politicians are equally desirous of becoming sponsors to ensure a wide base of electoral support.

A report on Filipino values commissioned by the Philippine senate in 1988 attempted to explain the reasons for the lack of democratic values. The major point was that Filipinos suffer from a colonial mentality that suggests that everything Filipino is second-rate and everything Western is first-rate. This report suggested that Filipinos have a feeling of national inferiority; hence, support for the nation's governmental system is weak compared to support for family and patrons. The report also suggested that Filipino elites are often alienated from their roots and from the masses of the people, most of whom they scorn. The elites' first value is to take care of themselves and not to concern themselves with the public good. Such values, of course, are not conducive to democratic rule, a form of government that requires mutual trust and respect for different points of view.

For democratization to take root in the Philippines, the formal institutions of government must become more than facades for oligarchical rule. Inasmuch as the overwhelming majority of newly elected senators and representatives are members of families who have dominated Philippine politics for centuries, the election of Corazon Aquino was more a restoration of certain families (and the demise of a few who had aligned with Marcos) than a revolution. Although the persons in charge of the government have changed, there has been no fundamental change in the character of the Philippine political system.

Economic Development

If Thailand has been the favorite case study for capitalist development of agricultural societies in the last several decades, the Philippines became the model for what not to do. On a par with Thailand in the mid-1970s, when each nation had an annual per capita GNP of just over $300, the Philippines later faltered, achieving a $720 GNP in 1989 in contrast to Thailand's $1,200. In the 1980s until the time Marcos left office, growth rates in the Philippines declined, making the republic the only ASEAN state not to share in this period of economic growth. Per capita GNP in 1984 had fallen to the levels of a decade earlier.

The Aquino government eventually achieved growth rates of 6.7 and 5.5 percent in 1988 and 1989, respectively, but these figures are far below Thailand's 10 to 11 percent rate. Moreover, the August 1990 Iraqi invasion of Kuwait brought about a rise in oil prices that affected the Philippines more than the other Southeast Asian nations. The Philippines imports almost all of its oil from the Middle East; thus, the crisis there doubled the oil import bill, worsened the trade deficit, dislocated 65,000 Filipino overseas workers, ended foreign exchange remittances from these workers, and added to the nation's already huge budget deficit.

Economic growth rates since Aquino, however, although more satisfactory than those under Marcos, ignore the 2.6 percent population growth, the highest in Southeast Asia. Real growth, then, was only 4.1 and 2.9 percent in 1988 and 1989, respectively. Moreover, the figures do not make it clear that the standard of living for laborers has decreased steadily for two generations due to the decline of the economy, high unemployment and underemployment, and inflation. (In 1989 unemployment was 9.8 percent and inflation 9.6 percent.) Concentration of wealth and land has long been more intensive in the Philippines than in any other Southeast Asian nation. The slight improvement in the economy has enriched the nation's higher-status economic classes but not the vast majority of the people.

The Philippine economy has been skewed since the days of Spanish colonialism, which thrust a feudal economic system upon the Filipinos. When Americans refined the system by their neocolonialism, the Filipino government and people lost control of their economy to outside forces, including multinational corporations, and to a group of incredibly wealthy Filipino families (mostly of Spanish or Chinese background). Philippine minerals and primary food crops were exported to U.S. markets, thereby integrating the economy into the capitalist world system. Neocolonial relations between Americans and Filipinos were of exploitation rather than cooperation for the mutual good, with the bulk of the profits gained by businesses in the Philippines going to Americans.

The Philippine economy at the end of World War II was in shambles because of widespread destruction in Manila and the infrastructure throughout the archipelago. The United States became the primary supervisor of the Philippine economy, and President Marcos later supported U.S. dominance of the Philippine economy while placing his cronies into positions of power.[14] Thus, the state became the major player in the economy, opening it to greater penetration by multinational corporations, foreign banks, and international funding agencies such as the World Bank. Only a small group of Marcos-centered industrialists and financiers benefited from this new form of state capitalism, while small businesses and labor groups were weakened.

As with most Southeast Asian nations in the 1950s, the Philippines adopted an import-substitution industrialization (ISI) strategy to develop the economy. In essence, the ISI strategy restricted imports of foreign goods in order to improve the balance of payments and to generate new industries to make the nation more self-sufficient. The United States had already penetrated the domestic Philippine economy, so this policy was not opposed by the Americans. Initially, the policy worked well in terms of benefiting domestic manufacturing industries, and between 1950 and 1980 the share of manufacturing in the total economy rose from 8 to 25 percent, while the share of agriculture declined from 42 to 23 percent.[15] Manufacturing accounted for more than half the value of exports in the 1970s, just a decade after accounting for only 6 percent. At the same time, however, every economic indicator showed the Philippines to have the least effective economy in the region.

The lack of success of ISI led international agencies such as the World Bank to change their advice and to recommend an export-oriented industrialization (EOI) strategy for economic development. EOI was the strategy used by Thailand to achieve high economic growth rates. However, interference by Marcos cronies kept protectionist measures intact so that the new strategy never worked effectively.

During the 1970s the rise in oil prices and the price collapse of the major Philippine exports, sugar and coconuts, caused a recession and a foreign trade deficit crisis. Unemployment rose, and the standard of living deteriorated. These economic predicaments occurred simultaneously with the people's growing disenchantment with the New Society's authoritarian ways and gross corruption.

The Philippines is characterized by a large tenant farmer population, which is prone to join revolutionary movements; thus, the failure of the Marcos land reform scheme to improve the farmers' lot further alienated a large sector of the population. Only a minuscule percent of potential recipients were awarded certificates of land after the 1972 land reform decree. By the early 1980s, farm prices had dropped so low that starvation was a real threat in the major sugar areas.[16] In contrast, the large majority of Thai farmers owned their own land and did not suffer the same degree of decline in their standard of living; consequently, they rarely engaged in radical political activities.

Similarly, urban laborers grew increasingly angry about the erosion of their wages and the deterioration of working conditions, while employers found themselves losing profits because of the increased costs of energy and pressure from the Marcos administration to raise wages. Both of these groups as well as the farmers could see that President Marcos's family and cronies were living in ostentatious luxury. Marcos had given his best friends monopoly control over the sugar and coconut sectors, which led to their amassing fabulous riches. These riches ended up in Swiss and U.S. bank accounts and real estate transactions throughout the world, a flight of capital that subverted the economy to an incurable state.

All these factors so undermined the economy that only a spark was needed to bring Filipinos to the streets to demand change. That "spark" turned out to be the return and assassination of Senator Aquino in August 1983. For Filipinos, the regime was not only a disaster economically but morally as well.

All of these difficulties kept foreign investment at a minimum, in contrast to Thailand where Japanese, Taiwanese, South Korean, and U.S. capital stimulated and sustained economic growth. The decline of Marcos led to increased international investment abroad, and six military coup attempts frightened away both trade and aid. The Multilateral Aid Initiative (MAI), known as the Philippine Assistance Program, budgeted $3.5 billion for the Philippines to be funded primarily by the United States, the World Bank, and Japan; it was to be an Asian equivalent of the Marshall Plan, which had been successful in rebuilding Europe after World War II. The money was to build an infrastructure, relieve the massive debt of the Marcos administration, and provide aid to the needy. However, the continued instability in the country slowed the pace by which MAI money reached the Philippines.

Corazon Aquino inherited a profoundly difficult and complex situation that was not easily resolvable by even the outstanding economists she was able to bring to her administration. The problems that beset the Philippines today are the same as those of the past: economic inequality, land disputes, monopolistic industries, corrupt leadership, and an elite class more concerned with self-interest than with the public good. These are problems that can be resolved only by fundamental changes in all areas of Filipino life, including the social, economic, cultural, and political realms.

For most Filipinos, the standard of living remains the lowest in ASEAN. That is a galling fact for a people who live in a country with rich natural resources, for the most literate and highly educated population in Southeast Asia with more experience with democratic rule than the other nations in that region.

The Philippine State

The Philippines is as interesting a case study as Thailand for analyzing the role of the state, but for different reasons. Thailand was known as a bureaucratic polity, where politics was enacted within the bureaucracy (including the military) and societal institutions were of secondary importance. Only in recent years have extra-bureaucratic groups become important in authoritative decisions that have an impact on the total society. The Thai legislature, political parties, and business associations have reduced direct domination by the military.

The Thai state lost some of its autonomy with the rise of competing groups and democratization. On the other hand, because of effective centralized administration, Thai authorities have shown a high degree of state strength by achieving their aims and meeting the needs of the citizenry. Thus, the Thai state has gained authority from its demonstrated high capacity to meet the needs of the people and by the legitimacy provided by the king.

If autonomy from societal institutions is a key variable for assessing strength, the Philippine state is weak because its authorities are integrated into a web of patronage networks that limits their authority. The Philippine state cannot set a coherent program because its authorities are not free from oligarchical connections that have been a major part of Philippine politics for five hundred years. In this respect, the Aquino years are not different from the Marcos years.

The Philippines is an example of a state that intervened in the economic system with devastating results. President Marcos undermined market forces by setting up incompetent cronies in businesses, then providing them with subsidies that relieved them of the need for accountability and efficiency. Marcos's crony capitalism was therefore different from that of his predecessors and successors only in degree. In contrast to Thailand, the Philippine state has critically hurt the economy through its corrupt intervention and its subservience to the economic dynasties. The result has been an economy of gross inequality, slow growth, resistance to change, and an inability to become part of the international economy (except in an exploited manner).

As discussed in the other country chapters, the first condition necessary for state strength is massive social dislocation. Unlike Thailand, which had no colonial heritage, the Philippines experienced two colonial regimes, both of which had a massive impact on every aspect of the country's life. Moreover, and again in contrast to Thailand, the Japanese interregnum was a period of dreadful trauma and devastation, and Manila was all but destroyed. In terms of this condition, then, the Philippines has the necessary background for development as a strong state.

A strong state is more likely to emerge when at a historical moment external political forces, such as a threat of foreign invasion, favor concentrated social control. In 1972 President Marcos used the internal threats of insurgency and civil war in the Moslem provinces to buttress his arguments for martial law. This insurgency and insurrection remained viable under his martial law as well as during Aquino's presidency. Thus, on this condition the experience of the Philippines is conducive to the rise of a strong state.

A social grouping that is independent of existing bases of social control and is able to execute the policies of state leaders is the third condition for a strong state. As if trying to fulfill this condition, the Philippine government has co-opted bureaucrats, technocrats, and business executives who identify their ultimate interests with those of the state. The dynastic families, on the other hand, have a separate power base (their regional clientele) that is often at odds with state authorities. The economically powerful Chinese also have not acted as an autonomous class. (Corazon Cojuangco Aquino is a descendant of a Chinese immigrant.)

More than Thailand, the Philippines has strong autonomous societal groups whose primary loyalties are with their religious, regional, and economic clienteles. Catholic church leaders play an important political role in contrast to Buddhist leaders in Thailand, who are apolitical. In their home provinces, the dynastic families carry out policies almost autonomously, independent of central government dictates. Intellectuals, students, and insurgents also have interests opposed to the central authorities. In this respect, then, the Philippine state is weaker than Thailand, lacking legitimacy and the capacity to integrate independent groups that are skillful enough to execute the designs of state leaders.

In terms of leadership, Philippine leaders have differed in strength and accordingly have either strengthened or weakened the state. Marcos collected great powers for himself and his clientele, but he was sufficiently incompetent to jeopardize the fabric of the republic. Aquino has reinstated democratic government, but she has been unable (or unwilling) to form policies that undermine the oligarchical form of government.

Thus, the Philippines has experienced the necessary conditions for the development of a strong state: massive social dislocation and external support. However, the state has remained personalistic with ineffective leadership and low capacity to meet the needs of the people.

Foreign Policy

The United States, the Philippines' closest ally, is also the republic's biggest foreign policy problem. Since the colonial period, the United States and the Philippines have had a "special relationship," a term that aptly describes the close and complex ties shared by the two nations for almost one hundred years.

The Philippines, as Asia's most Americanized country, shares a common Christian heritage and the use of the English language. In clothing, music, art, education, and politics, Filipinos have emulated Americans rather than their Asian neighbors. The result, therefore, has been a love-hate relationship. Many Filipinos look to the United States as their hope and even their future home at the same time that they demonstrate against U.S. interference in their affairs. The classic illustration of this ambivalence is the equal number of Filipinos demonstrating against U.S. policy in front of the U.S. embassy and the number of Filipinos waiting there in line for an immigration visa.

U.S. support of President Marcos, which was believed to have sustained and prolonged his rule, was applauded by some and denounced by others. The last-minute U.S. support of President Aquino, after it became clear that Marcos was finished, together with help in persuading Marcos to leave the country only partially helped to undo the damage.

Meanwhile, the presence of U.S. bases on Philippine territory has intensified the conflicting emotions Filipinos feel toward the United States. These sixteen facilities (later reduced to six) were negotiated in the 1947 Military Bases Agreement (MBA) to run for ninety-nine years. In 1966, however, the term of the MBA was reduced to twenty-five years (to 1991), to continue thereafter subject to one year's notice of abrogation by either party.[17] Negotiations commenced in 1990 to determine the future of U.S. bases in the Philippines.

The great importance that both nations place on negotiations has made a settlement difficult. For the U.S. negotiators, the issue is the continuation of the military's forward defense strategy in the Pacific. Moreover, as the Pacific Rim continues its dynamic economic growth and political development, that region will be increasingly important for the United States economically, politically, and strategically. The U.S. defense of the sea and air lanes in the Pacific is an important mission for Subic

Bay Naval Station and Clark Air Force Base in the Philippines in providing the U.S. Seventh Fleet maximum flexibility for operations throughout Southeast Asia, in the Indian Ocean, and in Northeast Asia (especially near Japan).[18]

This strategic factor increased in importance in 1975–1976 when the United States lost its bases in Thailand and Vietnam, leaving the Philippine bases the only facilities in Southeast Asia to deter the Soviet Union's buildup of forces in the Far East. This buildup occurred primarily at Cam Ranh Bay (which the Soviets say they will abandon) and Da Nang in Vietnam, bases built and operated by the United States before the Communist victory.

Subic is the largest naval supply depot outside of the United States, and Clark is the center of all air operations from Hawaii to the Indian Ocean and the Persian Gulf. Troops can be airlifted from Clark to the U.S. base at Diego Garcia in case of emergencies in the strategically and economically indispensable Persian Gulf.[19] From the vantage point of U.S. negotiators, the bases are an integral part of an interdependent global network of alliance relationships and strategic facilities among the non-Communist countries of the world.[20]

Those who support retention of the bases have also noted the economic benefits they provide the Philippines. Indeed, an estimated 3 percent of the Philippine GNP is generated, directly or indirectly, from the bases: from the 30,000 U.S. personnel, from the 45,000 Filipinos who work for the bases, and from Filipino businesses established near the bases, as well as from taxes paid by all these employees. An estimated $500 million, a huge amount in a poor country, is generated by the bases each year and fed into the local economy. In addition, compensation for use of the bases was $962 million over a three-year period between 1988 and 1991, an amount that will be renegotiated before the 1991 deadline.

Supporters of the bases argue that a U.S. presence guarantees a U.S. defense umbrella for the Philippines that keeps the military budget lower. If the United States were to withdraw, Philippine tax money would have to be diverted to the military, away from other needed programs. U.S. support for the multibillion-dollar, multiple aid initiative might also be jeopardized if the bases were no longer available. Moreover, U.S. withdrawal would make a military coup easier to carry out. U.S. air power was used to put down the December 1989 coup that came close to overthrowing the democratic government of President Aquino. Potential coup leaders would be less willing to attempt a takeover if the U.S. military could be quickly deployed.

U.S. negotiators have argued that alternatives to Subic and Clark exist but that the costs in money and reduced effectiveness are great. Besides, the United States has bases in Japan, on the island of Guam, and in South Korea, all of which could be updated or expanded to accommodate redeployed personnel. (Numerous political and technical obstacles would make redeployment difficult but not impossible.) None of the alternative sites equals Subic or Clark for proximity to the Persian Gulf and Southeast Asia or for sophistication of facilities.

Despite these problems, the United States may decide to move its bases to several locations in the area. Indeed, one advantage is that such a dispersal would make U.S. forces less vulnerable in war. Singapore, for example, has offered port facilities, and Guam could become a primary repair base, while Australia, South Korea, Japan, and Micronesia could provide air support facilities. These options would be acted upon only if the cost of retaining the Philippine bases is greater than the cost of relocation. Thailand, Malaysia, and Indonesia are reluctant to host bases, although they have supported U.S. bases in the Philippines.

For the Filipino negotiators, the crucial points are not strategic advantage but the issues of nationalism, constitutional principles, compensation, and social problems. Those who argue the nationalist issue state that because the Philippines is no longer threatened by an outside adversary, the U.S. bases are no longer necessary to protect Philippine security and sovereignty. From this viewpoint, the bases are an affront to Philippine sovereignty, a continuing illustration of the dependent relationship between the Philippines and the United States.

The importance of the "special relationship" has decreased as the international situation has changed from emphasis on security to emphasis on economics. From this perspective, the bases are not there to protect Philippine security but to protect U.S. and Japanese economic interests. Moreover, the December 1989 use of U.S. F-4 Phantom fighters stationed at Clark Air Force Base to defeat the coup by keeping rebel aircraft grounded is a reminder that the Philippines has not yet gained complete independence from its former colonial power.

Filipino negotiators have asked whether the bases do not act as a magnet, attracting the kind of catastrophe the bases are supposed to keep from happening. This view suggests that the Soviet Union (or some other adversary) would have to bomb the Philippine bases to be sure that those bases would not be used in a war against it. The bases can project weapons; thus, they would become targets of enemy fire. U.S. negotiators respond that the bases do not have a first-strike capability and hence would not be targeted.

Nationalist concerns also relate to restrictions made by U.S. authorities against Filipinos who work on the bases. In one embarrassing incident, President Marcos himself was not allowed in certain restricted areas. Indeed, the Philippine commandant of the bases is similarly restricted, despite the fact that the Philippine national flag flies over the bases. Limitations also exist on Philippine exercise of criminal jurisdiction in various areas.

The Philippine Constitution states that after the expiration in 1991 of the agreement between the Philippines and the United States, "foreign military bases, troops, or facilities shall not be allowed in the Philippines except under a treaty duly concurred in by the Senate and, when the Congress so requires, ratified by a majority of the votes cast by the people in a national referendum held for that purpose, and recognized as a treaty by the other contracting State."

This important provision requires a two-thirds vote of the Philippine Senate (the U.S. Senate must also approve a new treaty by the same majority). If the Philippine House and Senate so decide, a referendum could be held, but it is not clear if the referendum could precede rather than follow a senate vote. The statement that the MBA expires in 1991 is contrary to the 1966 agreement, which allows the MBA to go beyond that date subject to one year's notice of termination.[21]

A second constitutional provision states that "the Philippines, consistent with the national interest, adopts and pursues a policy of freedom from nuclear weapons in its territory." Although this provision appears to be a straightforward ban on nuclear weapons, the clause "consistent with the national interest" is sometimes interpreted as permitting exceptions for security reasons. The provision is important because the United States has nuclear weapons in its arsenal on Philippine territory, although the official U.S. policy regarding nuclear weapons is to "neither confirm nor deny" their presence. There is ambiguity, therefore, concerning nuclear weapons on ships that dock at Subic and on planes that take off and land at Clark, as long as these weapons are not actually (or literally) on Philippine territory.

The compensation issue is also contentious because it is related to questions of authority over the bases. The United States has rejected the term *rent*, for example, because it connotes Filipino ownership and sovereignty over the bases. There has been much confusion as well over the amount of money actually paid by the United States for use of the bases. Although the U.S. government makes a "best effort" to convince Congress to compensate the Philippines with military assistance grants, military sales, and economic aid, the annual sums are variable depending on U.S. congressional decisions. This variability has been termed unacceptable by the Filipino negotiators, who prefer an annual rent of a specified amount separate from other military and development assistance.

The other disputed issue is the impact the bases have on the quality of life in areas surrounding the bases. From one perspective, the bases have installed a "moral cesspool" in Olongapo and Angeles City. In Olongapo alone, some sixteen thousand prostitutes service sailors on rest and recreation, although AIDS and other sexually transmitted diseases have infected these prostitutes. Unfortunately, the economies of these towns are based on socially undesirable activities, a situation that has fostered a negative reputation for all Filipinos.

All of these issues will discussed by negotiators in the Philippine American Cooperation Talks before the 1991 deadline. The most likely outcome includes a phased withdrawal over a period of, say, ten years, with plans for transforming the bases into private enterprise sites or Philippine bases. A variation of this option is that the United States will stay at Subic but withdraw from Clark. Another option is that the negotiations will fail to reach an agreement satisfactory to the Philippine and the U.S. Congress, in which case the United States would withdraw from both bases forthwith.

In 1991 the war in the Middle East and the foundering Philippine economy softened the Filipino position on issues linked to greater sovereignty, greater Philippine access to base facilities, and more U.S. aid to the Philippine armed forces. Both Clark and Subic, as logistical support centers for the war in the Persian Gulf, created employment opportunities for thousands of Filipinos. By February 1991, the U.S. and Philippine negotiators tentatively agreed that the facilities could stay for another seven years in return for an $825-million-a-year compensation package—almost double the current U.S. rental commitment.

Conclusion

The contemporary Philippine political system is formally democratic, with structures and procedures conducive to an open polity. Informally, however, the system remains oligarchical, ruled by a self-perpetuating elite of landed families that has commanded the political and economic scene for centuries. Figuratively and literally, President Aquino symbolizes this grand contradiction: commitment to democracy versus loyalty to her wealthy family.

In contrast to Thailand, the Philippines has not assimilated modern values with traditional ways in a coherent or harmonious manner. The Philippines also has not brought legitimacy to its government; there is no Philippine parallel to the Thai king. Moreover, the Philippine polity has not met the needs of the people. Indeed, the standard of living of most Filipinos has deteriorated in the past several decades as a result of governmental mismanagement and the greed of the country's leaders. The Philippine capacity to cope with changing demands and to assert its own destiny is problematic.

Notes

1. This theme of development and decay is the focus of David Wurfel's *Filipino Politics: Development and Decay* (Ithaca: Cornell University Press, 1988). This book is the most comprehensive and balanced presentation of Filipino politics available.

2. William Overholt persuasively argues that contrary to the established view that the assassination caused the collapse of the regime or even accelerated Marcos's decline, the assassination was a successful strategem to delay the consequences of the Marcos regime's political, moral, and financial bankruptcy. See William Overholt, "The Rise and Fall of Ferdinand Marcos," *Asian Survey*, vol. XXVI, no. 11, November 1986, pp. 1137–1163.

3. The following paragraphs are taken from the author's *Politics in Southeast Asia* (Rochester: Schenkman Books, 1987).

4. Justus M. van der Kroef, "The Philippines: Day of the Vigilantes," *Asian Survey*, vol. XXVIII, no. 6, June 1988, p. 630.

5. *The Asian Wall Street Journal*, May 21, 1990, p. 18.

6. For a fascinating discussion of the lack of coordination among Philippine ministries, see Raul P. De Guzman, Alex B. Brillantes, Jr., and Arturo G. Pacho, "The Bureaucracy," in *Government and Politics of the Philippines*, ed. Raul P. De Guzman and Mila A. Reforma (Singapore: Oxford University Press, 1988).

7. The best overview of the evolution of political parties in the Philippines is by Luzviminda G. Tancangco, "The Electoral System and Political Parties in the Philippines," in *Government and Politics of the Philippines*, De Guzman and Reforma, eds. The following paragraphs are based on her analysis.

8. Felipe B. Miranda and Ruben F. Ciron, "Development and the Military in the Philippines: Military Perceptions in a Time of Continuing Crisis" in *Soldiers and Stability in Southeast Asia*, ed. J. Soedjati Djiwandono and Yong Mun Cheong (Singapore: Institute of Southeast Asian Studies, 1988), p. 169.

9. De Guzman, Brillantes, and Pacho, "The Bureaucracy," in *Government and Politics of the Philippines*, ed. De Guzman and Reforma, p. 180.

10. Ibid., p. 197.

11. Linda K. Richter, "Exploring Theories of Female Leadership in South and Southeast Asia," paper presented to the Association for Asian Studies, Chicago, April 1990, p. 7.

12. David Joel Steinberg, "The Web of Filipino Allegiance," *Solidarity*, vol. 2, no. 6, March–April 1967, p. 25.

13. Mary R. Hollnsteiner, *The Dynamics of Power in a Philippine Municipality* (Manila: Community Development Research Council, 1963), p. 75.

14. S. K. Jayasuriya, "The Politics of Economic Policy in the Philippines During the Marcos Era," in *Southeast Asia in the 1980s: The Politics of Economic Crisis*, ed. Richard Robison, Kevin Hewison, and Richard Higgott (Sydney: Allen and Unwin, 1987), p. 82.

15. Ibid., p. 83.

16. Ibid., p. 102.

17. Fred Greene, ed., *The Philippine Bases: Negotiating for the Future* (New York: Council on Foreign Relations, 1988), p. 4. Much of the material in this section comes from this comprehensive and balanced account of Philippine–U.S. negotiations over the bases.

18. Gregory P. Corning, "The Philippine Bases and U.S. Pacific Strategy," *Pacific Affairs*, vol. 63, no. 1, Spring 1990, p. 6.

19. Ibid., p. 12.

20. Greene, *The Philippine Bases: Negotiating for the Future*, p. 94.

21. Ibid., p. 22.

5

INDONESIA

With over 180 million inhabitants, making it the fifth most heavily populated nation in the world, Indonesia presents different challenges in its quest for economic and political development than its less populated, more homogeneous neighbors. Almost half of all Southeast Asians live in Indonesia, which has thousands of islands and thirteen major and hundreds of minor ethnic groups. Two-thirds of all Indonesians live on the island of Java, one of the most densely populated areas of the world, while a minority lives in the larger outer islands. Although 90 percent of the population is at least nominally Muslim, the variety of religious beliefs within this Islamic ambiance suggests diversity more than unity. Indonesia is characterized by geographic, linguistic, ethnic, and social heterogeneity; thus, the population has overcome almost insuperable obstacles in achieving nationhood.

In contrast to Thailand and the Philippines, Indonesia experienced a daunting struggle for independence at the end of World War II. Having lived under Dutch colonialism for three hundred and fifty years and then Japanese occupation during the war, during the postindependence period Indonesians looked for a leader who could forge unity within diversity. As spokesman for Indonesian independence, leader of the revolutionary struggle against the Dutch from 1945 to 1949, and first president of independent Indonesia, Sukarno became the charismatic "solidarity maker"—destined, it seemed, to forge a "new Indonesian person." Neither Thailand nor the Philippines needed such a leader because their societies had not been as devastated or torn asunder as Indonesia's.

Postindependence Indonesia can be divided into three periods: (1) parliamentary democracy 1950–1957 (followed by a transition period, 1957–1959); (2) "guided democracy," 1959–1965 (followed by a transition

87

period, 1965–1967); and (3) "new order," 1967 to the present. The first period featured multiple political parties, parliamentary government, and elections. These Western-style governmental forms—adopted to prove to Indonesians that they could govern themselves in a "modern," democratic manner—did not fit well with Indonesian culture, which traditionally placed little value on representation, group formation, and majority-plus-one governance. Eventually, the westernized institutions were blamed for the government's inability to meet the economic needs of the people.

As liberal democracy floundered, Sukarno moved toward a political system based on Indonesian traditions, with Western-style voting replaced by *musjawarah-mufakat*—a traditional method of deliberation-consensus—with Sukarno himself as the ultimate and unchallenged arbiter. The essence of guided democracy was *gotong rojong* (mutual benefit), where in an environment of cooperation and tolerance (rather than competition) decisions could be arrived at with unanimous approval.

To rally support for his guided democracy, Sukarno made nationalism the cornerstone of his ideology. Nationalism was defined as the submergence of regional and ethnic loyalties in favor of national ones, allegiance to Sukarno, indigenous patterns of governance (free from the mentality of colonialism), and the annihilation of neocolonialism. After Sukarno banned most political parties, reduced the power of parliament, and suspended civil liberties, he moved ideologically to the left—embracing the Communist Party of Indonesia (PKI)—and then to the right—strengthening the armed forces—when the PKI became too dominant. Sukarno tried to balance the demands of numerous groups including the PKI, Chinese entrepreneurs, students, rightist Muslims, outer-island groups, and the army.

Although guided democracy was initially supported as an Indonesian antidote to a failed Western system, the deterioration of the economy and the administrative chaos that ensued undermined the unity Sukarno had established. Corruption was flagrant, and the cost of living index rose from a base of one hundred in 1957 to thirty-six thousand in 1965. Unemployment was rampant, and Communists were gaining strength as peasants and workers were armed with Chinese weapons.

In 1965, in one of the most far-reaching events in contemporary Southeast Asia, a group of dissident army officers planned a purge of their high command, which led to an attempted coup d'etat. The result changed Indonesia's political structure fundamentally, decimated the PKI, led to one of the worst bloodbaths in history, and brought into power a military government that has ruled ever since.[1] The precise roles of the PKI, the army generals, the dissident army rebels, and President Sukarno himself in the September 30–October 1 Gestapu coup may never be known, as the evidence is inconclusive and contradictory. What is clear, however, is that General Suharto, the commander of the Strategic Army Reserve, assumed command of the army and captured the leading participants within hours. The coup failed when the army united against the rebels and the population failed to rise in support of the dissidents.

Within a year, the slaughter of hundreds of thousands of Indonesians—mostly suspected Communists—occurred, with the encouragement of the army. During this transitional time (1965–1967), Suharto reduced Sukarno's power, banned the PKI, ended the policy of confrontation (*Konfrontasi*) against Malaysia, rejoined the United Nations, and by 1967 had taken all power for himself. Sukarno died June 21, 1970, at the age of 69, while living under house arrest.

Suharto proclaimed a new order for Indonesia, ending the twenty-year postindependence charismatic, ideological, and ultimately catastrophic leadership of Sukarno and beginning a period of pragmatic, development-oriented, authoritarian, and stable rule that has endured to the present. The first task of the new order was to create a stable and legitimate political system with control throughout the archipelago; the second task was to rehabilitate the shattered economy.

To achieve the first task, the army was purged of pro-Sukarno forces and made the basis of Suharto's power base. Suharto then set up a "government party" called Golkar (an acronym for *golangan karya*, or functional group), which was dominated by the military and administered by officials at every level of government, from national to village. All government officials had to become members, so Golkar developed a nationwide apparatus. Suharto further strengthened Golkar by forcing four Muslim political parties to merge into the United Development Party (PPP), while three secular parties and two Christian parties merged with the Indonesian Democratic Party (PDI). These two parties, which became the formal opposition to Golkar, did not have access to the resources available to Golkar and consequently were not able to challenge Golkar's political dominance.

To give legitimacy to his regime, Suharto agreed to elections for members of the People's Consultative Assembly (MPR), which in turn elected a president and vice president for five-year terms. In these elections, in 1971, 1977, 1982, and 1987, Golkar won 63, 62, 64, and 73 percent of the vote, respectively. Golkar's success is due largely to its ability to mobilize the governmental bureaucracy on its behalf and to persuade voters that the nation's continued economic growth and political stability require the continuation of its rule.

Suharto was as successful in rehabilitating the economy as he was in stabilizing and legitimizing the political system. Assembling a group of Western-educated economic technocrats and listening to their advice, he cut government and defense spending, reduced inflation (from thousands percent during the Sukarno regime to less than 10 percent), greatly increased per capita income, reaped revenues from the sale of oil, and sustained an average annual GNP growth per capita of about 4.8 percent during his tenure in office.

The availability of food improved in Indonesia more rapidly than in comparable developing countries so that the country is now self-sufficient in rice. An Indonesian born in 1985 can expect to live 23 percent longer than one born in 1965.[2] Out of 135 million Indonesians in 1976, 54 million—or 40 percent—were below the poverty level. By 1987, out of 172 million people, only 30 million—or 17 percent—were below the poverty line.

The success of the Indonesian economy (relative to that in the Sukarno period) was the principal cause of widespread support for the Suharto administration. Economic growth brought Suharto legitimacy and undercut allegations by his detractors about the authoritarian nature of his regime. The strength of the economy was integrally related to the regime's political stability.

Institutions and Social Groups

Constitution

Contemporary Indonesia has been ruled under two constitutions: the 1945 constitution for the periods 1945–1949 and 1959 to the present, and the 1950 provisional constitution of 1950–1958. The present constitution calls for a People's Consultative Assembly (MPR) as the highest governmental body in the land. The MPR elects the president and vice president, and each holds office for a term of five years. The president, although responsible to the MPR, is the executive head of the government, in charge of its day-to-day administration. He has overall power over the armed forces, appoints ministers and governors, and promulgates laws.[3]

The MPR consists of 920 members, including the 460 members of the parliament (DPR). One-third of the DPR is appointed by the government from the Indonesian military and from "functional groups," ostensibly to ensure political stability by guaranteeing executive dominance of the legislature.[4] In brief, the constitution was fashioned around a centralized government led by a strong president. Suharto has been able to use the powers delegated to him by the constitution to dominate virtually every aspect of political life in Indonesia.

Military

In no other Southeast Asian nation, with the possible exception of Burma, has the military so pervasively intervened in politics. Now enshrined in state doctrine, the military has set forth the notion of *dwi fungsi*, or dual function, providing the military with both a security and a sociopolitical role in Indonesian society. Through legislation, this dual role has legitimated the military's involvement as members of the cabinet, governors of provinces, members of the legislative body, and leaders of Golkar. It is impossible to imagine in the short term an Indonesian administration without the active participation of army generals.

The Armed Forces of the Republic of Indonesia is characterized by a generational split between veteran soldiers who fought against the Dutch in the 1945–1949 war and younger soldiers who did not. The new generation was educated in Indonesia, and its military training stressed professional subjects. Younger officers, who have gradually taken over most of the top military positions, have supported Suharto (a 1945-generation officer) despite their ambivalence about the legitimacy of dual function. General Try Sutrisno is the first armed forces commander of the new generation.

Although the generational difference will be manifested most clearly when a succession decision occurs, these differences are muted while Suharto is in power because of the universal support he receives from his military subordinates. However, when he chooses not to remain president, both generations will attempt to replace him with a leader who supports their respective groups.

Bureaucracy

Suharto's Indonesia has been characterized as a bureaucratic polity: "a political system in which power and participation in national decisions are limited almost entirely to the employees of the state, particularly the officer corps and the highest levels of the bureaucracy, including especially the highly trained specialists known as the technocrats."[5] Since the beginning of the new order, the president, his personal advisors, selected technocrats, and top-level generals exercise decisive control over national policymaking. This wielding of power has rarely been draconian (the period from 1965 to 1967, when suspected dissidents were executed, was an exception). Instead, bureaucratic leaders have relied on co-optation, manipulation of the electoral process, selected repression, persuasion, and success in meeting the needs of large numbers of Indonesians.

Initially after independence, the bureaucracy was weak because the Dutch had not trained an effective corps of Indonesian officials. However, the establishment in the 1970s of a new corps of civil servants known as *Korpri* made the bureaucracy far more efficient and eventually established its authority throughout the nation. *Korpri* is centralized, with the president appointing the governor in each of the twenty-seven provinces. In contrast to other Southeast Asian countries, the military holds the majority of bureaucratic positions, including most of the governorships.

Suharto is responsible for seeing that a large number of Western-educated technocrats hold important positions in the civil service. They have been responsible, in turn, for much of the success of the economic development programs. A majority of ministers are also viewed as technocrats. As Indonesian universities improve, a new group of indigenously educated civil servants will play increasingly important bureaucratic roles as well.

Political Parties

Since the late 1960s, no party has been able to compete with Golkar, the official party of the government and the military. Golkar functions simultaneously as the principal support of the government and as the representative of the Indonesian people. Golkar was originally established by the military to oppose Communist organizations; thus, the party developed a national apparatus down to the village level.

The other important parties are the PPP and the PDI, two conglomerates of smaller parties that were banned by Suharto. By forcing Muslim parties into the PPP and secular parties into the PDI, Suharto neutralized them as threats to his regime, requiring the new parties to declare the state ideology of *Pancasila* (the five principles of nationalism, democracy, internationalism, social justice, and belief in one God) as their sole ideology. They could no longer set forth an ideologically unique program. Moreover, the government had the power to screen proposed leaders of political parties, exercising veto power over those found unacceptable.

The fifth election since independence and the fourth scheduled election since 1971 occurred in 1987 to choose members of the DPR, the elected body that forms an important element of the MPR. With 90 percent of the population voting, Golkar candidates won 73 percent of the vote, PDI 11 percent, and PPP 16 percent. Golkar candidates ran on a platform calling for the strengthening of democratization within the context of economic development. PDI candidates stressed the needs of the poor, while PPP candidates stressed education, the unequal distribution of resources, and bureaucratic corruption. Because of the requirement that *Pancasila* be the sole principle of the party, the PPP lost support because its claim to represent Muslim interests was diluted. Indeed, the Muslim group, known as *Nahdatul Ulama*, defected from the PPP to become an educational, nonpolitical organization and gave its permission to Muslim adherents to vote for Golkar.

Golkar's overwhelming victories are explained by the party's access to unlimited government funds, which Suharto distributed to his candidates. Also, there was sincere support for Suharto's generally successful endeavors to bring economic stability and growth to Indonesia. Golkar candidates persuaded the electorate that an alternative to their rule jeopardized economic growth. Golkar's victories are also attributable to the nation's civil servants, who used their positions to mobilize the countryside. Further, a prohibition against other parties organizing in rural areas in interelection periods and an injunction against certain criticisms of the government limited free debate on the issues.

If these factors did not prove sufficient, Suharto had set up the legislative body in such a way as to ensure support for his retention of power. He appointed a large number of the members (representing group interests), including military officials who owed their positions to Suharto. Thus, even if a majority of elected members represented the opposition, they could not outvote the appointed members, who were unanimously supportive of Suharto. Having acceded to calls for democratizing his administration by means of this so-called vote, he enhanced his regime's legitimacy in the eyes of the Indonesian citizenry and the world community.

Although there are limitations on campaiging, there is not as much blatant voting fraud as existed in the Philippines under Marcos. Although the results of elections are clear even before a campaign even begins, elections do influence government policy. If only for a short time, Indonesians participate in the political system, expressing their complaints, opinions, and aspirations through subtle forms of communication at campaign rallies, in newspaper letters and editorials, and in public and private interaction.[6]

Women

Indonesian women have not played major political roles at the top levels of the polity. Nonetheless, it would be incorrect to infer that women do not exert some influence on public affairs.[7] As with Malaysian women, Indonesian women are active in political party auxiliaries, but their influence appears to be more indirect than direct. As in most of Southeast Asia, women act as the overall managers of the family unit, while men dominate in the public sphere.

Democratization

Liberal democracy has not flourished in postindependence Indonesia. The one attempt to fashion such a system, which lasted from 1950 to 1957, featured multiple political parties and a parliamentary government. However, that period was a time of great political unrest as the country moved from dependence on its colonizers, the Dutch, to independence. Sukarno, who was president during the transition, paid little attention to the necessary day-to-day administrative tasks; nevertheless, the democratic system was blamed for the collapse of the economy and infrastructure. Consequently, Sukarno's notion of a unique, indigenous form of democracy was readily embraced as more fitting for Indonesia.

Sukarno argued that "50 percent-plus-one" Western parliamentary practices exacerbated rather than solved problems. Therefore, he advocated a "democratic practice" of the villages for Indonesia, where deliberations are held until consensus emerges, in the spirit of *gotong rojong* with himself as the trusted elder.[8] This notion of democracy appeared to fit traditional Javanese value systems in which power is bestowed on one person, usually a sultan. Indonesian political culture is essentially hierarchical and authoritarian: Central authorities cannot tolerate an opposition or any individual gathering power resources independently, as this will endanger the potency of the state.[9] From an Indonesian perspective, therefore, guided democracy is the most effective way to make policy, even if that process is not compatible with Western notions of representative and accountable government.

From a Western perspective, on the other hand, guided democracy assured perpetuation of Sukarno's power at the expense of the liberties and openness available under liberal democracy. From this vantage point, real democracy was not destroyed by a traditional culture but by corrupt, power-hungry politicians who initiated repression and authoritarian institutions to retain their positions. Suharto's new order is viewed from this perspective as the archetypical authoritarian administration that mouths the virtues of democracy but practices the politics of dictatorship.

Rejecting both of these extreme positions, a younger generation of educated officials suggests that, indeed, Western-style democracy is difficult to sustain in a nation that has had virtually no experience with such practice except during a period of grave economic instability. Nevertheless, accountability and civil liberties are not exclusive values of the West, and as Indonesia's population is educated, informed, and economically developed, there is no reason why Western democratic arrangements cannot be adapted. Officials who support Suharto have stated that during his twenty-five years as leader, Indonesia has evolved to where Indonesian-style democracy can begin to be meaningful. The argument is that slow progress toward democracy, institutionalizing each step to make sure it holds, is the most effective way of ensuring continuation of democratic processes.

Those who support an "opening" of the Indonesian system are reacting to the forces of democratization in the region from the Philippines to Burma as well as in Eastern Europe and throughout the Third World. The Indonesian leadership does not want its country to be viewed as having an anachronistic political system in an era of democratization. Hence, Suharto has allowed more and more discussion of the role of parliament and political parties, of the press, and of how to develop a participatory culture.[10] These topics have complemented discussions on how to achieve a more open, stable economy. Such discussions have thus far taken place with the understanding that the military's role in the political life of the republic will continue. Thus, contemporary Indonesia is a classic case of a nation seeking to balance the advantages of an open political and economic society with the advantages of an authoritarian system purportedly based on indigenous values.

Economic Development

Although the Indonesian economy is the largest in Southeast Asia in gross national product, it ranks the lowest among ASEAN countries in annual per capita GNP ($520). Having averaged a 4.8 percent growth rate each year since 1965, the country's current per capita figure reflects the strikingly low base of under $100 when the new order began. Sukarno's "revolutionary" economic system under his guided democracy was isolationist and xenophobic and was skewed to meet ideological goals rather than the needs of the citizenry. Suharto's new order economics sought to provide order to replace the disorder and rationality to replace the irrationality so that economic development would become the yardstick by which the legitimacy of his regime would be measured.

For the most part, the yardstick measured steady although not spectacular growth, but it was enough to buy a substantial share of popular support and political stability. The means to this end were a series of five-year plans to improve the public welfare, a financial bonanza from oil revenues, the advice of economic technocrats, the repair of the infrastructure, and an emphasis on the private sector for necessary capital, structural change, and productivity.[11] Although the results were generally

positive, some difficulties occurred, including widespread income dispar-
ity, corruption, and mismanaged industries.

The most badly managed company was the government-owned oil
industry, Pertamina, which went bankrupt in the 1970s. Led by President
Suharto's colleague, General Ibnu Sutowo, Pertamina incurred huge debts
from lavish spending on useless projects. When oil prices dropped pre-
cipitously from $34 per gallon in 1981 to $8 in the mid-1980s, economic
growth fell correspondingly, ending a decade of greatly increased government outlays for education, infrastructure, and communications.

The importance of oil to the Indonesian economy in the early 1980s
can be seen by noting that oil exports accounted for 78 percent of export
earnings and oil revenues for 70 percent of government revenue at that
time.[12] In 1969, in contrast, oil revenues accounted for only 19 percent of
government revenues. Development budgets grew 2,000 percent between
1973 and 1989 as a result of oil revenues. Oil, no longer the largest share
of exports, has been replaced by manufactured items in this capacity.

When oil prices fell again in 1986, the government was forced into
drastic reforms to keep the economy from slackening. Suharto mobilized
his technocrats to bring order to the economy by making it less reliant
on oil revenues, forcing austerity in budget expenditures so as to reduce
the deficit, and opening the economy to foreign investment and joint
ventures. A series of reform measures was established such as duty-free
zones, liberal investment laws, and less bureaucratic red tape, all designed
to encourage foreign investment. Despite these reforms, the foreign debt
rose to about $50 billion in 1989, the largest in Asia, with a debt service
ratio of about 38 percent. Debt servicing now constitutes a major portion
of the national budget.[13]

The policy of promoting foreign investments and Indonesian exports
replaced the former policy of import substitution, which had been characterized by protectionism and heavy government intervention in dis-
tributing capital. The success of the new policy is shown by the fact that
foreign investment commitments rose more than threefold in a three-year
period, from $1.4 billion in 1987 to $4.7 billion in 1989.

Part of the reason for the great increase in foreign investments is that
Indonesia, like Thailand, has become a major assembly area for manufacturers from Hong Kong, Singapore, Taiwan, and South Korea. Most
investments have been in labor-intensive, low-technology industries such
as footwear, food canning, textiles, and wood processing where Indonesia's
low wages attract entrepreneurs from higher-wage countries.[14] In addition,
the indigenous Chinese, who have long been active in the economy (like
the Chinese throughout Southeast Asia), have been given greater leeway
in return for their support of Golkar. Officials and military officers have
provided Chinese business executives with protection and useful legis-

lation, while the Chinese have supplied capital and access to profits from their businesses. These Chinese, called *cukong* (boss), are resented by Indonesian entrepreneurs who view the *cukong* system as corrupt and exclusive.

The Suharto government initiated its fifth five-year plan in 1989, emphasizing income equity instead of economic growth that ignored the distribution of resources and wealth. These reforms have generally been successful, although income disparities continue to grow. Agriculture, which is still the slowest growth sector in the economy, accounts for 25 percent of the GNP and employs the greatest number of persons, fully 55 percent of the population. Indonesia has reached self-sufficiency in rice, partly as a result of the "green revolution," which provided fertilizers, new seed varieties, and pesticides, but more importantly because of the technological sophistication that farmers throughout the republic learned from outreach programs.

The Indonesians' quality of life has improved in numerous ways. Life expectancy has increased significantly in just one decade: from 50 years in 1980 to 60 years in 1990. (Thailand's life expectancy, however, is 65; the Philippines' is 66; Malaysia's is 67; Vietnam's is 64; and Singapore's is 73; whereas Burma's is 58 and Cambodia's is 48.) Infant mortality rates have also improved: In 1971, 132 of 1,000 newborns died before their first birthdays, but by 1985 the rate had declined to 71 deaths in 1,000 births (compared to 45 deaths in the Philippines, 39 in Thailand, and 24 in Malaysia).[15]

These improvements are a major factor in explaining the stability of the economy and the polity and the high level of legitimacy accorded the Suharto administration. Accordingly, contemporary Indonesia is a good example of a nation whose economic performance is largely responsible for the legitimacy of the regime. At the same time, its high level of economic development is the most important force moving the country toward a more open political system.

The Indonesian State

The diversity of its population and its demographic character make Indonesia a difficult state to control. Nevertheless, a strong, autonomous state has emerged in new order Indonesia. The state controls all aspects of political and economic life and has co-opted all institutions that could even potentially challenge the state. Even so, the Indonesian state enjoys a legitimacy known by few other states because of its capacity to meet the economic needs of the citizenry and its protection of the country's security, both internally and externally.

The new order administration in Indonesia intervened in the economy with generally positive results. This contrasts with the situation in the Philippines, where the Marcos administration brought the economy to ruin through corrupt and self-interested policies, and in Thailand, where the state intervened only minimally. Thus, the Indonesian model lies between the activist (but corrupt) interventionist Philippine model and the laissez-faire Thailand version.

The Indonesian state, unlike that in the Philippines, is not subservient to particular societal forces. Instead, all potentially powerful groups have been integrated into the bureaucratic polity. However, the military plays the most important role in the bureaucracy in determining public policy. Most political institutions, such as the legislature and the primary political party, Golkar, are creatures of the bureaucracy and are led by President Suharto. Even the Chinese support Golkar in return for political protection and market monopolies.

The most prominent societal groups that are not integrated into the Indonesian state are the Muslim parties, although most of these have been emasculated under Suharto. The insistence that all parties adopt *Pancasila* was a successful attempt to depoliticize Islamic groups. When a group of prominent retired generals, known as the *Petisi Kelompok 50* (Group of 50 Petition), criticized Suharto and his administration for using *Pancasila* to undermine political opposition, the government-dominated parliament ignored the petition.[16] This autonomy from societal groups defines the Indonesian state as strong.

Indonesia has had a history of social dislocation, which is the first condition for the development of a strong state. Like the Philippines, Indonesia experienced a long colonial rule (three hundred and fifty years as the Dutch East Indies) during which its economy served Dutch interests through the exploitation of Indonesia's natural resources. The impact of the Spanish and Americans on the Philippines was greater than that of the Dutch on the Indonesians, perhaps because the Indonesians' values were more deeply ingrained.

The Japanese occupation of Indonesia, while not as devastating as in the Philippines, was an important event. Indonesia and the Philippines present a striking contrast to Thailand, where there was neither colonialism nor occupation. Moreover, Indonesia waged a four-year war against the Dutch, who returned to retake their former colony after the defeat of the Japanese; thus, a revolutionary war led to rebellions and civil wars between contenders for power.

More recently, the Indonesian state experienced a major bloodbath when, following the Gestapu coup of 1965, about half a million Indonesians were killed. Despite their enormity, the killings did not become an international story or a focus of worldwide attention, perhaps because the new government in Indonesia was allied with the United States and was anti-Communist during the height of the cold war. The violence spread as racial, religious, ethnic, social, economic, and political differences were judged to be sufficient cause for mass killings. What began as a political cleansing to oust Communists became an orgy of killing and a breakdown of law and order. The PKI, which had once had nineteen million members, was virtually annihilated. Together, these episodes suggest that Indonesia has had the necessary dislocations for the development of a strong state.[17]

Strong states may also arise when external forces take advantage of crises to concentrate state control. For instance, the Indonesian state was strengthened during the era of the new order when the United States and international agencies poured aid and grants into the country to ensure that the republic would not become Communist. Indonesia was often named as one of the "dominoes" if Vietnam fell to the Communists; thus, Western countries strengthened the state under Suharto to preclude such a fall. Suharto himself often referred to outside threats as a reason for the necessity of authoritarian rule.

Suharto brought various groups of people into his rule who were independent of existing bases of social control yet skillful enough to execute the designs of his administration. The technocrats fit nicely into this category; they brought order to the economy and thereby managed to strengthen Suharto's claim to power. Even more important have been the military leaders who were loyal to Suharto and who consolidated their power around the regime. The prominence of these independent, skilled groups also led to a strong Indonesian state.

Clearly, Suharto qualifies as an able leader who brought Indonesia into the modern world, rationalized the economy, and is responsible for twenty-five years of political stability. His capability does not come from charisma, which he decidedly lacks. On the contrary, his strength has come from his capacity to provide effective government and economic development. In this sense he has succeeded, at least as long as the economic indicators remain positive. From all these perspectives, then, Indonesia has met the conditions for a strong state but primarily because of its capacity to cope with changing demands and conditions.

Foreign Policy

As in other Southeast Asian nations, the primary goal of Indonesia's postindependence foreign policy has been to sustain the republic's security.

Sukarno's means to this end have included anti-Western nationalism, opposed to the old established forces (OLDEFOS) and allied with the newly emerging forces (NEFOS). OLDEFOS is also defined as neoimperialist nations and their allies, and the United States symbolizes this grouping. NEFOS, on the other hand, stands for "progressive" Third-World and Communist nations, struggling against OLDEFOS. Sukarno's *Konfrontasi* against Malaysia, which began in 1962 and ended in 1965, was described as a classic example of a NEFOS struggle against an OLDEFOS lackey. Supporting Sukarno's foreign policy against the agents of neocolonialism, colonialism, and imperialism was the PKI.

When his new order was inaugurated, Suharto ended *Konfrantasi*, banned the PKI, and reentered the international arena with a pro-Western, anti-Communist foreign policy. New order Indonesia's quiet support for ASEAN and the Zone of Peace, Freedom, and Neutrality in Southeast Asia reflected its leadership's lower profile in international relations. During the twenty-five years of the Suharto regime, Indonesia has played only a minor role in international affairs, despite the fact that the nation is the fifth largest (in population) in the world and is of immense importance economically, geographically, and strategically.

The major exception to Indonesia's nonintrusive participation in foreign affairs was Suharto's decision to invade the former Portuguese colony of East Timor within the Indonesian archipelago. Suharto feared that an independent, possibly Communist Timorese republic would become a base for destabilizing Indonesia. Accordingly, he annexed East Timor in 1975–1976, and made it Indonesia's twenty-seventh province. This action exacerbated a vigorous guerrilla insurgency movement, which has continued since the annexation.

Indonesia, which has played a quiet role in attempting to resolve the Cambodian crisis, hosted the Jakarta Informal Meetings in 1989 and 1990. However, these talks proved unsuccessful in settling the many issues among all the nations involved. Then, as relations between Indonesia and the People's Republic of China improved after two decades of conflict following the Gestapu coup, Indonesian foreign policy moved closer to that of the other ASEAN countries. Thailand in particular had made accommodations with China, viewing Vietnam as the major threat to Southeast Asia's security. Indonesia, on the other hand, saw China as the primary threat and had numerous ties with Vietnam. Its improved relations with China provided Indonesia with a more balanced regional foreign policy. In August 1990, the two countries formally established diplomatic relations, ending twenty-five years of hostility. The United States, Japan, South Korea, Taiwan, and Western European nations continued to be Indonesia's main markets and sources of investment and development assistance.

Conclusion

President Suharto will be eligible for a sixth five-year term in 1992. Because he has been the only leader of most Indonesians, the succession question is of increasing interest and concern. In fact, succession discussions revolve around the issues of political stability, economic development, and democratization. Indonesians have lived under Suharto's new order strong state with its generally high capacity for effective governance, albeit an authoritarian rule that is dominated by the military.

Indonesia's modernization has opened the society to the rise of a more educated and economically well-off middle class with information about Western ways. The populace will therefore seek a fit between its indigenous values and those of the Western world. Moreover, the people will seek leadership that can cope with the problems of uneven distribution of income, urban growth, the concentration of population on the island of Java, the integration of ethnic minorities, corruption at all levels of the administration, and the rise of Islamic militants. The military, of course, will insist that it play a major role in resolving these problems.

In 1989, U.S. Ambassador Paul Wolfowitz caused a national debate by calling for greater political openness to accompany the progress made in economic liberalization. That is the crucial task for future governments: to create a process that will allow democratic openness while ensuring political stability and continued economic growth.

Notes

1. For varied views of the Gestapu coup, see Benedict Anderson and Ruth T. McVey, *A Preliminary Analysis of the October 1, 1965, Coup in Indonesia*, Interim Report Series, Modern Indonesia Project (Ithaca, N.Y.: Cornell University Press, 1971); Arnold C. Brackman, *The Communist Collapse in Indonesia* (New York: Norton, 1969); Peter J. Dommen, "The Attempted Coup in Indonesia," *China Quarterly*, no. 25, January/June 1966, pp. 144–170; John Hughes, *Sukarno: A Coup That Misfired, A Purge That Ran Wild* (New York: McKay, 1967); Justus van der Kroef, "Origins of the 1965 Coup in Indonesia: Probabilities and Alternatives," *Journal of Southeast Asian Studies*, vol. 3, September 1972, pp. 277–298; Tarzie Vittachi, *The Fall of Sukarno* (New York: Praeger, 1967); W. F. Wertheim, "Suharto and the Untung Coup—The Missing Link," *Journal of Contemporary Asia*, vol. 1, no. 2, Winter 1970, pp. 50–57.

2. Donald Emmerson, "The Military and Development in Indonesia" in *Soldiers and Stability in Southeast Asia,* ed. J. Soedjati Djiwandono and Yong Mun Cheong (Singapore: Institute of Southeast Asian Studies, 1988), p. 109.

3. For a detailed discussion of the constitution and formal structures of government in Indonesia, see Colin MacAndrews, ed., *Central Government and Local Development in Indonesia* (Oxford: Oxford University Press, 1986).

4. Leo Suryadinata, "Indonesia," in *Politics in the ASEAN States,* ed. Diane K. Mauzy (Kuala Lumpur: Maricans, 1986), p. 120.

5. Karl D. Jackson and Lucian Pye, eds., "Bureaucratic Polity: A Theoretical Framework for the Analysis of Power and Communications in Indonesia," in *Political Power and Communications in Indonesia,* ed. Karl D. Jackson (Los Angeles: University of California Press, 1978), p. 3.

6. Harry Tjan Silalahi, "The 1987 Election in Indonesia," in *Southeast Asian Affairs 1988* (Singapore: Institute of Southeast Asian Studies, 1988), p. 98.

7. Ann Ruth Willner, "Expanding Women's Horizons in Indonesia: Toward Maximum Equality with Minimum Conflict," in *Asian Women in Transition,* ed. Sylvia A. Chipp and Justin J. Green (University Park: Pennsylvania State University Press, 1980), p. 187.

8. Ulf Sundhaussen, "Indonesia: Past and Present Encounters with Democracy," in *Democracy in Developing Countries: Asia,* ed. Larry Diamond, Juan J. Linz, and Seymour Martin Lipset (Boulder, Colo.: Lynne Rienner Publishers, 1989), pp. 448–449.

9. Ibid., p. 455.

10. Gordon Hein, "Indonesia in 1988," *Asian Survey,* vol. 29, no. 2, February 1989, p. 124.

11. Geoffrey B. Hainsworth, "Indonesia: On the Road to Privatization?" *Current History,* vol. 89, no. 545, March 1990, p. 121.

12. H. W. Arndt and Hal Hill, "The Indonesian Economy: Structural Adjustment After the Oil Boom," *Southeast Asian Affairs 1988* (Singapore: Institute of Southeast Asian Studies, 1988), p. 107.

13. Gordon Hein, "Indonesia in 1989," *Asian Survey,* vol. 30, no. 2, February 1990, p. 227.

14. *Far Eastern Economic Review,* April 19, 1990, p. 42.

15. Ibid., p. 46.

16. Suryadinata, "Indonesia," in *Politics in the ASEAN States,* ed. Mauzy, p. 127.

17. Many of the ideas in this section come from Donald K. Emmerson, "Beyond Zanzibar: Area Studies, Comparative Politics, and the 'Strength' of the State in Indonesia," paper presented to the Association for Asian Studies, Chicago, April 1990.

6

MALAYSIA

Malaysia has emerged as Southeast Asia's strongest open polity and economy. With a per capita income of over $2,000, Malaysia is Southeast Asia's next NIC. Only the citizens of the city-state of Singapore have a higher standard of living than Malaysia's seventeen million people. This is especially noteworthy because of the country's ethnic and geographic diversity. Malaysia consists of the peninsula (formerly Malaya), which is connected to southern Thailand, and Sabah and Sarawak on the island of Borneo, which the South China Sea separates from the peninsula by more than one thousand miles.

There is no more powerful force in Malaysian society than communalism: division of the country into ethnic communities, 48 percent Malay, 36 percent Chinese, 9 percent Indian, and the rest smaller minorities. The Malays are Muslim, mostly agricultural, rural *bumiputera* ("sons of the soil"), while the non-Malays are urban non-Muslim immigrants usually employed in industry, trades, and textiles.

Immigrants to Malaysia from 1860 to 1940 were mostly impoverished workers and peasants from South China who came during the British colonial administration to work the tin mines and perform labor Malays scorned. Their separateness was reinforced even as they expanded their economic roles, becoming money lenders, middlemen, contractors, and manufacturers. Their primary stress on education and ambition provided mobility so that at present the Chinese are the wealthiest business executives in every area of the economy. These facts parallel the condition in other Southeast Asian nations, except that they are magnified in Malaysia because the number of Chinese is almost 50 percent of the population in contrast to 10 percent for the rest of the region.[1]

Communalism has resulted in stereotyping Malaysia's ethnic groups. Malays view the Chinese as aggressive, acquisitive, unscrupulous in business dealings, ritually unclean, and politically suspect. Chinese, on the other hand, view themselves as hardworking, progressive, competitive, and faithful to their families. To the Chinese, the typical Malay is lazy and superstitious and without motivation for hard work or personal advancement, whereas Malays view themselves as scrupulous in their dealings with others and as more concerned with the quality of human relationships than with material acquisition.[2]

To mitigate ethnic differences, the British arranged the Bargain when they relinquished colonial authority over Malaya (not yet Malaysia) in 1957. The Bargain included constitutional advantages to the Malays; support for a Malay as head of state (*Yang diPertuan Agong*), chosen from the nine Malay sultans; Malay as the country's official language; and Islam as the official religion. Also, the constitution provided special privileges to Malays in land acquisition, educational assistance, and civil service employment.

To meet the terms of the Bargain, the leading Malay, Chinese, and Indian political parties formed an alliance with the understanding that non-Malays would prevail in the economic sector while Malays would control the political sector. As long as that formula was accepted by all groups, the Malaysian political system was stable. When the formula was challenged in May 1969 following a national election, rioting ensued, causing the deaths of at least 196 persons and precipitating declaration of a state of emergency that lasted almost two years.

Britain continued to exercise influence over Malaya; over Britain's self-governing colony, Singapore; and over the dependencies of North Borneo (now Sabah), Sarawak, and Brunei (all situated on the island of Borneo). In 1963 Malaya joined with Singapore, Sabah, and Sarawak to form the Federation of Malaysia. All of these areas shared a common colonial heritage under Great Britain, and all feared that without collaboration, they could not function as viable and autonomous nation-states. To offset the integration of three million Chinese from Singapore into the federation, Sabah and Sarawak were brought in to maintain a favorable proportion of non-Chinese in the population. Singapore was given wide-ranging autonomy over its domestic affairs.

The federation lasted only two years until August 1965, when Malaysia's first prime minister, Tunku Abdul Rahman, expelled Singapore for many complex reasons inextricably bound up with communal problems. The prime minister of Singapore, Lee Kuan Yew, called for a "Malaysian Malaysia"—that is, for a Malaysia with equal participation from all areas and groups. His call opposed and contrasted with Tunku Abdul Rahman's design for a "Malayan Malaysia," with special privileges reserved for the dominant ethnic group. When Lee Kuan Yew attempted to influence the larger area of Malaysia, Tunku Abdul Rahman regarded the attempt as a direct threat to continued political dominance by the Malays.

The 1969 communal riots were a watershed event in Malaysia's post-independence era, and their immediate cause was erosion of support for the Alliance party in the 1969 elections. In the preceding two elections, in 1959 and 1964, the Alliance party won an overwhelming majority of the parliamentary seats. In 1969, for the first time the opposition parties won a majority (51.5 percent) of the votes against the Alliance party's 48.5 percent. Although Alliance candidates still controlled a majority in the parliament despite losing twenty-three seats, the 1969 election showed that the Alliance party's capacity to govern was seriously impaired. To celebrate their "victory," anti-Alliance forces paraded in the streets of the capital, Kuala Lumpur. Later, on May 13, Alliance supporters paraded, which led to communal tensions to the point of provoking mob action that raged for four days.

The Malaysian government viewed the riots as a threat to the ethnic Bargain which had been the formula for civic stability. To ensure that Malays retained political power, a state of emergency was proclaimed, parliament was temporarily disbanded, civil liberties were curtailed, and total authority was granted to a National Operations Council (NOC). The NOC worked to restore order and the eventual return to parliamentary democracy. The rights of Malays were extended by reserving for them a proportion of positions in higher education and certain businesses, and sedition acts were passed that prohibited discussion of such "sensitive issues" as the prerogatives of Malay rulers, special rights for Malays, and official status for the Malay language. This twenty-one-month period was a time of suspended democracy.

Believing that economic tensions were mainly responsible for the communal riots, Tun Razak, the new prime minister, proposed a new economic policy to promote national unity and a just society by attacking poverty and "reducing and eventually eliminating the identity of race with economic function." In essence, this meant that Malay participation in the economic sphere was to be increased by granting special privileges in terms of business ownership, tax breaks, investment incentives, and employment quotas.

By 1972 parliamentary democracy returned, albeit within the constraints of the sedition acts and the reworking of the Alliance into a National Front (*Barisan Nasional*). Tun Razak established the National Front to assure dominance of the political system by Malays and to preclude upheavals such as the 1969 riots. His National Front, having co-opted most of the opposition parties, won 90 percent of the parliamentary seats in the 1974 election.

When Razak died in 1976 he was succeeded by Tun Hussein Onn who, like his predecessors, came from a prestigious ancestry and great wealth and had a Western education. He continued front policies until 1981 when, following a serious illness, he resigned and was succeeded by Deputy Prime Minister Dr. Datuk Seri Mahathir bin Mohamad. Mahathir, the first commoner prime minister, with no aristocratic ancestry or family wealth and with a local education, symbolized the new Malaysian technocrat. His brash and confrontational style was the opposite of his refined predecessors.

Mahathir became an articulate spokesman in modern Malaysia's bid to develop economically. His Look East policy argued that Western nations were not appropriate models for Malaysia. He believed that Malaysia should emulate the methods of Japan, South Korea, and Taiwan, all Asian countries whose values were more in tune with those of Malaysia. He also introduced the idea of Malaysia Incorporated, whereby business and government leaders would work together as in a modern corporation. His policy of privatization of public utilities, communications, and transportation is an example of his attempt to bring the profit motive and increased efficiency to the Malaysian economy.

In the 1982 parliamentary election, Mahathir and the National Front triumphed, winning 132 of 154 seats. Again in 1986, the National Front won a landslide victory, winning 148 of the 177 parliamentary seats, but this election marked the beginning of a period of political and economic difficulties. Strife among the leaders of the major parties in the Front occurred as the country underwent a major recession, which brought a negative economic growth for the first time since independence.

The major problem was within the United Malay Nationalist Organization (UMNO), the dominant party of the National Front and the "home" of Mahathir (as well as all former prime ministers). Strife in UMNO led to the resignation of high-ranking officials, some of whom joined a faction known as Team B, who then challenged the leadership of Mahathir and his followers, known as Team A. In the elections for leadership of UMNO in April 1987 (the most important elections in Malaysia because they determine the top party and government leadership), Mahathir barely beat his challenger, Team B leader and Trade and Industry Minister Tunku Razaleigh Hamzah, when of the 1,479 voting UMNO delegates he won by only 43 votes, 761 to 718. In a shocking display of internecine factionalism, Team B officials accused Mahathir of blatant abuse of power, authoritarian leadership, economic mismanagement, and corruption.[3]

Razaleigh had run against Mahathir following five years of a recessionary economy, including a 1 percent decline in the GNP, which disillusioned the Chinese and the new Malay middle class. Mahathir's confrontational administrative style had also become controversial. The challenge to Mahathir was especially noteworthy because it is the custom of Malays not to challenge their leaders; generally, Malaysians believe in *taat setia* (absolute loyalty) to their rulers. It is considered a case of *kurang ajar* (impropriety) to question the leadership. This electoral challenge undermined this important custom in Malay politics.[4]

In response, Mahathir purged Team B members from his cabinet and from UMNO leadership, and he invoked the Internal Securities Act, ordering the arrest of persons critical of government actions. Also, three opposition newspapers were closed, and Operation Lallang was ordered: a sweep by the Malaysian police (on October 27, 1987) that detained 119 persons who had been accused of threatening internal security by provoking communal conflict. All those arrested were members of religious, political, and social organizations that, merely by criticizing regime policies, had qualified themselves as "thorns in our side."[5]

In still another stunning incident related to UMNO factionalism, the Malaysian high court decreed that since unregistered regional branches had participated in the UMNO elections, UMNO was an illegal organization. The high court's decision was a shocking development because UMNO had won every election since independence. Immediately, there was a scramble to register a new party with UMNO in its name and to lay claim to the party's considerable assets. After the rejection of Team B's applications, Mahathir was able to get *UMNO Baru* (New UMNO) registered. A dissident faction, again led by Razaleigh, formed a new party, *Semangat '46* (Spirit of '46, the year of UMNO's birth), and allied itself with other opposition groups to form an alternative party known as *Angkatan Perpaduan Umnah* (APU). In subsequent by-elections, the National Front, led by *UMNO Baru*, won six of eight against APU as well as winning the national election in October 1990.

Because of high court decisions that Mahathir believed were against the interests of the National Front, he reduced the power of the courts by taking away their right to judicial review of executive decisions on internal security and matters concerned with the administration and running of political parties. Indeed, in 1988 he forced a constitutional amendment through parliament that eliminated the constitutional basis of judicial review and replaced it with "such powers as parliament shall grant." Ostensibly, this reduction was to ensure that in threats to the nation's security, an executive could move with dispatch rather than having to wait for the cumbersome courts to deliberate. Eventually, at Mahathir's instigation, a specially created tribunal removed a majority of court justices from office.

In early 1989 Mahathir suffered a heart attack and underwent a successful multiple coronary by-pass. His rapid recovery restored him as the central figure of contemporary Malaysian politics, and he moved toward the 1990 elections with confidence as the National Front began to recover from factional struggles and as the economy recovered from recession.

The strong economy (estimated economic growth rate of 9 percent in 1990) was the principal factor in the overwhelming election victory Mahathir and the multiracial National Front coalition achieved in October 1990. After only a ten-day campaign, the shortest in any Southeast Asian nation, he won a two-thirds majority, thus ensuring control over constitutional amendments. The National Front won 127 of the 180 seats in parliament despite the strongest opposition campaign in modern Malaysian history.

Institutions and Social Groups

Political Parties

The Alliance (in the pre-1969 period) and the National Front are coalitions of parties, joined together by the common goals of winning elections and securing societal stability. These goals have for the most part been achieved. Three parties composed the Alliance: UMNO, the Malayan Chinese Association, and the Malayan Indian Congress. Representing the three major ethnic groups, these parties accepted the Alliance formula to legitimize the interests of these ethnic groups. The formula required that each group accept the basic societal division: Malays dominate the political sphere, and Chinese and Indians dominate the economy.

When the formula broke down in 1969, the Alliance was transformed into the National Front, which consisted of the three Alliance parties as well as a further coalition of former opposition parties led by *Partai Islam Se-Malaysia* (PAS), the country's strongest Islamic party, and the Democratic Action Party (DAP), the principal Chinese opposition. Thus, the Front has eleven component parties, but UMNO is the senior partner and has the final say over coalition decisions.[6] Every Malaysian prime minister has been a member of UMNO.

In 1988, when the courts found UMNO unlawful on the grounds that delegates sent to the assembly had not been properly chosen, the country was stunned. For most Malays, UMNO had embodied their culture, aspirations, and belief in the Malays' right to rule their country. The rapid transformation of UMNO into *UMNO Baru* (with *Baru* subsequently deleted) was important to retain the country's legitimacy. For the first time since independence, UMNO was challenged by a party organization, *Semangat '46*, led by a Malay and strong enough to defeat the National Front. Having allied with APU (which included PAS and DAP), the opposition provided the first viable alternative to the UMNO-dominated Front.

However, APU's strength was found wanting in the 1990 elections when some eight million registered Malaysians voted. For the first time, a multiracial opposition coalition led by a Malay (Razaleigh) was in a position to challenge the Front. Candidates representing the National Front capitalized on the issues of economic growth and political stability to achieve their electoral victory. They also warned the populace against the unwieldy alliance of the main Chinese opposition party (DAP) with a fervent Muslim party (PAS) that wanted Malaysia to become an Islamic state. The opposition's focus on issues of human rights, press freedom, lower taxes, and Mahathir's combative personality were not as credible to the voters.

The other advantage of the National Front has been UMNO's access to funds. UMNO has transformed itself into a huge business conglomerate with assets in numerous corporations. Although conglomerates throughout Southeast Asia rely on government patronage, no assemblage of companies owned directly by a political party appears to have benefited from government largesse to the same extent as UMNO's holdings.[7] Neither opposition nor allied parties in the Front have access to such funds.

Compared to political parties in Thailand and the Philippines, UMNO is highly institutionalized as a party, which makes it a potent instrument of government. Every Malaysian prime minister has reached that position because he has led UMNO, whereas Thai and Filipino leaders have reached the top governmental position in other ways, reflecting the lesser importance and institutionalization of their parties and party systems.

Bureaucracy

In Thailand, the bureaucracy has been the core of political action; in Malaysia, however, the politicians have dominated the decision-making process with the bureaucrats in the role of implementors. There is no bureaucratic polity in Malaysia despite the bureaucracy's strength, which was built up under the British. The role of extra-bureaucratic institutions, especially political parties, has impinged upon the centrality of the bureaucracy. Malaysia's bureaucracy includes Southeast Asia's most sophisticated and highly educated technocrats.

State Royalty

Malaysia's means of choosing its monarch is unique. Nine states have hereditary rulers known as sultans, and the *Yang diPertuan Agong* is elected from this body of nine (usually on the basis of seniority) for a term of five years. This king, who has ceremonial and religious duties and powers of appointment, can delay certain legislative bills (although this power has been circumscribed). The king is not held in the same awe as the king of Thailand, who is venerated by virtually all Thais; nevertheless, he plays an important symbolic role as the Malay head of state.

Legislature

Malaysia's political system is based on the British model, with a bicameral parliament that elects one of its own members to the prime ministership. The prime minister must sit in the lower house of representatives (*Dewan Ra'ayat*) and must command majority support. The upper chamber, the senate (*Dewan Negara*), has fifty-eight members, twenty-six elected and thirty-two appointed by the king after recommendation by the prime minister. Senators hold office for six years; representatives serve five years unless parliament is dissolved sooner than that. Although representation is based on single-member constituencies, a weighting of constituencies in favor of rural areas enhances Malay representation—in effect almost guaranteeing Malay political power.[8]

Military

In contrast to Thailand, Indonesia, and Burma, the Malaysian military has not played a major role in politics. In the early years of independence, priority was given to socioeconomic development goals rather than to building large armed forces.[9] When it received its independence, Malaysia had less than one army division, no air force, and no navy. Instead, it relied on a defense arrangement, the Anglo-Malayan Defence Agreement, which was superseded by the Five-Power Defence Arrangement (with Singapore, Great Britain, Australia, and New Zealand). The average 13 percent government expenditure for the military is lower than that in most of the other nations of Southeast Asia.

Modernization of Malaysia's armed forces helped bring "the Emergency" to an end in 1960 after a twelve-year struggle between Communist-controlled insurgents and government troops. Malaysian forces were also strengthened during the era of Indonesia's *Konfrontasi* policy against Malaysia in the 1960s when Indonesian President Sukarno sought to bring down the "neocolonial" Malaysian government. When Vietnam invaded Cambodia in December 1978, once again the Malaysian military perceived a threat to the nation's security.

Opposition Groups

In Malaysia, all Malays are Muslim by legal definition. Islam provides both legal and political privileges to Malays that if lost are tantamount to renunciation of the Malay way of life. Islam, which does not separate secular from religious activities, is tightly organized from the village up to the state level; hence, Muslims can be easily mobilized. Muslim youth groups (*Dakwah*), which tend to be fundamentalist and anti-Western, call for rigid codes of conduct and the implementation of Islamic law, and this increase in Islamic militancy is viewed as threatening by the non-Muslim population. Mahathir has attempted to defuse the Islamic resurgence by a program of "absorption of Islamic values," but this issue fans the contentious flames of communalism.

The religious element is central to the political party orientations of Malaysians. In the independence period, parties were formed that were defined almost exclusively in terms of their degree of Islamic orthodoxy. Although thus far moderate Islamic parties have been dominant in the ruling alliance, the principal opposition parties (such as DAP) are made up of Islamic fundamentalists, and they use their religious doctrines for political objectives.

Chinese citizens also join political parties that reflect their ethnicity. Most Chinese have joined moderate parties such as the Malaysian Chinese Association (which has affiliated with the National Front), but radical parties have arisen among the Chinese as a result of fear of Islamic militancy and economic policies that threaten the leading Chinese role in the economy.

Communist guerrillas have fought against Malaysian administrations since 1948 when members of the Malayan Communist Party, having participated in the war against the Japanese, took arms against a state they saw as fascist and anti-Chinese. Known as "the Emergency," this struggle threatened Malayan sovereignty until 1960 when the military prevailed, although sporadic fighting continued up to 1989. At that time, the MCP agreed to disarm. As the insurgency was carried out primarily by ethnic Chinese, their actions further worsened racial relations and raised questions about Chinese loyalty to the government.

Women

Women's roles in Malaysian politics have been subordinated to those of men because of Moslem teachings and traditional customs, which taught that women were to be modest and to stay in the background. If publicly active, women were regarded with amusement and then indignation. In the past, women have not been able to occupy high public office.[10]

With the increase in influence of conservative Islam, women's roles in politics will continue to be circumscribed. Nevertheless, westernization has brought more women into professional and business positions. Moreover, the present minister for trade and industry, Puan Rafidah, has been a highly visible woman in national affairs and an active representative of Malaysia internationally.

In party politics, women have formed auxiliary groups to ensure separate involvement. These auxiliaries have provided women with a way to involve themselves in the affairs of the parties while holding to Islamic customs that separate the public activities of men and women.[11] The separateness has guaranteed that women would not be brought into the internal workings of the political parties and that they would not participate in public activities.

Democratization

Compared to its neighbors in Southeast Asia, Malaysia has managed to sustain the institutions of democratic rule. The major exception, following the riots of 1969, was a temporary state of emergency, carried out less as a coup d'etat than as an interlude during which to rebuild parliamentary democracy.

In contrast to the Indonesians and Vietnamese, from their beginning as a nation Malaysians had the advantage of not having to struggle against the return of their colonialist ruler, Great Britain. The granting of independence was carried out peacefully and was received with some reluctance by the Malaysians, who feared their country's viability would be jeopardized without the support of Great Britain. Nevertheless, the Malaysians adopted the Westminster model of governance, including regularized competitive elections, a representative parliament, separation of powers, and civilian supremacy and civil liberties. This is especially noteworthy because Malaysian elites tend to hold a formalized view of democracy, which crumbles when it faces more deeply held values; stability and security, for example, take precedence over democratic values.[12] The best example of this phenomenon is the universal acceptance of emergency rule in 1969.

Since independence, Malaysia has witnessed eight national elections—in 1959, 1964, 1969, 1974, 1978, 1982, 1986, and 1990. Opposition candidates won about 40 percent of the votes, although their numbers in the parliament were few. In the same period there have been four orderly successions of power. Despite this record, Malaysia is generally regarded as a quasi- or semidemocracy because of limitations on civil liberties.[13] Its Official Secrets Act, Internal Securities Act, and Sedition Act have imposed a culture of silence on citizens and prohibited all discussion of "sensitive issues." Newspapers, television, and radio are government or UMNO controlled and are generally compliant vis-à-vis all communalism issues. Newspapers that raised "sensitive issues" after the 1987 split in UMNO were shut down when Mahathir invoked the Internal Securities Act.

The explanation for the necessity of quasi-democracy rather than full, Western-style democracy is that the polycommunal situation in Malaysia is unique. Such a society cannot carry out its affairs in a fully democratic way if one segment of the society must be given special privileges of governance. For example, under such a system the loss of an election is tantamount to total defeat. In the context of communal issues, an election loss by the Alliance and then by the National Front would mean the perceived end of the primary rights of the Malays. That is why emergency rule was necessary in 1969 once the leadership realized that the prospect of an election loss was possible.

The rules for Malaysian democracy, which had to be modified after 1969 to ensure the continuation of Malay political supremacy, were changed to include opposition parties in the Alliance.[14] Dividing the nation along ethnic lines between those in power and those not in power would only worsen communal issues. To mitigate divisiveness, the National Front was created to include a wider range of parties. Even the Islamic-based PAS was initially included in the National Front, but it later withdrew to join the Chinese-oriented DAP in leading the opposition. The Front formula was uniquely Malaysian, reflecting the difficult ethnic sensitivities that have long been the core of Malaysian politics.

In 1987 the formula broke down when factionalism arose in the National Front and Prime Minister Mahathir responded harshly. The eruption of serious problems led to the end of the "Malay way."[15] This Malay way, similar to that in Indonesia, emphasizes the avoidance of conflict and direct confrontation and the acceptance of courtesy, compromise, and broad consultation before decisions are made. Openings for reconciliation are always pursued. Mahathir's administrative style, however, has been more toward confrontation than consensus, and his opponents have responded in kind, thereby departing from the traditional ways of leading the nation.

Economic Development

Malaysia has been one of the few success stories of economic development in the Third World. With a per capita GNP of $2,000, Malaysia has surpassed Portugal and Hungary in the world's rankings.[16] However, the picture is not all positive. Large pockets of poverty, widening income inequality, and excessive dependency on world prices for primary products are major problems. The extent of Malaysia's dependency on the world economy became strikingly clear in the mid-1980s when the decline in the world price of primary products brought about a recession.

Despite these problems, there has been a clear improvement in the standard of living since independence in 1957. In 1966 only 18 percent of households in a typical Malaysian village had piped water. By 1978 the percentage was 71. Electricity was available to 45 percent of households in 1966; this increased to 79 percent in 1978 and to 100 percent in 1987. In 1966 only 29 percent of men and 4 percent of women had completed more than four years of schooling, but a decade later these figures were 48 percent and 34 percent, respectively. In 1966 4 percent of Malay families owned a television; in 1987, the figure was 90 percent. In this period, dirt roads were paved, telephone lines were installed, and mosques were built.[17] These figures, valid throughout the country, show a rapid economic development achieved by few Third-World nations.

In 1971, by means of an unprecedented new economic policy (NEP), the Malaysian government initiated an extraordinary twenty-year plan designed to eradicate poverty and to eliminate race as a function of economic prosperity. The plan was meant to change the fundamental structures and ethnic divisions of Malaysia by directing the increments of rapid economic growth disproportionately to the Malay sector without expropriating Chinese assets or weakening the vigor of Chinese enterprise.[18]

The NEP was the government's response to the 1969 riots and the perceived need for a dramatic attack on the ethnic divisions in the economy. The government's data indicated that in 1971 the ownership of share capital was 63 percent foreign, 34 percent non-Malay, and less than 3 percent Malay. The goal was to raise the Malay share of capital ownership to 30 percent and reduce the foreign share to 30 percent, while allowing the Chinese share to rise to 40 percent.[19] The means to this end were the granting of special privileges in business ownership, tax breaks, investment incentives, and employment quotas. The government required all banks to earmark a significant proportion of their business loans to Malays.

The NEP was to end in 1990; however, as the target of 30 percent capital ownership by Malays had not been met (the estimate in 1989 was about 20 percent), the government appointed a commission to design a new twenty-year policy. The foreign share had fallen from 63 to 33 percent, and the difference was taken up by non-Malays, whose share increased from 34 to 47 percent. Other goals were substantially achieved, including reduction of the poverty level, which had fallen from 30 percent in 1977 to 17 percent by 1987. Many more *bumiputera* Malays were in businesses in which they had formerly been underrepresented. Investments in agricultural programs and rural development had increased manyfold during the twenty-year NEP.

Under Mahathir, Malaysia emphasized a market-oriented economy, featuring the privatization of public utilities, communications, and transportation; at the same time it also featured state-owned heavy industrialization. Mahathir's Look East policy stressed adoption of the work ethic and methods of Japan and South Korea and increased trade with Asian neighbors. The success of these programs, including 8 percent economic growth in both 1988 and 1989, has led economists to predict that Malaysia will be the next NIC, joining Singapore, Taiwan, South Korea, and Hong Kong as Asia's fifth "tiger."

As the world's largest exporter of semiconductors and one of the largest exporters of room air conditioners, textiles, and footwear, Malaysia has become integrated into the world capitalist system. Manufacturing accounted for one-half of total exports in 1990, compared to just 20 percent ten years ago. These increases in manufacturing output, stimulated largely by export-oriented industrialization, have resulted in a much broader-based economy.[20] New foreign investment in Malaysia in 1989 was $3.2 billion, an increase of 76 percent over 1988. Despite these achievements, Prime Minister Mahathir has declined to label the nation an NIC because he does not want to lose benefits as an underdeveloped country, including concessionary import tariffs under the generalized system of preferences.

The Malaysian State

Malaysia received independence by peaceful means and adopted and adapted British governmental institutions; thus the country emerged in its postindependence period with a strong and stable political system. Because of the communal character of their society, Malaysian leaders adapted Western democratic structures in the nation's attempt to provide Malays with dominance of the political realm. That attempt required that the principal institutions of the society be merged with the state.

The clearest example of this close association is the integration of the Alliance (before 1969) and the National Front with the state. As in Indonesia, where Golkar is in essence a state institution, the National Front (led by UMNO) has merged with the state—dominating the bureaucracy, the parliament, the media, and the courts. This sets Malaysia apart from Thailand and the Philippines, where political parties are relatively autonomous from the state and have minimal influence.

One characteristic of strong states is their ability to project their power into the countryside. Through co-optation of local Malay elites and the provision of roads, credit, medical facilities, recreational programs, and other development activities, the Malaysian state has succeeded in tying local power brokers to the central authorities through either UMNO or local-level governmental agencies.[21]

In economic affairs as well, the Malaysian state has asserted its control. No facet of the economy is excluded from governmental intervention in order to meet the goals of the NEP and to provide resources to the leading party (UMNO) in the National Front. The state has co-opted most of those who could challenge it. Indeed, oppositionists are established supporters of the state, differing only in terms of their desire to replace its political leaders. Thus, the Malaysian state is not subservient to societal forces, such as an autonomous military or insurgency, or to such external national powers as a former colonial ruler.

Malaysia's status as a relatively strong state can be explained only partially in terms of its history of social dislocation (a major condition for the development of a strong state). In contrast to Indonesia, which experienced a traumatic colonialism and later had to struggle for independence, Malaysia's colonial situation led to less dislocation. However, the Japanese interregnum; the evolution toward independence; the federation with Singapore, Sabah, and Sarawak; the ouster of Singapore; and the May 1969 ethnic riots provided sufficient dislocation for the development of a strong state.

Dislocation is more likely to lead to a strong state if it occurs at a moment in which external political forces favor control. For Thailand in the postwar period, the United States played the role of supporter as a means to keep it from becoming Communist. The Thai military also played a primary role in state control, ostensibly to protect Thai security although an invasion of Thailand was never a real possibility. Malaysia, even less than many other Southeast Asian nations, was not endangered by external powers, nor did the nation rely on a particular foreign or domestic guarantor of its sovereignty. Thus, in terms of this condition, the Malaysian state was not strengthened.

As with Thailand and Indonesia, Malaysia has bureaucrats, technocrats, and ethnic leaders who identify their interests with those of the state. Chinese business leaders have joined groups and parties that have been integrated or co-opted into the state system through the Alliance and the National Front. These ethnic leaders have strong constituencies outside the bureaucracy, but they do not constitute a separate power base that opposes the interests of the authorities in power. Instead, they rely on the state to provide them with protection and access to needed resources. Even the NEP, ostensibly a plan to upgrade the status of Malays in the economy, did not attempt to usurp the dominant position of the Chinese in the economy; indeed, the Chinese flourished during the twenty years of the NEP. In this respect, Malaysia meets the condition of a strong state requiring societal groups that can implement the designs of the state.

The last condition for strong state status is skillful leadership to take advantage of the conditions to build a strong state. Suharto in Indonesia clearly qualifies as such a leader. Malaysia has also experienced strong leadership, beginning with Tunku Abdul Rahman, the father of Malaysian independence, through the present prime minister, Mahathir. Except for the brief period of the state of emergency in 1969 and the assault on the judiciary by Mahathir in 1988, Malaysian leaders have not undermined the institutions of the state in a manner similar to that of Marcos in the Philippines. On the contrary, each prime minister has strengthened state institutions as a means to promote political stability, economic development, and ethnic harmony. In short, all these perspectives provide a context for assessing the Malaysian state as strong.

Foreign Policy

Malaysia has not been an interventionist country, nor has it participated prominently in international affairs since its independence in 1957. However, support for ASEAN has long been a first priority for Malaysia as a means to enhance both the nation's security and its economic objectives. Conflict with the Philippines over territory in Sabah has not precluded overall support for ASEAN. Thai-Malaysian relations improved in 1989 when Communists in the border area ended their insurgency.

As the primary initiator of the Zone of Peace, Freedom, and Neutrality (ZOPFAN), a policy adopted by ASEAN to reduce major power and intraregional confrontation in Southeast Asia, Malaysia has attempted to reduce its military involvement in Southeast Asia. When Singapore offered to station U.S. air and naval facilities on its land, Malaysia argued that the establishment of such a base was against the spirit of ZOPFAN. Nevertheless, Malaysia has supported U.S. military bases in the Philippines.

Malaysia's main adversary has been China because of the support the People's Republic gave to Communist insurgents during the Emergency and because of distrust of Malaysia's indigenous Chinese. In 1974, nevertheless, Malaysia normalized relations with China, although such ties are tenuous because of the domestic communal situation. Malaysia has looked skeptically at Thailand's moves toward closer relations with China and Vietnam.

To gain greater international stature commensurate with its economic strength, the Malaysian government pursued and won a seat on the Security Council of the United Nations, and in 1989 Malaysia hosted the Commonwealth heads of government meeting. This latter event improved relations between Malaysia and Great Britain after a period of tension due to British policy regarding tuition rates for Malaysian students in England and Great Britain's refusal to impose sanctions on South Africa.

Conclusion

The October 1990 parliamentary election continued the established mode of authoritative decision making, with the National Front leading an alliance of parties. These parties have continued the Bargain, negotiated at the time of independence, which calls for Malay political dominance and non-Malay economic dominance. They have continued to support a refurbished NEP to end poverty and provided Malays with special privileges.

After the decline of the Malay way in 1987, all leaders, including Mahathir, attempted to return to the traditional modes of political negotiation, emphasizing consensus rather than confrontation. The continued economic vibrancy of the country is important for providing a buffer for the Malaysian government, as an economic decline could bring ethnic tensions to the surface. However, the universal desire for stability, especially now that a large number of citizens have an economic stake in the society, will ensure the continued capacity of the state to cope with changes.

Notes

1. Milton J. Esman, "Ethnic Politics and Economic Power," *Comparative Politics,* vol. 19, no. 4, July 1987, p. 402.

2. Milton J. Esman, *Administration and Development in Malaysia* (Ithaca: Cornell University Press, 1972), pp. 20–22.

3. Diane K. Mauzy, "Malaysia in 1987," *Asian Survey,* vol. 28, no. 2, February 1988, p. 214.

4. Hari Singh and Suresh Narayanan, "Changing Dimensions in Malaysian Politics," *Asian Survey,* vol. 29, no. 5, May 1989, p. 517.

5. Stephen A. Douglas, "How Strong Is the Malaysian State?" paper presented to the Association for Asian Studies, Chicago, April 1990, p. 2.

6. Zakaria Haji Ahmad, "Stability, Security and National Development in Malaysia: An Appraisal," in *Durable Stability in Southeast Asia,* ed. Kusuma Snitwongse and Sukhumbhand Paribatra (Singapore: Institute of Southeast Asian Studies, 1987), p. 125.

7. Doug Tsuruoka, "UMNO's Money Machine," *Far Eastern Economic Review,* July 5, 1990, p. 48.

8. Zakaria Haji Ahmad, "Malaysia: Quasi Democracy in a Divided Society" in *Democracy in Developing Countries: Asia,* ed. Larry Diamond, Juan J. Linz, and Seymour Martin Lipset (Boulder, Colo.: Lynne Rienner Publishers, 1988), p. 373.

9. Zakaria Haji Ahmad, "The Military and Development in Malaysia and Brunei, with a Short Survey on Singapore," in *Soldiers and Stability in Southeast Asia,* ed. J. Soedjati Djiwandono and Yong Mun Cheong (Singapore: Institute of Southeast Asian Studies, 1988), p. 235.

10. Virginia H. Dancz, *Women and Party Politics in Peninsular Malaysia* (Singapore: Oxford University Press, 1987) p. 6.

11. Ibid., p. 226.

12. For an in-depth analysis of this point, see James C. Scott, *Political Ideology in Malaysia* (New Haven: Yale University Press, 1968).

13. Ahmad, "Malaysia: Quasi Democracy," in *Democracy in Developing Countries: Asia,* ed. Diamond, Linz, and Lipset, p. 349.

14. Ibid., p. 358.

15. Mauzy, "Malaysia in 1987," p. 213.

16. Charles Hirschman, "Development and Inequality in Malaysia: From Puthucheary to Mehmet," *Pacific Affairs,* vol. 62, no. 1, Spring 1989, p. 72.

17. All these figures come from Marvin Rogers, "Patterns of Change in Rural Malaysia: Development and Dependence," *Asian Survey,* vol. 29, no. 8, August 1989, pp. 767–770.

18. Esman, "Ethnic Politics and Economic Power," p. 403.

19. Ibid., p. 403.

20. Mauzy, "Malaysia in 1987," p. 116.

21. Douglas, "How Strong Is the Malaysian State?" p. 12.

7

SINGAPORE

The quest for survival, order, and prosperity is a dominant theme of contemporary Singaporean politics. Surrounded by nations some hundreds of times larger with populations twenty to one hundred times greater, this city-state island is in many respects a speck in a region of giant nations. As a primarily urban entrepot with virtually no agricultural base, Singapore stands alone, bereft of the resources and land of its neighbors.

Singapore's principal resource is its people. Multiethnic and multi-cultural, Singapore's 2.6 million citizens are about 77 percent Chinese, 14 percent Malay, 7 percent Indian, and 2 percent other minorities. Singaporeans, who live in a densely populated city, are the wealthiest, best-educated, best-housed, and healthiest group in Southeast Asia. Literacy, for example, is over 90 percent, and among those under 30 years old it is 99 percent.

Singaporeans enjoy the most westernized conveniences and public services of the region as well. Having achieved the highest standard of living in Southeast Asia, Singapore's leaders are now attempting to counter the worst aspects of growing westernization (hedonism, materialism, and self-centeredness) by creating an Asian meritocracy.[1] The importance of creating a quality society is illustrated by the republic's concern about the emigration of about two thousand persons each year (but almost five thousand each year in 1988 and 1989). The primary reasons emigrants give for leaving Singapore are the great emphasis on work and competition, the restrictive regulations that permeate every facet of life, and the concern that their children will not pass the requisite exams to attain elite positions. Singaporean authorities are attempting to find the formula that emphasizes order and merit while it reduces the stress brought about by the pervasive competitive spirit.

No non-Communist society in Southeast Asia regulates its citizens' behavior as much as Singapore. For example, rules on traffic, street cleanliness, shops and markets, housing, landscaping, and food preparation are strictly enforced by the authorities and rigorously followed by the citizenry. Less corruption exists here than in any other Southeast Asian nation. Although a part of the political system, patronage is less salient in political recruitment and policymaking than is the case in the systems of Singapore's neighbors.

To achieve order, Singapore has fashioned one of the world's most effective and efficient governments. Characterized by democratic institutions but within the context of authoritarian order, Singapore's government has been controlled by a single party, the People's Action Party (PAP), since full independence was obtained in 1965. Singapore has known only one leader, Lee Kuan Yew, who has led the nation since 1957.

The themes of survival, quality, and order have become fused in Singapore to produce a unique style of politics and economic life.[2] The fusion stems from colonial times when the British controlled Singapore, making it dependent on British economic policies. After achieving limited independence in 1957, Singapore granted Britain control over external affairs and security matters out of fear of a seizure of power by the Communists or by external intervention. To achieve full independence, the Singaporean economic system established interdependence in the global economic system, and the country allied with its northern neighbor, Malaysia, which complemented Singapore economically.

The concern for survival was the major impetus for the decision by Malaysia and Singapore to forge a Federation of Malaysia in September 1963, to include peninsular Malaya, Sabah, Sarawak, and Singapore. Tunku Abdul Rahman, Malaysia's founding prime minister, feared that Singapore would become Communist, an "Asian Cuba." The solution was to accept Singapore as a member of the federation. From the Singaporean perspective, the agricultural resources of Malaya were necessary for the development of the urban city-state. Lee Kuan Yew did not believe that Singapore was viable by itself.

The federation lasted only two years, until August 1965, because the Alliance government in Kuala Lumpur perceived that the Chinese in Singapore were threatening the privileged political position of the Malays. Lee Kuan Yew had called for a "Malaysian Malaysia," with the implication that all Malaysians, regardless of race, could participate equally in all phases of life. This view was contrary to the Tunku's belief that a "Malay Malaysia" was in the society's best interest.

After being ejected from the federation, Singapore again faced the challenge of survival in an era of grave tensions, which stemmed mostly from the cold war and the *Konfrontasi* threat from Indonesia. Rather than seek a complementary alliance to achieve security, Singapore fashioned policies designed to achieve rapid and far-reaching economic development to ensure its sovereignty. By 1969 the government had consolidated the republic's independence, stability, and viability, a consolidation that has lasted to the present. This success has depended on continued economic development and the inculcation of values supportive of a unified, highly educated, quality-oriented Singapore in people from diverse backgrounds.

Since gaining full independence in 1965, Singapore has been ruled by the PAP under the leadership of Prime Minister Lee, who is now one of the world's longest ruling leaders. In 1990 at age sixty-six, he turned power over to the new generation of leaders in preparation for his full retirement. His chosen successor, Deputy Prime Minister and Defense Minister Goh Chok Tong, has recommended that Lee be accorded special ministerial privilege following his stepping down or, alternatively, be elected to the ceremonial post of president. Goh was making the important policy decisions by 1990.

At age forty-nine, Goh represents the new generation of leaders in Singapore after almost thirty years of the founding generation. Goh promised a continuation of disciplined rule and the continuation of Lee Kuan Yew's presence as leader of the PAP. Lee's son, Lee Hsien Loong, as industry and trade minister as well as deputy defense minister and deputy prime minister in Goh's cabinet, is in line to replace Goh in the near future.

Institutions and Social Groups

Lee Kuan Yew

Few leaders in Southeast Asia have had the impact on their societies that Lee Kuan Yew had in some thirty years of dominating Singapore. Ho Chi Minh, Sukarno, Suharto, Ne Win, and Sihanouk had comparable influence, but none ruled a society with as much effectiveness as Lee. First in his class at both Cambridge and Oxford, Lee is a brilliant and pragmatic politician with more popular support than almost any other world leader.

By placing highly educated and technically proficient officials in charge of his development programs, Lee relied on his subordinates to establish effective policies free from corruption. By combining the advantages of Western-style democratic institutions with an Asian-style hegemonic political party system, Lee was able to dominate the country's politics and still achieve universal support and legitimacy.

In the late 1980s, Lee's consummate political skill lost some of its edge, as he moved toward authoritarian and away from open and pragmatic policies. In a series of decisions concerning the jailing of dissident politicians and the restriction of newspapers printing articles critical of his administration, Lee veered from the careful balance he had achieved between civil liberties and order during the previous decades. Lee rationalized the new direction toward increased order as necessary for the continued stability of the country and as appropriate for Asian culture.

Since 1988, Singaporeans have expected that Lee would resign as prime minister. However, his often reiterated vow to turn power over to the new generation has been repeatedly postponed because of fear that his successors could not carry out their governmental duties as effectively as he. Nevertheless, he has turned most of the major decisions over to the second-generation leaders, while acting as a "goalkeeper" and intervening only to block egregious errors.[3] Indeed, of the original cabinet and parliament members, only Lee remained in 1990.

Political Parties

The PAP is almost synonymous with Lee Kuan Yew and with governance in Singapore. PAP has been in power since 1959. More striking than its noninterrupted rule is the fact that since 1968 PAP has won all but four seats (of hundreds), with its percentage of party votes ranging from 63 to 84.

The only party ever to provide credible opposition was the left-wing *Barisan Sosialis* (Socialist Front), which had split from PAP, in the 1960s. Since that time, opposition parties have been allowed to function, but none has provided meaningful competition to PAP. The reasons for PAP's dominance include the factionalization of the opposition, the effectiveness and incorruptibility of most PAP politicians, the ability of PAP to meet the needs of the people, and the rigid rules that circumscribe the activities of political parties and opposition groups, which were especially important in the late 1980s when newspapers were censored and suspected Communists arrested. The other major reason for the success of PAP is the apprehension of the electorate at undoing a system that is working and thereby risking alternative leadership. To many Singaporeans, PAP is indispensable for continuation of the extraordinary economic development and societal stability the city-state has gained since independence.

In contrast to most hegemonic parties, PAP does not have a large staff to perform research and mobilizing functions.[4] Instead, civil bureaucrats outside the party perform these functions, leaving PAP visible only before general elections. To ensure its continued dominance, PAP has prepared for succession through its self-renewal program, choosing young candidates who are more in tune with the electorate. In the 1988 election, virtually every PAP candidate was from the younger generation. Nevertheless, the percentage of votes won by PAP candidates has decreased since 1980, when the party won 77.7 percent of the votes, to 64.8 percent in 1984 and to 63.1 percent on September 3, 1988. In the 1988 election, campaigning on a slogan of "more good years," PAP won 80 of 81 parliamentary seats.

Legislature

Singapore's parliamentary system is a legacy of British colonialism, even though the practice is much different from that of today's Great Britain. In contrast to the British bicameral system, the Singaporean parliamentary system is unicameral and has had no meaningful opposition to present an alternative rule. Legislators have five-year terms unless the prime minister dissolves parliament before the term ends.

To ensure a semblance of bipartisanship, in 1984 the parliament provided for three opposition seats, to be awarded even if opposition candidates did not win in any constituency. These three nonconstituency members would be appointed from among the highest-polling opposition candidates as long as they won at least 15 percent of the votes cast in the constituency.[5] Nonconstituency oppositionists were not accorded full voting rights; they were prohibited from voting on motions relating to constitutional amendments, money bills, or votes of no confidence in the government. The opposition saw this change as tokenism rather than a meaningful commitment to open politics.

Another major change in the procedures of parliament is the Team MP scheme. Beginning with the 1988 election, in certain constituencies the electorate voted for a team of candidates instead of only one candidate. Certain constituencies are declared Group Representation Constituencies (GRCs), and each is represented by three members of parliament. Not more than half of the total number of constituencies can be GRCs. At least one of the three candidates in a GRC is required to be an ethnic minority. The team that wins a plurality of the total vote is elected.[6]

The purpose of Team MP is to institutionalize multiracial politics by ensuring that minorities will be represented in parliament by getting minority candidates elected on the coattails of others.[7] PAP was confident that the change would not threaten its ability to win. Indeed, in the 1988 election PAP won all but one parliamentary seat. Only one election has been held under the new system; thus, it is not yet clear if the Team MP plan will either guarantee minority representation or enshrine racial consciousness and division.

In another attempt to bring alternative ideas to parliament and to sustain traditional values, six distinguished individuals from the community, academia, the military, the professions, and trade unions will be selected to serve as nonvoting members of parliament. This innovation, however, will not imperil PAP's dominance.

Democratization

The case of Singapore raises the question of whether a one-party state can be democratic. From a Western perspective, the governmental system of Singapore does not meet the criteria of full civil liberties and competitive choices of leaders. From the Chinese perspective, the paternalistic nature of the government is appropriate, providing, as it does, law and order as well as economic achievements without oppression. Lee Kuan Yew agrees with Sukarno's rationale for guided democracy in Indonesia and has said that Western-style majority rule leads to chaos, instability, dissension, and inefficiency.

Prime Minister Lee has argued that in the Chinese tradition there is no concept of a loyal opposition. For example, it is not possible to support an opposition candidate without withdrawing total support from the government. This tradition stems from Confucian philosophy, which stressed the principles of centralized authorities. Obligation to those in authority were the cement of the Confucian order. As long as the authorities are meeting the needs of the people and leading according to moral principles, the ruler is considered to have the mandate of heaven and is therefore deemed legitimate by the public. Singaporeans do not swing back and forth from opposition to support for PAP. Given this cultural perspective, a strong one-party system is most conducive to effective rule.[8]

One-party systems can provide policy alternatives if there are differences in opinion among the party leaders. Moreover, if two-way communication between the government and the people is established, the citizenry can assert influence over public policy. In Singapore, a high degree of intra-party factionalism occurs, with varying points of view aired publicly. In addition, PAP has established grassroots organizations, including Citizens' Consultative Committees designed to elicit ideas from the public. Singapore's semidemocracy has provided the republic with effective and accountable government, consistent with its traditions and history and supportive of the goals of development, order, and merit.

Economic Development

It is impossible to make generalizations about Singapore's economic development because its city-state status is fundamentally different from every other Southeast Asian nation. With no agricultural base, Singapore is destined to become increasingly interdependent with the world economic system to ensure its survival.

Singapore is a mixture of capitalist and socialist economics, with emphasis on the former. PAP leadership inherited a capitalist economic system from the British and has created state institutions such as the Housing and Development Board, which houses about 80 percent of the population.

With the exception of two years in the mid-1980s when the economy suffered negative growth, Singapore has consistently posted the region's highest growth rates. The 11 and 9 percent rates in 1988 and 1989, respectively, accompanied by an inflation rate of less than 3 percent, are indicative of this growth. These growth rates are largely the result of an outward-looking, export-oriented strategy begun after 1965 to accelerate the growth of manufactured products, obtain needed outside capital, and reduce unemployment. Foreign investment increased from $0.3 billion in 1967 to $2.3 billion in 1972 and to $8 billion in the mid-1980s. Unemployment dropped from 13 percent at the beginning of the 1960s to under 3 percent in the 1980s. Singapore now hires foreign nationals to supplement its work force.

Singapore's major manufacturing export, electronic products, accounts for over 30 percent of domestic exports. Such a large percentage makes the Singaporean economy dependent on continued good prices for its products. The republic has one of the highest trading-to-gross-domestic-product ratios in the world; thus, an international recession could devastate Singapore as happened briefly in 1985.[9] Today, Singapore's primary trading partner is the United States, followed by Japan, Malaysia, Hong Kong, Thailand, Australia, and West Germany.

In anticipation of changes in the world economy, Singapore launched a Second Industrial Revolution in 1979, designed to restructure the economy toward high-tech industries. The plan was to make Singaporean exports of superb quality, win higher salaries for workers, upgrade job skills, and reduce dependence on foreign workers. The economy emphasized automotive components, machine tools, computers, electronic instrumentation, medical instruments, and precision engineering.

The revolution was a success until 1985, when protectionist tendencies of developed countries hurt Singaporean exports. Low petroleum prices dealt a sharp blow to the ship repairing and ship building industries (which made up one quarter of the manufacturing sector), and the high wage costs were not matched by productivity growth.[10] Finally, the continued high rate of national savings (42 percent of gross domestic product [GDP]) could not become a part of productive domestic investments.

Through state intervention to correct each of these difficulties, the economy responded rapidly, leading Singapore to a period of remarkable growth. As the economy diversified, financial and business services displaced manufacturing as the leading sectors of the economy. Not content with the level of economic development, Lee Kuan Yew set forth a controversial program to improve the gene pool. He determined that the quality of the people was the most important factor responsible for the country's rapid development, and he arranged a program for the marriage and procreation of the well-educated populace, giving incentives for educated mothers to have more children. However, the negative response from Singaporeans undermined the program's goals.

The Singapore economy is interdependent with the world economic system. With a more diversified economy, some of the best transportation infrastructures in the world, superb medical care, the highest standard of living in all Southeast Asia, a highly educated and technologically proficient population, and good relations with its neighbors, Singapore's prospects for continued high levels of economic development are excellent.

Given these achievements, it is surprising that many Singaporeans decide to leave the city-state. The explanation is that for many citizens Singapore's traditions and culture have been swallowed by the forces of economic development. Huge housing projects have undermined the traditional extended family. Massive modern skyscrapers have replaced traditional Chinese architecture. Impersonal rules and regulations have supplanted personal relations as the arbitrator of behavior. For many Singaporeans, the city has become devoid of spirit, heart, and vitality, which have been displaced by a materialistic coldness symbolized by ubiquitous rules.

The Singaporean State

By most reckoning, Singapore does not have the requisites for a strong state. Geographically, the country is minuscule and has no important natural resources. Although it boasts the highest per capita income in Southeast Asia (except for the anomaly of Brunei), its total GNP is far smaller than that in Indonesia, the Philippines, Malaysia, or Thailand.

Singapore's military is capable of only minor defense operations. Viewed in these terms, Singapore does not have the wherewithal to be a strong state.

Nevertheless, using different criteria, Singapore's state can be considered strong. Its leaders use the agencies of the state to get people in the society to do what they want them to do. In no other Southeast Asian society do the citizens follow the dictates of the state with the same regularity as in Singapore. Taxes are paid, young men accept compulsory military conscription, and traffic rules are followed. Few autonomous groups compete for influence in the society. Indeed, the state has co-opted the bureaucracy, the military, and interest groups, while the hegemonic PAP—itself a creature of Lee Kuan Yew—has co-opted the state.

In explaining or understanding the high capacity of the state in Singapore, it happens that the country's small size is a major factor in strengthening the state. Although Singapore is heterogeneous in the ethnic sense, a more important fact is that its society is quite homogeneous culturally. All Singaporeans are urban and united in their goals for their society. Living in fewer than 700 square miles (smaller than the city and urban environs of Jakarta), citizens have little room for nonconformity. One need simply compare Singapore with Indonesia—where 180 million people live on 5,000 miles over thousands of islands and speak hundreds of languages—to get a rough idea of the differences between the two countries.

A necessary condition for a strong state is massive social dislocation that has weakened the capacity of a people or a society sufficiently to inhibit or preclude state strength.[11] This condition, so clearly evident in Indonesia, has not occurred in Singapore. Singapore's post–World War II history has generally been stable, including its peaceful transition from colonial status to independence. Its expulsion from Malaysia was wrenching, strengthening the politics of survival, but it was not as traumatic as the anti-colonialist wars fought by Indonesia, Burma, or Vietnam. Rather than massive dislocation, continuity characterized Singapore's transition to full independence.

States are strengthened when external forces favor concentrated social control. As in most of Southeast Asia, where the international modus operandi in the postwar era was cold war politics, Singapore was a recipient of Western aid to ensure that communism would not prevail. Also, in the period of the Vietnam war and in the 1980s, a tremendous growth in external investments occurred. The impact of aid and overseas investment was important for strengthening the role of the Singaporean state.

Serious military threats, whether they be internal or external, also facilitate the emergence of a strong state, and this condition was supportive of the strong state in Singapore. In the 1960s when PAP was factionalized into left-wing and moderate groups, Lee Kuan Yew's victory over the Left was interpreted as a victory over communism and, therefore, as a victory for the survival of the country's democratic system. Lee justified his "administrative state" as necessary for the concentration of power and for repressing internal and external enemies of the state.

Another condition conducive to state strength is the presence of a social grouping, independent of existing bases of social control, that is skillful enough to execute the designs of state leaders.[12] The technocrats in Singapore are among the most educated and skilled in Southeast Asia, and Prime Minister Lee has turned policymaking over to these officials. Incorruptible and effective, they appear to not be beholden to particular societal groups. Instead, they are integrated into the state through PAP or the ministries. Their lack of any mass political base reinforces their loyalty to the state.

The final condition for a strong state is skillful leadership, and here Singapore is the quintessential example. For many Singaporeans, Lee Kuan Yew is the state. His strength comes less from charisma or repression than from his extraordinary capabilities to fashion an effective state. This condition alone appears to have moved Singapore into the ranks of the strong states, despite the absence of what was thought to be the necessary condition of massive state dislocation.

Singapore is the most disciplined society in Southeast Asia, in part because of its citizens' fear of being fined or punished and in part because they believe lawful obedience to be in the public interest.[13] Certainly, the government has set forth extraordinary measures to ensure orderly behavior such as installing devices that detect urine in housing bloc elevators and that, if urine is detected, lock the elevator door until authorities arrive. While the Chinese heritage is one of discipline for the common good, at the time of independence Singaporeans behaved similarly to present-day Southeast Asians. The difference is that the Singaporean state has had the capacity to exploit that heritage to help it achieve its aims of survival, economic development, meritocracy, and order. The price it has paid is no meaningful participation in the affairs of state by the Singaporean people and a sanitized society that has lost much of its soul.

Foreign Policy

Singapore did not take charge of its foreign relations until 1965 when the republic was expelled from Malaysia. Since then, the basic foreign policy theme has been survival. As a small city-state with only minimal military capacity, Singapore has looked to Western powers and Japan to balance the Soviet Union and China in Southeast Asia. Unabashedly anti-Communist, Singapore supported the U.S. war in Vietnam and has been the main spokesman for a hard-line policy toward the present Vietnamese government.

Despite its pro-U.S. stance, Singapore has enunciated a policy of neutrality, avoiding embroilment in major power conflicts. Nevertheless, particular issues have strained Singapore–U.S. relations. In 1988 Singapore accused Washington of interfering in its domestic affairs and expelled a U.S. diplomat who allegedly encouraged a famous dissident to organize a group of opposition candidates, thereby interfering in Singapore's internal affairs. Bad feelings also arose when President Reagan removed Singapore from the GSP, effective in 1989. The GSP had allowed selected goods to enter the United States duty free, but Singapore had reached the status of an NIC and was no longer eligible for this benefit. Relations improved when Singapore offered to host an increased U.S. military presence as a response to the prospect that the United States would be expelled from the Philippines.

ASEAN was the main instrument of foreign policy for trade matters and for security from outside aggression or internal subversion. Singapore was the only ASEAN nation that did not have diplomatic relations with China, although an increasing number of trade missions between the two countries suggested that such ties were imminent. Today, Singapore has become China's fourth largest investor after Japan, the United States, and Hong Kong.

By 1990 Singapore had achieved its goal of survival. It was no longer threatened by internal insurgency or external intervention, and it was surrounded by large nations that had no capacity or desire to intervene in the affairs of the republic. As the cold war diminished and as regional and international ties improved, Singapore's security was strengthened accordingly.

Conclusion

Singapore's singularity does not allow meaningful comparisons between it and other countries. Indeed, Singapore is an anomaly in Southeast Asia in terms of culture, ethnicity, geography, state capacity, and level of economic development. Thus, the island-state is not a useful model for Southeast Asian nations to emulate because its conditions are so different from those of every other country. A smooth succession from Lee to second-generation leaders will bode well for the continued stability and development of Singapore.

Notes

---

1. Thomas J. Bellows, "Singapore in 1989," *Asian Survey*, vol. 30, no. 2, February 1990, p. 202.
2. Lee Boon Hiok, "Political Institutionalization in Singapore" in *Asian Political Institutionalization*, ed. Robert A. Scalapino, Seizaburo Sato, and Jusuf Wanandi (Berkeley: Institute of East Asian Studies, University of California, 1986), p. 202.
3. Bellows, "Singapore in 1988," p. 145.
4. Hiok, "Political Institutionalization in Singapore," in *Asian Political Institutionalization*, ed. Scalapino, Sato, and Wanandi, p. 207.
5. Chan Heng Chee, "The PAP in the Nineties: The Politics of Anticipation," in *ASEAN in Regional and Global Context*, ed. Karl D. Jackson, Sukhumbhand Paribatra, and J. Soedjati Djiwandono (Berkeley: Institute of East Asian Studies, University of California, 1986), p. 173.
6. Bellows, "Singapore in 1988," p. 146.
7. Lee Lai To, "Singapore in 1987," *Asian Survey* vol. 28, no. 2, February 1988, p. 203.
8. *Far Eastern Economic Review, Asia Yearbook, 1990* (Hong Kong), pp. 214–215.
9. Chan Heng Chee, "Singapore: Domestic Structure and Foreign Policy," in *Asia and the Major Powers: Domestic Politics and Foreign Powers*, ed. Robert A. Scalapino, Seizaburo Sato, Jusuf Wanandi, and Sung-joo Han (Berkeley: Institute of East Asian Studies, University of California, 1988), p. 284.
10. Jon S.T. Quah, "Singapore in 1987," in *Southeast Asian Affairs 1988* (Singapore: Institute of Southeast Asian Studies, 1988), p. 249.
11. Joel Migdal, *Strong Societies and Weak States: State-Society Relations and State Capabilities in the Third World* (Princeton, N.J.: Princeton University Press, 1988), p. 269.
12. Ibid., p. 274.
13. Donald K. Emmerson, "Beyond Zanzibar: Area Studies, Comparative Politics, and the 'Strength' of the State in Indonesia," paper presented to the Association for Asian Studies, Chicago, April 1990, pp. 28–29.

8

NEGARA BRUNEI DARUSSALAM

Negara Brunei Darussalam is the official name of the country known informally as Brunei. Overlooking the South China Sea, Brunei is located on the island of Borneo and is divided into two sectors surrounded by the Malaysian state of Sarawak. With a population of only 300,000 and the highest per capita income in Southeast Asia (estimated to be between $12,000 and $22,000 per year), Brunei, like Singapore, is unlike other nations in the region.

About 70 percent of the people of Brunei are ethnically Malay, and most of this group works in the public sector. The Chinese community, which makes up nearly one third of the population (but for the most part does not have Bruneian citizenship), supplies most of the nonpublic workforce. Islam is the state religion.

Brunei received full independence from Great Britain on January 1, 1984. Ironically, however, the sultan of Brunei was reluctant to accept independence because he feared his new nation would be vulnerable to attack from its larger neighbors, Indonesia and Malaysia. Brunei achieved internal self-government in 1959 when the sultan promulgated Brunei's first constitution, thereby ending British rule and ensuring that power would be transferred to the ruling dynasty rather than to the people. Foreign and military affairs were still handled by the British, however, until full independence was achieved.

Brunei's reluctance to have full independence also stemmed from the monarch's fear that externally supported revolts could undermine the royalty's prerogatives. Therefore, British security was needed to shore up the royal family's absolute rule. The most threatening incident occurred in 1962 when the Azahari revolt, favoring popular representation, convinced the royal family that its continued rule was in jeopardy.

Following independence, Brunei achieved political stability and economic development primarily because of enormous revenues from oil and natural gas. These funds allowed the government to establish a cradle-to-grave welfare system (facetiously known as the shellfare state) that provided, among other things, free education and health programs as well as subsidies for housing, cars, funerals, and pilgrimages to Mecca. Moreover, there is no income tax. These benefits are partially responsible for the high degree of legitimacy accorded the absolute monarchy and for the continuity of governmental institutions.

Institutions and Social Groups

Sultanate

The sultanate is the embodiment of the state, and Sultan Sir Muda Hassanal Bolkiah—the twenty-ninth ruler in a dynasty that originated in the thirteenth century—is an absolute monarch whose legitimacy derives from his heredity, not from popular elections or accountability to Bruneians. He is the son of Sultan Haji Omar Ali Saifuddien Sa'adul Khairi Waddien, ibni Almarhum Sultan Mohammad Jamulul Alam, who was known as the Sultan Seri Begawan. The capital city, Bandar Seri Begawan, is named in his honor. Although the Seri Begawan abdicated in favor of his son in 1967, he attempted to keep ultimate power for himself so that the present sultan was not able to rule unconditionally until the death of his father in 1986.

At age 44 (in 1990), the sultan lives in a palace with 1,700 rooms and rules in the style of classic potentates. There is no distinction between the wealth of the state and the personal riches of the sultan; thus, he is reputed to be the richest man in the world. All the state's revenues and reserves are his, and he alone decides what portion goes for state expenditures.[1] The sultan has shed his playboy image and has attempted to create a new image of a responsible, benevolent ruler.

The sultan has ceremonial responsibilities and, as the nation's prime minister, administrative duties in which he has total control over the day-to-day affairs of the state. There is no parliament, the cabinet is made up principally of members of his own royal family, and there is no dissent from the populace because the sultan has absolute powers. His power is enhanced by the fact that he oversees the government bureaucracy, which employs an estimated two-thirds of Brunei's eighty thousand-person workforce.

Military

The Royal Brunei Armed Forces (RBAF), with about four thousand members (the strength of a brigade group with support elements), is the smallest military force in ASEAN. This voluntarily recruited, highly paid national defense force represents a state that spends a higher proportion of its budget on defense than any other ASEAN nation. The RBAF is augmented by such mercenary forces as a battalion of British Army Gurkhas and is directly at the disposal of the sultan. This force helps to ensure that there will be no revolt against the sultan's rule.

Political Parties

Brunei has no viable political parties, nor has the government mobilized its own party as is the case in Indonesia and Burma. In 1985 the *Partai Kebangsaan Demokratik Brunei* (Brunei National Democratic Party) was established, with moderate principles based on Islam and liberal nationalism, in order to achieve a system of parliamentary democracy under a constitutional monarchy. During 1986 leaders of the party called for elections and for the sultan to give up his position as prime minister so that his royal position would not be sullied by involvement in politics. Not surprisingly, these leaders were arrested in 1988, and the party was deregistered by the sultan.

Democratization

There is no democracy in Brunei. Its political system is an absolute monarchy with no representative form of government. The 1984 constitution consolidated the power of the monarchy by suspending parliamentary institutions. All communications throughout the country are controlled by the sultan; for example, the only newspaper is strictly monitored by the royal family.

In the absence of democratic institutions, the sultan has initiated a visit the people program in which he encourages his subjects to state their grievances. In 1989, more than a thousand residents attended a meeting at which they were allowed to express their views on government policy. However, it is not clear if this "town hall" meeting will be regularized or the grievances addressed.[2]

Economic Development

Vast oil reserves make Brunei's dynamics different from the agriculturally based economies of other Southeast Asian nations. Oil and natural gas represent 60 percent of the GDP (down from 80 percent in 1985) and 95 percent of export earnings. In view of the estimated twenty-year limit to Brunei's oil resources, the nation's Fifth National Development Plan (1986–1990) emphasizes diversification of the economy by developing small industries based on agriculture, forestry, and fisheries. The government has identified industries that can eventually offer replacement for employment and revenue as the oil reserves are depleted. These alternative industries include pharmaceuticals, cement, steel, chemicals, ceramics, and high technology.[3]

The oil economy has no direct developmental effects or linkages with the rest of the economy. Its capital and technology are acquired from abroad and have little impact on the other sectors of the economy. Most of the oil is exported, so the major result is that the state is provided with income; hence, any developmental effects that are derived from the oil sector depend on what is done with the profits. Brunei has chosen to use the profits to develop infrastructural facilities and a comprehensive welfare system.[4]

The recession in 1985—when Brunei, like Singapore, suffered a negative economic growth—resulted from the cutback in oil production to conserve reserves and stop falling oil prices. The recession also emphasized the need for alternative employment opportunities.[5] Moreover, Brunei's dependency on other countries for its food has reduced the nation's autonomy. One of the priorities of the latest development plan is to produce about 30 percent of Brunei's rice needs locally. Brunei's welfare state mitigates the impact of recessions, as the citizens' basic educational and health needs are provided free and their housing, religious, and cultural needs are subsidized.

The Bruneian State

Brunei's small size makes governing it far easier than is the case in the large and more diverse countries in other parts of Southeast Asia. Moreover, the state has brought virtually all institutions into its fold, leaving no autonomous societal groups to compete with the state apparatus. There is an essential identity between the state and the person of the sultan. The welfare state covers all basic needs of most Bruneians; thus, there is little dissension with the absolute powers of the sultan. His lineage and royal aura and his leadership of Islam in Brunei further strengthen his position. Nevertheless, there have been moves to establish groups that have called for the formation of democratic institutions and the relegation of the sultan to ceremonial rather than administrative functions.

Brunei has not experienced massive social dislocation in the contemporary period that would explain its strong state status. The government has pointed to Indonesian and Malaysian support for past revolts as a major reason for the constraints imposed on the people's right to establish political groupings. However, the sultan's supreme role does not constitute a catastrophic event that clears the way for the installation of a new, statesponsored strategy for survival. Brunei has experienced no event equivalent to the independence struggle in Indonesia, the destruction in the Philippines during World War II, or the Indochina war.

Brunei has received considerable aid and support from its former colonial ruler, Great Britain, and the presence of the Gurkhas has strengthened the state by intimidating potential dissidents. There is no major external threat to Brunei's security today, nor has there been since 1962 when the Azahari revolt was supported by Indonesia. No dissident groups have been allowed to reach a stage at which they pose a meaningful threat to the regime. Thus, Brunei's experience contrasts with that of Indonesia, where the internal Communist threat was considered sufficient to allow mass bloodletting and repression.

Every official, technocrat, and military officer in Brunei is related— directly or indirectly—to the sultan, his family, and his advisors. These persons do not have another base of social control independent of the state; the sultan is the state, and all officials are part of his entourage. The lack of any mass political base in Bruneian society has reinforced these officials' loyalty to the state. Nevertheless, they are skilled and highly educated. Even the Chinese community is loyal to the state, despite the fact that most Chinese in Brunei are not even citizens. However, their businesses depend on the sultan's continued largesse and support.

Sultan Sir Muda Hassanal Bolkiah has grown in his position. He was in the shadow of his father until 1986 and has only recently shown his leadership skills. His plan to diversify the economy in anticipation of the time when oil revenues will not be available is far-reaching. However, his unwillingness to move toward a more democratic government is effective in the short run but problematic in the long run as increased communications and economic development bring the modern world to Brunei.

Foreign Policy

Just one week after receiving its independence in 1984, Brunei joined ASEAN, strengthening its relationships with former adversaries such as Indonesia and Malaysia. Today, Brunei's foreign policy is pro-West and anti-Communist, and its central theme is security attained through international legitimacy. ASEAN membership was the primary means to that end.[6]

Brunei's relations with the United States have been close since its independence. Indeed, according to media coverage, Brunei channeled some $10 million to help the U.S.-backed Contras in Nicaragua after depositing the money in a Swiss bank account in 1986, and the Bruneian government confirmed that "His Majesty the Sultan of Brunei Darussalam . . . had made a personal donation to the United States to be used for humanitarian purposes in Central America."[7] This incident became part of the "Irangate" imbroglio; thus, it became the only information most Americans ever read about Brunei.

To help defend the nation and to discourage any attempt to challenge the sultan's absolute rule, the Bruneian government pays the full costs of stationing a British Gurkha brigade in Bruneian territory. At present, however, perhaps because Brunei is not threatened by any external power, the country has adopted a low-key foreign policy that is more reactive than proactive. Its main concerns are participating in ASEAN programs and building its diplomatic missions abroad to ensure future investments in the Bruneian economy.

Conclusion

As is true of most other Southeast Asian states, there are discrepancies in the explanation of conditions for a strong state in Brunei, whose absolute monarchy is increasingly an anachronism in the changing world of Southeast Asia. As the world moves toward open societies and governmental accountability to the people, Bruneians continue a nineteenth-century version of rule more akin to Middle East kingdoms than to modern Southeast Asia. The country's capacity to sustain absolutism results from the great wealth brought in by the sale of oil and gas. In a country surrounded by agricultural societies in which most of the people are poor, the sultan has "bought" his legitimacy by providing his subjects with the necessities and, indeed, with luxuries.

Notes

1. D. S. Ranjit Singh, "Brunei Darussalam in 1987: Coming to Grips with Economic and Political Realities," in *Southeast Asian Affairs 1988* (Singapore: Institute of Southeast Asian Studies, 1988), p. 63.

2. Bruce Burton, "Brunei Darussalam in 1989: Coming of Age Within ASEAN," *Asian Survey*, vol. 30, no. 2, February 1990, p. 198.

3. *Asia 1990 Yearbook* (Hong Kong: Far Eastern Economic Review, 1990), p. 91.

4. K. U. Menon, "Brunei Darussalam in 1986," in *Southeast Asian Affairs 1987* (Singapore: Institute of Southeast Asian Studies, 1987), p. 86.

5. Ibid., pp. 87–88.

6. Ibid., p. 97.

7. Ibid., p. 99.

9

BURMA

On June 18, 1989, the martial law government of Burma declared that the country's official name (in English) would henceforth be Myanmar.[1] Myanmar is a transliteration of what has been the country's official name in the Burmese language since its independence in 1948. The disadvantage of the name Myanmar (as well as of the name Burma) is that it has ethnic connotations, implying that the country is the land of the majority ethnic group—the Burmans. About a dozen minority non-Burman groups make up more than one-third of the total population of forty million; thus, there has long been ethnic sensitivity to the dominant position of the Burmans.

As most of the nations of Southeast Asia move toward economic development and democratization, Burma is a clear exception. Characterized by ethnic conflict, economic stagnation, and political oppression, Burma has been unable to achieve *pyidawtha*—the ideal peaceful, happy, and prosperous society. Failure to reach this goal has been all the more tragic because the nation is rich in natural and human resources and because the Burmese came close to securing their political rights in 1988 when they revolted against their military leaders. Carrying out their version of "people's power," the Burmese exalted in a short "Rangoon Spring" before the military brutally quelled the uprising.

The 1988 revolt was not the first time the Burmese have struggled for their rights. In January 1948 the Burmese won their independence after several years of demonstrations and often violent opposition to British rule. The independence struggle was led by the Thankin movement, a group of anti-British nationalists headed by Aung San, the father of modern Burma and a fiery nationalist who received his training in Japan during World War II when the Japanese occupied Burma. Subsequently, the movement turned against the Japanese as their occupation became increasingly repressive. Aung San, who was expected to be Burma's first head of state, was assassinated in 1947 and thus became the nation's martyred hero.

The Thankin movement served as the core for the Anti-Fascist People's Freedom League (AFPFL), a united front group opposed to the Japanese. AFPFL forces cooperated with the British to oust the Japanese, then turned against the British in the struggle for independence. AFPFL negotiated independence and formed the first parliamentary government in 1948 under the leadership of U Nu.

The period from 1948 to 1958 was known as the Time of Troubles. The well-organized minority ethnic groups opposed the government's move toward a national state and instead supported the establishment of autonomous states for each group. The Shans and Karens in particular rose against the central authorities, precipitating a struggle that came close to becoming a full-scale civil war.

The second major postindependence problem concerned the poorly trained civil service, which was not able to carry out government programs effectively. U Nu's government had proclaimed a Socialist policy that required a high degree of centralized administration, but the Burmese bureaucracy floundered, causing severe political and economic disturbances. By 1958 Burma's political condition was so chaotic that U Nu turned the functioning of the government over to the military, led by General Ne Win, a leader of the Thankin independence force and a compatriot of Aung San. Following this "constitutional coup," a caretaker administration succeeded in stabilizing the cost of living and controlling the black market. Exports were increased, and corruption was temporarily halted. Ne Win's government reorganized the bureaucracy to make it more efficient and restored a semblance of law and order.

Despite the success of the caretaker government in a number of areas, in 1960 the electorate chose to return to U Nu for leadership. Again, however, he was not able to control the economy. U Nu's leadership was based on his charismatic religious qualities and a reputation for impeccable honesty, but he was a poor day-to-day administrator. The nation was reeling from multiple rebellions among minority groups; therefore, a large share of the central budget was allocated to internal security, but U Nu concentrated on making Buddhism the state religion. His program to reach an idealistic vision of a Burmese welfare state based on the teachings of Buddha was not matched by a parallel plan for implementation and administration.

The military, which perceived that the civilian government was weak and dependent upon Western-style political institutions that were incompatible with Burmese culture, carried out a coup on March 2, 1962, led by Ne Win. This seizure of power, which was rapid, nonviolent, and without major challenge, began an era of military rule that has continued for twenty-nine years. Ne Win disbanded the Western-style parliament, banned political parties, and restricted civil liberties. He also devised a program of radical economic and political policies called the Burmese Way to Socialism, which included the nationalization of major industries, schools, rice mills, small and large businesses, and financial institutions. His program of a centralized state monopoly of the means of production was designed to ensure control of a united Burma.

To mobilize support for the Socialist program, Ne Win established the Burmese Socialist Program Party (BSPP), organized to reach down to the village level along hierarchical lines but with all the power at the party's military-dominated top echelon. The party's main function was to legitimize army rule. To keep Western "bourgeois decadent" ideas from infiltrating into Burma, Ne Win arrested those who opposed his policies, restricted travel to Burma by foreigners, and ended academic freedom at the universities. His move toward a neutralist foreign policy took the form of isolationism. By rejecting all forms of westernization, Burma—unique in Southeast Asia—has not accepted or encouraged the Western model of development.

In January 1974, Burma became the Socialist Republic of the Union of Burma after the new Socialist constitution had been passed by the electorate. Although Ne Win discarded his military uniform in 1971 and became the "civilian" president of the new government, the military continued to be the dominant political force. Ne Win stepped down as president in 1981 but retained his more powerful position as head of the BSPP. In that position he was able to continue his dominance over political and economic policymaking. In the summer of 1988, hundreds of thousands of farmers, urban workers, students, monks, and civil servants took to the streets of Burma's major cities to demonstrate against their government leaders.[2] This revolt was the culmination of years of frustration and disgust at the failures of the military government to bring development to Burma. Although rich in natural resources, Burma had been humiliated by the U.N. decision in 1987 to declare it one of the world's least-developed nations. The revolt was also a response to the pervasive persecution of the people's political rights since 1962 when the military had taken all power for itself.

A more immediate cause of the revolt was the decision of Ne Win's administration to declare valueless some 80 percent of the Burmese money in circulation. Any *kyat* note over $1.60 in value became instantly worthless. This demonetization, justified as a measure to undermine black marketeers and to control inflation, adversely affected the entire population, rich and poor. The bulk of the working economy was sustained by the black market (the government's Socialistic economy having collapsed), so the demise of the black market was seen as a great disaster. Moreover, no recompense was given holders of *kyat* notes above the maximum allowed; in effect, then, the savings of the entire population were wiped out.

The precipitating incident of the revolt occurred in a tea shop, where students and other patrons squabbled over the choice of music tapes being played. When the police arrived, a student was killed. Thousands of his schoolmates later returned to avenge their colleague's death, but they were met by weapons and security police. In a particularly dreadful incident, forty-one students were herded into a police van, where they suffocated in the intense heat. The head of the security police, General Sein Lwin, was held responsible for these and other deaths by the students and their sympathizers. More and more demonstrations and deaths occurred in the ensuing weeks. Unofficial estimates of student deaths from beatings, bayonet stabbings, and suffocation were in the hundreds, but the government blandly announced a total of only two student deaths.[3]

To defuse the threat to the army's continued political domination, Ne Win announced his resignation as BSPP party chairman and advocated a popular referendum for a multiparty system, implicitly admitting the failure of the Burmese Socialist experiment. The party rejected the idea of the referendum but agreed to accept his resignation. In an incredible decision, the BSPP appointed as chairman Sein Lwin, the head of the despised security police (*lon htein*), who was known as "the butcher" for his role in violently quelling student demonstrations in 1962, 1974, and 1988. His appointment set off even more demonstrations and more killings by the police.

After only several weeks as leader of the country, Sein Lwin was replaced by the civilian Dr. Maung Maung, an academic scholar and biographer of Ne Win. His appointment, however, came too late to stop the growing power of the people. In fact, his toleration of a free press and free assembly swelled the ranks of the demonstrators in the Rangoon Spring, as this period became known, as newspapers criticized the government. The U.S. government was one of the first to protest the military and police violence and was also the symbol of democratic government; thus, the grounds of the U.S. Embassy became an important site for antigovernment demonstrations. Demonstrations in the capital city of Rangoon and in Mandalay involved more than a million people.

With the knowledge that the military's dominance was in jeopardy, army commander-in-chief General Saw Maung, ostensibly on orders from Ne Win, crushed the revolt and restored the military (*Tatmadaw*) to power on September 18, 1988. The military's coup was not against an opposition government, as none existed, but was against the army's own creation of a civilian facade government under Maung Maung. The violent coup was followed by the arrest of demonstrators, the censorship of all forms of communication, and the flight of tens of thousands of students to the nation's borders to escape the military and to organize for a future rebellion. Altogether, some three thousand Burmese lost their lives in their attempt to end military rule.

Saw Maung, taking his orders from Ne Win, established the State Law and Order Restoration Council (SLORC) to endure "until anarchy and demonstrations could be brought under control." SLORC consisted of generals who were loyal to Ne Win and who were given responsibility for administering the state. Ruling by martial law, SLORC brutally suppressed all dissent. At the same time, but only for brief periods, SLORC allowed more open politics than during the Ne Win years. For example, political parties were able to apply for official recognition in anticipation of an election to be held in May 1990. However, when opposition party leaders spoke out against the regime, they were arrested.

SLORC argued that its harsh policies were necessary because of an alleged collusion between the Burmese Communist party and the U.S. Central Intelligence Agency, which was the cause of demonstrations and antigovernment dissidence. For example, Aung San Suu Kyi, the highly respected daughter of Aung San and head of the major opposition party, National League for Democracy (NLD), was placed under house arrest for having been "manipulated" by Communists and foreign intelligence agencies. SLORC also argued that a highly centralized, military-oriented administration was necessary to ensure the country's continued unity in the face of potential rebellion by minority ethnic groups. None of these explanations was accepted by the vast majority of Burmese, who were extremely angry that their people's revolt had been crushed. The *Tatmadaw*, once a symbol of stability in Burma, became a hated organization.

Reports from Burma were few during 1989 and 1990 because SLORC did not allow foreign journalists or scholars into the country. However, sketchy reports suggested that SLORC was violating the human rights of the Burmese by silencing writers, banning assemblies, and forcefully moving some half a million people from their homes with the aim of breaking up prodemocracy neighborhoods. The relocation of urban residents in late 1989 from urban cities to satellite towns was particularly egregious but was justified, according to SLORC, as a "beautification measure." A large number of people were also moved from constituencies believed to be favorable to opposition leader Aung San Suu Kyi.

Despite these violations of human rights, SLORC organized the May 27, 1990, election to choose legislators in the *Pyithu Hluttaw* (People's Assembly), the sole organ of legislative authority. Under the election law, each constituency was to elect one representative to the *Pyithu Hluttaw*.

Some 492 constituencies, defined by population, were to choose representatives; seven constituencies of ethnic minorities, however, were not allowed to vote because of "security" threats in the regions. SLORC believed that the election could be controlled to ensure that progovernment forces would prevail. In fact, the government was given the power to censor the speeches and publications of parties and candidates. Television time was limited to one ten-minute period per party during the entire campaign, and statements had to be submitted for approval seven days in advance. Candidates who gave speeches that had not been scrutinized and approved by the authorities were imprisoned.

Popular opposition leaders were harassed and kept from participating in the election. Aung San Suu Kyi, for example, was disqualified, as were former Prime Minister U Nu and another prominent opposition leader, former General Tin U. All of these leaders were placed under house arrest. Progovernment candidates who joined the successor party of the BSPP, the National Unity Party (NUP), received government funds for campaigning, but funds were not available to oppositionists. The authorities banned outdoor assemblies and relocated citizens from their voting constituencies to ensure a progovernment vote.

In spite of these measures and in an extraordinary display of independence, the oppositionist National Democratic League won more than 80 percent of the seats (396 of 485) in the National Assembly. The NUP won only ten seats, losing even in areas dominated by the army. Such a sharp rebuke of the martial law government was unexpected. Even months after the election, the military still refused to turn the government over to the newly elected legislators, even though the latter were ready to install a new constitution based largely on the country's last democratic constitution of 1947. Although the Burmese had expressed their anger toward the military government and their support for democratic rule through their vote, the regime in power was unwilling to act in compliance with the people's will.

Institutions and Social Groups

Since independence, the Burmese military has played the central role in governmental affairs. No other institutions or social classes have even been available to compete with the military. With the exception of Brunei, where the monarchy controls every aspect of society, no nation has been ruled by a single institution to the same degree as Burma.

General Ne Win

Eighty-nine years old in 1990, Ne Win has been commander of the armed forces, deputy prime minister, prime minister, minister of defense, chairman of the Revolutionary Council, president, and chairman of the state's only legal political party. His current title while he is in semiretirement is Patron of the War Veterans' Organization. Ne Win's power has been so great because power is personal in Burma; loyalty within the government is to the person, not the institution. As the supreme patron in a land of patron-client relationships, Ne Win received the undivided loyalty of government officials and common citizens.[4] Only when his abuse of power went beyond acceptable limits did his clientele rise against him. Even after the 1988 revolt when he became more reclusive, Ne Win continued to rule as he had for the preceding thirty years.

Legislature

The People's Assembly, a unicameral body, is elected by the people in single-member constituencies. Prior to 1989, the only legal party was the BSPP, which controlled the nomination of candidates so that there would be no deviation from party policy. Twenty-nine members of the legislature were chosen to the Council of State, the supreme executive authority, whose chairman, Ne Win, served as president of the republic. The Council of State nominated a Council of Ministers for the National Assembly to approve. The council chose the prime minister and carried out day-by-day governing responsibilities. The role of the legislature under a new constitution was not clear immediately after the 1990 elections.

The Military

In the early 1960s, the 190,000-member *Tatmadaw*, which began as a popular pro-independence force, was the only credibly unified force in the country. Ne Win, identified as the leader of the military, took over state power as a guardian who was above party politics. He ran the government by assigning leading governmental positions to military comrades.

In the postindependence period, the army has intervened to take power on three occasions. In 1958 the army was asked by U Nu to step in temporarily, but in 1962 it took power without an invitation. From then until 1988, the military dominated Burmese politics until demonstrations threatened to oust it, whereupon the army intervened once again, this time under Saw Maung who was fronting for Ne Win.

Political Parties

The only party allowed to function during the period of military dominance was the BSPP. Committed to Socialist policies, the BSPP became a national mass organization dedicated to supporting Ne Win as leader. In 1988 when the BSPP changed its name to the National Unity Party, the NUP—with its symbol of the rice stalk—inherited a strong organization and generous funding from BSPP. NUP has had access to government resources, including transportation, and to government officials who support NUP. During the 1990 election campaign, NUP candidates were the only ones not harassed by government and military bureaucrats.

When political parties were sanctioned in 1989, more than two hundred parties registered. Most political parties were ethnically or regionally based and supported a particular person. Many small parties were formed, however, in order to qualify for access to telephones and rations of gasoline provided by the government to political parties. Registration as a political party conferred the right to display a signboard, hold gatherings of fewer than five persons, and obtain extra gasoline. Nevertheless, governmental decrees made it impossible to hold meetings, print and distribute party literature, and say anything that might be construed as criticism of the military.[5]

The most important opposition party was the NLD, with its symbol of the farmer's hat. Initially, the party was led by Aung Gyi, Tin U, and Aung San Suu Kyi. Aung Gyi had become famous for a series of letters he wrote to Ne Win deriding the military regime, which he argued had brought great suffering to the people. Aung Gyi later alleged that Communists and pro-Communist elements had infiltrated the NLD. When he could not substantiate the charge, he was asked by the other party leaders to resign.

Aung San Suu Kyi, the daughter of independence hero Aung San, was schooled in Burma during her first fifteen years. A member of a prominent family, she was then sent to England to study politics, philosophy, and economics at Oxford University. She later published books on Burmese history and literature. Prior to 1988, she had no direct political experience and was known primarily as the daughter of Aung San.

Shortly before the beginning of the rebellion, Aung San Suu Kyi returned to Burma from England to care for her ailing mother. She joined the opposition and, because of her name and superb oratorical ability, began to draw large crowds. Burmese women copied her hair and clothing style. She was cheered for her straightforward attacks against the government and against Ne Win. Her military adversaries, frightened by her popularity, suggested that she was manipulated by Communists. On July

20, 1989, the military placed her under house arrest for one year, a term that was renewable each year, and cut off all communications with her followers and the outside world. She was not freed the following July 20, when the government chose to renew the sentence.

Minority Ethnic Groups

During the postindependence period, Burma's minority groups have continued to view themselves primarily in terms of ethnicity rather than nationality. The Karens, Shans, Kachins, and other groups that fought for state autonomy do not trust the government. In their struggle for minority rights, these groups have joined the National Democratic Front (NDF), an organization of nine groups, in revolt. The NDF assumes, first, that the peoples of Burma are members of ethnic-linguistic communities that came together in 1947 and formed a voluntary Union of Burma.[6] In this union, equality of communities was to be reflected in their organization as political units, each having power to govern itself, a reasonable share of the nation's resources, an equal right to develop its lands and societies, and equal representation in the national government.[7] In this projected union, the states were to be strong and the central government weak. In reality, however, and despite promises to state leaders at the time of independence, the central government became strong and the separate states weak.

In order to achieve the goals of minorities, armed insurgencies have been organized by the ethnic groups to protect their territories and to pressure the central government to accept a federated Burma, with ethnic states having autonomy under a federal umbrella government. Many opposition parties in the 1990 elections supported a federal system of government.

Another problem is opium, which represents a form of culture in an area in which it has grown for more than a century and now involves criminal elements.[8] The insurgents as well as the Burmese Communist party rely on opium profits to finance their guerrilla activities. Also, the illicit drug trade is lucrative for Thailand, which is the marketing channel for opium grown in Burma. If the opium trade dried up, Thailand would sustain an economic loss.

Women

Aung San Suu Kyi is the first woman in contemporary Burma to be seriously considered for national leadership. Like Corazon Aquino in the Philippines, she is the relative of a martyred hero. As the daughter of Aung San, the nation's founder, Aung San Suu Kyi is not a typical Burmese woman. In addition to having instant name recognition, Aung San Suu Kyi has qualities that explain her immense popularity. She is an eloquent orator, has impeccable character, is brilliant, and has the courage to oppose the military government. Like Aquino, her incorruptible character stands in striking contrast to the leaders in power. Stymied by her great influence and her commitment to democratic values as opposed to their autocratic ways, the nation's military leaders decided to silence her by placing her under house arrest.

Women have experienced a large degree of equality with men at the family level. They are household managers, have equal inheritance rights, and retain their own names during marriage. However, at the national level women have played subordinate roles compared to men, who have held virtually every position of political power. No woman in contemporary Burma has held a major military position or served in the cabinet.

Democratization

For almost all of its history, Burma has been ruled by autocratic monarchs and military leaders. Burma's only experience with democracy was a short period under the 1947 constitution after independence, when U Nu supported representative institutions, free elections, and civil liberties. The ineffectiveness of U Nu's rule was used as a rationalization for the government takeover by the military in both 1958 and 1962. Since that time, democratic institutions and behavior, said to be "foreign to the traditions" of the Burmese and a rejected legacy of Western imperialism, have been suppressed.

Burmese political culture, with its emphasis on hierarchy and status, is not conducive to democracy. Paternalistic authority is inconsistent with democracy's reliance on equality of opportunity, freedom of speech and assembly, and representative institutions. Burmese leaders, like those in Thailand during periods of military rule, argue that the quest for modernization and for security from outside aggressors demands strong, effective governments.

The inability of the Burmese government to develop the nation economically together with its oppression of human rights led to the people's rebellion against their leaders. The "supreme patron" was not fulfilling his obligations to his clients to meet their economic needs and to provide them with security. Ne Win lost his *pon* (grace) and therefore the respect of the Burmese people. The government became the problem rather than the solution.

Events in the summer of 1988 suggest that despite their isolation from world events, the Burmese desire the same freedoms and opportunities demanded by the peoples of Eastern Europe, China, and the Third-World nations, whose countries have moved from authoritarian to democratic regimes in the past decade. Hearing about the higher standard of living in Thailand, Burmese people know that the government's claim that authoritarian governments are necessary for economic development is false. In the past, at the moment when the nation's leaders could no longer meet the people's needs, they were believed to have lost their unquestioned authority and their apparently magical powers. That moment occurred in the summer of 1988.

Economic Development

The similarities between Burma and Thailand are striking. Both nations have had histories of absolute monarchy; both have practiced Therevada Buddhism; and both have similar natural resources and fertile soils for agriculture. In the 1950s, Burma and Thailand also had similar GNPs. In view of these similarities, why has Thailand had success in its quest for economic and political development while Burma has failed?

One answer stems from the most obvious difference between the two nations: The Burmese were colonized by the British, whereas the Thais have been independent throughout their history. The Thais, who did not develop an inferiority complex toward the West or antipathy to Western ways, were therefore more flexible about adopting and adapting westernization. In contrast, the Burmese consciously eschewed Western ways including the materialism and commercialism of Western culture, which the Burmese believe have ruined Bangkok.

Another answer is that the postindependence governments of Burma chose to isolate the nation from the world economic system, relying on indigenous government-controlled Socialistic economics. Thailand, on the other hand, "opened" its economy through a policy of free enterprise and export-driven growth. The results are dramatic: Thailand went from a per capita GNP of $100 in the 1950s to over $1,000 in 1990 while in the same period Burma went from a $100 per capita GNP to one less than $200. This latter figure does not include the black market—Burma's unofficial, underground trade, which covers about 80 percent of the economy and acts as a safety valve for an otherwise explosive situation. This large "free market" within the Socialist system has helped check the Burmese people's frustration.

Burma's economy reached its nadir in 1987 when the United Nations granted the once prosperous nation the ignoble status of Least Developed Country, placing Burma in the same category as Chad, Ethiopia, Nepal, and Bangladesh. Whereas Burma once controlled 28 percent of the world rice trade, by 1970 the figure had decreased to 2 percent.[9] The brutal suppression of demonstrators in 1988 ended the few ongoing Western development projects, reducing the external capital that had been available to the government. To counter this cessation of aid, in November 1988 Burma promulgated its most liberal foreign investment law to date. It permits foreign investors to form either wholly owned enterprises or joint ventures in which the foreign partner is required to hold a minimum 35 percent stake. However, little investment was induced by the government's policy because of the country's political instability.

SLORC has opened the economy slowly, hoping to rejuvenate the private sector. Civil servants have been given large pay raises, but much of those has been wiped out by an annual inflation rate of 40 percent. Burma has also opened its border trade with Thailand and China and has granted oil exploration agreements to South Korean, Japanese, Australian, and U.S. firms. (It is believed that Burma possesses significant oil reserves.)[10] However important these changes are for achieving higher levels of economic development, they will be limited by the continuation of a closed and tightly controlled political system.

The Burmese State

In a very real sense, the Burmese state has been dominated by few persons and institutions. Absolute monarchs followed by a military general have made the authoritative decisions that have affected the Burmese citizenry. In the postindependence period, General Ne Win and the state have become one and the same. Ne Win and his subordinates constitute the officials who decide public policy that is binding on the society. His domination of the state has been impressive, but his capacity to meet the needs of the people has been weak.

Burma has not developed institutions outside the military and its subsidiary organization, the BSPP. Essentially, the plethora of political parties established in 1989 was tailor-made for individuals and had no institutionalized structure. External institutions, such as a parliament, political parties, and interest groups, have had little influence over the state's policy decisions. In that sense, the Burmese state has been strong and autonomous, independent of societal organizations.

Whereas in Thailand the integration of the military into the political process increased governmental capacity, in Burma the integration reduced capacity. In Thailand, the military worked in conjunction with the bureaucrats, the monarchy, and interest groups to meet the demands of the citizenry. Also in Thailand, the military-dominated state managed the political-economic affairs of the kingdom effectively, thereby co-opting opposition groups and reducing challenges to the authorities. In Burma, on the other hand, the military used force rather than co-optation and coordination to retain its power.

In Thailand, the state authorities managed to achieve one of the highest economic growth rates in the world, primarily by allowing the nation's entrepreneurs to promote economic development. In Burma, however, the state authorities intervened in every aspect of the economy—nationalizing public utilities, industries, and agribusinesses and placing numerous obstacles in the path of entrepreneurs. The Burmese state has shown little adaptability to changes in the international and regional spheres and in the worldwide movement toward democratization. This lack of adaptability has undermined the legitimacy once enjoyed by the *Tatmadaw* and by Ne Win himself. The military is no longer the respected unifier of the nation; instead, it has become a symbol of stagnation and oppression. In this regard, the Burmese state at present is viewed as weak. It is a patronage operation with low capacity and legitimacy levels.

Like the Thai state, the Burmese state can be viewed as strong or weak. Burma, like all the other Southeast Asian nations except Thailand, underwent colonialism and Japanese occupation, both of which created severe social dislocations. These experiences favored concentrated social control to ensure that the nation would be secure from similar aggressions. Surrounded by strong nations, Burma has accepted its centralized rule as a means to thwart foreign invasion. Under similar circumstances, Thailand strengthened its state by receiving large amounts of foreign aid, especially from the United States. Burma fashioned its state primarily with its own resources. Those resources were few, and the strength of the state withered.

Burma's postindependence government has not invited technocrats, politicians, intellectuals, and socioeconomic elites to participate in state affairs to the same degree as has Thailand. The few outsiders brought into the polity had no autonomous political base or constituency. The economically powerful Chinese minority has not participated in Burmese politics, and the ethnic minorities have struggled against the state for decades. In contrast to Thailand where there are no strong autonomous groups whose primary loyalties are with regional or ethnic sects, fully one-third of Burma's population has such loyalties. In this respect, Burma does not meet a condition for a strong state, requiring groups that are skillful enough to execute the grand designs of state leaders.

Ne Win has used his leadership abilities to concentrate social control. Since 1962, Burma has had only one leader. In that same period, Thailand has had more than ten leaders. In 1988 the Burmese people rose against their aging leader, who they believed no longer had the capacity or legitimacy to rule.

Foreign Policy

There are many good reasons why the Burmese have felt insecure about their nation's security. Their colonial heritage and the Japanese occupation are reminders that Burma has been a victim of both imperialism and aggression. Surrounded by nations with far greater populations and military strength, Burma shares a thousand-mile-long border with China and equally long borders with India and Thailand. Burma's ethnic minorities, who live in the northern half of the country, have been supported by outsiders and are linked with the drug trade and with elements of the Burmese Communist party. Moreover, the nation's Indian and Chinese minorities have an influence in the Burmese economy disproportionate to their numbers. Finally, the government views westernization as a threat to Burmese traditional culture.

The government's response to this insecurity has been a policy of nonalignment. Burma has attempted a quasi-isolationist foreign policy by forgoing membership in ASEAN, refusing to participate in the Indochina conflict, and eschewing aid from various nations. However, this policy did not prevent China from providing military and political support to rebels along the border, although that support apparently ceased under China's more pragmatic post-Mao administration, which was more concerned with economic relations. Burma was one of the few nations in the world that expressed support of the Chinese government for its handling of the Tiananmen Square demonstration, possibly because Burma's 1988 rebellion was quelled in a similarly brutal manner.

Relations with Thailand have always been tense because of the history of wars between the two nations. However, relations improved following the 1988 revolt when General Chavalit Yongchaiyut visited Burma to negotiate logging and fishing deals for Thai companies. Desperate for foreign capital, Burma acceded to Thai requests to exploit its teak forests. Thai firms could no longer log in Thailand due to new environmental regulations not practiced in Burma. Concessions to Thai companies in

Burma permit extraction of 1.2 million tons of logs annually.[11] For the first time in decades, official and legal border trade was established between Thailand and Burma. The two nations resolved another obstacle to improved relations when the Thai military granted the Burmese military permission to use Thai territory to attack ethnic minority camps from the rear.

Relations with Burma's other major neighbor, India, remained cool, especially when the Indian government expressed support for the Burmese people's resolve to achieve democracy. India's support for Burma's opposition movement was shared by most Western democracies, and Japan, West Germany, the United States, Great Britain, and Australia suspended their aid programs after the mass killing of demonstrators in 1988.[12] The United States protested human rights violations in Burma but did not break relations, at least partially because of the need to continue coordinating policies to stem the narcotics trade. In 1989 Japan and Australia resumed aid to Burma.

Burma's policy of modified isolationism will be tested as the cold war recedes and international interdependence becomes the means by which economies grow. As economic development becomes the primary goal of successor regimes to the military, Burma will undoubtedly expand its international involvement.

Conclusion

Burma's future is unclear because the state is in a period of traumatic transition. Although the move from socialism to capitalism appears to have taken hold, the move from authoritarian military rule to democracy is still problematic. The main point is that the Burmese will continue to resolve their problems at their own pace, refusing to become dependent on outsiders. At the same time, they will carefully merge into the world system in order to achieve their primary goals of economic and political development without succumbing to the worst aspects of westernization. Without Ne Win in power, the state will be freer to broaden its constituencies. At the same time, the country will not have the stabilizing force of a known leader. The remarkable support accorded Aung San Suu Kyi suggests that the Burmese are willing to accept the notion that the military is not indispensable.

The Burmese polity will not lose its personalistic character overnight, nor will Western-style democracy flourish immediately. Patron-client politics, factionalism, and oligarchy have been essential elements of Burmese politics and will continue to be important factors. A politically balanced democracy is not the sole alternative for Burma. Military control, however, is no longer acceptable to the Burmese people.

Notes

1. The "r" in Myanmar is not pronounced but serves to lengthen the "a" sound. The word is pronounced approximately as Bamah. As Burma has been the correct English language name of the country until 1989, as the government that changed the name may be temporary, and to reduce confusion resulting from using two names, this chapter will use the name Burma throughout.

2. Maureen Aung-Thwin, "Burmese Days," *Foreign Affairs*, vol. 68, no. 2, Spring 1989, p. 143.

3. Burma Watcher, "Burma in 1988," *Asian Survey*, vol. 29, no. 2, February 1989, p. 174.

4. David I. Steinberg, *The Future of Burma: Crisis and Choice in Myanmar* (Lanham, Md.: University Press of America, 1990), p. 1.

5. Josef Silverstein, "Aung San Suu Kyi: Is She Burma's Woman of Destiny?" paper presented to the Association for Asian Studies, Chicago, April 1990, p. 10.

6. Josef Silverstein, "National Unity in Burma: Is It Possible?" in *Durable Stability in Southeast Asia*, ed. Kusuma Snitwongse and Sukhumbhand Paribatra (Singapore: Institute of Southeast Asian Studies, 1987), p. 80.

7. Ibid., pp. 80–81.

8. Ibid., p. 88.

9. Aung-Thwin, "Burmese Days," p. 150.

10. Robert H. Taylor, "The Evolving Military Role in Burma," *Current History*, vol. 89, no. 545, March 1990, p. 108.

11. James F. Guyot and John Badgley, "Myanmar in 1989," *Asian Survey*, vol. 30, no. 2, February 1990, p. 191.

12. Far Eastern Economic Review, *Asia 1990 Yearbook* (Hong Kong, 1990), p. 97.

10

VIETNAM

Stretching some twelve hundred miles from its border with China to its southernmost point in the South China Sea, Vietnam is like two rice baskets at the ends of a pole. The bulk of the population lives in the two baskets: the Red River Delta in the north and the Mekong River Delta in the south. The "pole" is the mountains in the central, sparsely populated regions of the country.

The majority of Vietnam's sixty-five million people work in agriculture. Eighty percent are Mahayana Buddhists and 7 percent are Roman Catholics, a religion to which they converted during the French colonial period. Many indigenous minority religions exist in Vietnam, including the Cao Dai and the Hoa Hao sects, each with about one million adherents. Since independence, Vietnamese society has been secularized so that most residents do not actively practice or pursue their religious beliefs. Confucianist principles from the nation's Chinese heritage stress centralized political authority and the notion of duties of subordinates to superiors: ruled to ruler, son to father, and pupil to teacher.

Nationalism has been the key concept for understanding Vietnamese politics. Indeed, Vietnam's search for a national identity received its greatest impetus during the thousand-year Chinese domination (111 B.C. to A.D. 939). The ability of the Vietnamese to emerge from that period with many of their traditions intact is proof of the nationalist urge that has pervaded the country's history. Similarly, the struggle against French colonialism, Japanese occupation, and U.S. intervention reflects the importance of that nationalism.

Vietnam has not always been united. During the era of French colonialism, the country was divided into three areas: Tonkin in the north, with Hanoi as the capital; Annam in the middle, with Hue as the capital;

and in the south, Cochin China, whose capital was Saigon. Traditionally, the northerners have seen themselves as modern, progressive, and efficient, and they have viewed the southerners as lazy. The Annamese have seen themselves as highly cultured, the northerners as grasping, and the southerners as rustic. Southerners have regarded themselves as pacifistic and their northern neighbors as aggressive and violent.

In addition to these differing cultural perceptions, national unification had to overcome the cultural and political dichotomy between the rural areas and the cities. Such interaction as there was consisted largely of the exploitation of the peasantry by the mandarin class. Moreover, Vietnam is populated by minority groups that have traditionally been treated with disdain by the Vietnamese majority.

Despite the divisiveness that has characterized much of Vietnamese history, a nationalist continuity has remained in the form of anti-colonialism and anti-neoimperialism. Following the Japanese World War II defeat in 1945, Ho Chi Minh—the leader of the League for the Independence of Vietnam, known as the Vietminh—proclaimed the country's independence and set up a provisional government headed by himself. The French and the representatives of the newly established Democratic Republic of Vietnam led by Ho initially agreed that a new independent state existed and that the French would not move to reclaim their former colony. However, the agreement broke down, and a series of clashes ignited the French-Indochinese War, which lasted eight years.

The military defeat of the French led to the Geneva Agreements of 1954, which sought to separate the rival French and Vietminh forces by setting up a temporary military demarcation line at the 17th parallel. This line was not intended to be a political or territorial boundary. In addition, the Geneva Agreements called for eventual national elections for the purpose of unification. During the Geneva conference, an anti-Vietminh administration emerged below the 17th parallel, initially led by the former Annamese emperor Bao Dai and subsequently by the strongly anti-Communist, Catholic-mandarin Ngo Dinh Diem. On October 26, 1955, Diem proclaimed the Republic of Vietnam with himself as the first president. He repudiated the Geneva Agreements, specifically the provision for national elections.

Ho Chi Minh had agreed to the Geneva Accords at least partly because he believed national elections would ensure reunification under Communist Vietminh leadership. Ho, who was both a nationalist and a Communist, saw the two ideologies as inseparable. His goal of a united Vietnam was scuttled when it became clear that Diem had no intention of merging with the north. Diem, with the support of the United States, had established a separate regime known as South Vietnam, with its capital in Saigon.

During Diem's increasingly repressive rule in the late 1950s, South Vietnam became the site of guerrilla insurgency against his government. The political arm of the guerrilla activity was the National Liberation Front (NLF), which was initially an autonomous southern-based movement. The military arm was known as the Viet Cong (Vietnamese Communist). A large number of northerners who had moved to the south following the Geneva Agreements joined these guerrillas. In the early 1960s the North Vietnamese provided increasing military support to the NLF. The People's Revolutionary party—the Communist party of South Vietnam—which was controlled by North Vietnam, gradually dominated the NLF until ultimately the two were indistinguishable.

To counteract insurgency, Diem relied on U.S. advisors, weaponry, money, and soldiers. U.S. support began in 1954 with one thousand advisors, which increased to five thousand by 1960 and stood at half a million in 1968. Despite this support Diem's position deteriorated until President John Kennedy acquiesced to a coup d'etat against Diem by South Vietnamese generals. The coup, which took place in October 1963, and Diem's concurrent death paved the way for a dozen ineffective and unstable military governments, which were less interested in economic or social reforms than in a military victory over the Viet Cong and North Vietnamese.

U.S. involvement continued to escalate. In February 1965 the United States began massive bombing of the north in order to interdict North Vietnamese supply lines, erode morale, and provide time for the south to strengthen its forces. None of these purposes was achieved. The massive 1968 Tet offensive by the north, which included attacks on all major cities and towns in the south, showed the ineffectiveness of the U.S. bombing policy and led to Lyndon Johnson's decision not to run for the presidency again.

South Vietnam had increasingly become a client state of the United States. To reduce this dependency and to blunt rising U.S. protests against the war, in the early 1970s President Nixon began a policy of "Vietnamization"—that is, the gradual withdrawal of U.S. troops from Vietnam while escalating the bombing against the north. In May 1970, U.S. and South Vietnamese troops invaded Cambodia, ostensibly to stop Viet Cong use of Cambodian "sanctuaries." The result, however, was a massive escalation of the war to all of Indochina, unparalleled demonstrations against the war in the United States, and the unification of insurgent forces in Cambodia.

Following the 1972 Christmas bombing of Hanoi (in which forty thousand tons of bombs were dropped), the Paris Peace Accords were signed by the contending powers in January 1973. North Vietnam agreed to a ceasefire, while the United States agreed not only to a cessation of bombing in the north but to withdrawal of its troops. The Paris Peace Accords were essentially a victory for the north because North Vietnamese troops were able to stay in place. Without U.S. bombing support and financial aid (the United States had spent over $112 billion in Vietnam since the 1950s), South Vietnam could not withstand the pressure from the north.

The rationale for U.S. intervention had several foundations. The first concern was the perceived national interest of the United States itself. Most U.S. policymakers saw the fall of Vietnam to communism as one more stage in a cancer that could eventually spread to the United States. Thus, South Vietnam became a testing ground for Communist wars of national liberation. It was believed that anything less than a committed stand against Communist aggression would be tantamount to an invitation for further aggression in other parts of the world. U.S. credibility as a world power was also seen as being at stake. U.S. policymakers cited the commitment of four presidents, the terms of SEATO, and agreements with South Vietnam as proper sanctions for U.S. involvement.

Decisions regarding Vietnam were also a function of internal pressure. Each president feared a political backlash if he were seen to be responsible for the defeat of South Vietnam. Therefore, Vietnam became the test of presidential strength, especially for Presidents Johnson and Nixon—both of whom articulated the need for total victory.

U.S. policy in Vietnam was also the product of several small steps, each insignificant in itself but in sum representing a giant leap. In this sense, U.S. intervention was almost inadvertent, a policy of gradual escalatory moves that by themselves seemed restrained but in sum committed the United States to a war in which over fifty-eight thousand U.S. soldiers died, over two million Vietnamese were casualties, over two million U.S. soldiers fought, and more bombs were dropped and exploded than in all past wars combined.

In April 1975 North Vietnamese troops moved swiftly through the south, conquering province after province and eventually capturing Saigon. A war that had endured for three decades came to a swift close. The immediate causes of the Communist victory included the corruption of the South Vietnamese army and the end of U.S. support. Long-range reasons for the Communist success included the artificiality of the south's political system. The South Vietnamese government, which did not meet the needs of the people, was viewed by many southerners and northerners as a lackey state of the United States. The war was also never fully understood by U.S. policymakers, who underestimated the importance of Vietnamese nationalism and the tenacity of a people to withstand great pressure. Moreover, the war never received the wholehearted support of the U.S. public or of even a large element of the government. As the war continued, more and more Americans believed that the means used by the U.S. government were disproportionate to the stated goals.

The North Vietnamese moved swiftly to consolidate their power. The newly united nation was named the Socialist Republic of Vietnam. Ho Chi Minh's goal of a united Vietnam under Communist rule was reached, and in his honor Saigon was renamed Ho Chi Minh City (although local residents continued to call the city Saigon). Hanoi became the nation's capital. Plans were carried out to transform the south into a Socialist economy, and "reeducation camps" were established to indoctrinate former partisans of the South Vietnamese government with Socialist values. An estimated 2.5 million Vietnamese have gone to these camps and been released following "rehabilitation."

The southerners did not take well to the economic programs of their new rulers. They resisted efforts to collectivize and redistribute the land. Moreover, the Vietnamese economy deteriorated, worsened by drought and the diversion of resources to its military in Cambodia and along the Chinese border. Poor management and planning by the central authorities were also responsible for the economic catastrophe faced by the new revolutionary government.

As the Vietnamese government ended the traditional free-market system in the south, the indigenous Chinese—the mainstay entrepreneurs in Ho Chi Minh City—fled the country. The government's reform of the monetary system had wiped out the savings of these shop owners. The result was a second wave of refugees, this time ethnic Chinese who became boat people. During 1978 and 1979, arrivals on the shores of Thailand, Malaysia, Singapore, and Indonesia finally overwhelmed those countries' resources, as seventy-five thousand refugees per month fled Vietnam.[1] Close to one million Vietnamese have left Vietnam since the Communist takeover. Ho Chi Minh City in particular suffered from the loss of Chinese shopkeepers and the resulting inflation and unemployment.

On December 25, 1978, with the concurrence of the Soviet Union, Vietnamese troops invaded Cambodia and established a new government led by an unknown Vietnamese-trained Cambodian named Heng Samrin. The Vietnamese claimed their invasion was launched to restore order and security in border areas by punishing Cambodia for a long series of border incursions and for intransigence in negotiations. The Vietnamese also insisted they were liberating Cambodians from the genocide and repression of the Pol Pot regime. The invasion acted as an impetus for the subsequent Chinese invasion of Vietnam in February 1979. The Chinese hoped that their own offensive would force Vietnam to withdraw its occupation force of two hundred thousand troops from Cambodia. China desired to "teach Vietnam a lesson," to convince the Vietnamese that

China was not a paper tiger, to punish the country for its harsh treatment of overseas Chinese, and to send a signal to the Soviet Union that China would not acquiesce to increased Soviet influence in Southeast Asia. Neither country was able to claim a clear-cut victory.

Vietnamese expectations that independence from foreign exploitation for the first time in over one hundred years would bring them a better life were dashed by the continued deterioration of the economy. In the 1980s, a decade after their defeat of the United States—the world's mightiest and most technologically sophisticated nation—the Vietnamese people's standard of living was worse than before the war. Indeed, the economy had advanced little since the French colonization of Vietnam in the late nineteenth century.[2]

The sixth congress of the Communist Party of Vietnam (CPV) realized the seriousness of the economic malaise and met in December 1986 to implement a plan to remedy the problems. Nguyen Van Linh, a prominent reformer, was named CPV general secretary. His appointment and the retirement of such old-guard Communist revolutionary leaders as President Truong Chinh, Premier Pham Van Dong, and Foreign Minister Le Duc Tho signaled a significant turn in Vietnamese politics. The leadership shift to the more pragmatic, social welfare-oriented, reform-minded younger officials from the ideologically conservative, security-minded party leaders was the first major break in leadership patterns since Ho Chi Minh came to power after World War II.

The succession to Nguyen Van Linh was carried out smoothly, just as a smooth succession had occurred in 1969 when Ho Chi Minh died. After Ho's death, a collective leadership had arisen with Le Duan the first among equals. No one could replace Ho, for his legend was too immense to be inherited by one man. When Le Duan died in 1986, the succession to Linh again proceeded without purges, despite the desperate state of the nation's economy.

At the December 1986 party congress, Linh set forth a policy of renovation (*Doi Moi*), a plan publicly approved by the Communist party leaders, all of whom agreed that the policies of the previous eleven years— since the end of the war—should not be repeated. Renovation called for major economic and political changes with the proviso that the party-led dictatorship of the proletariat remain sacrosanct.

Nevertheless, renovation was difficult because a strong coalition of conservative party leaders felt threatened by the changes. Communist party leaders feared that the party's dominance would be lost, and military leaders—who play an important role in the politburo—believed that renovation threatened national security because it diminished the importance of military strength in favor of economic development.[3]

The changes included rapid movement away from the centrally planned economy and development of a more market-oriented model. The change built upon the economic reforms that had begun in the late 1970s when a contract system was introduced and decentralization of various aspects of the economy carried out. The contract system allowed peasants to sell a small portion of their crops after meeting their obligations to the government. That system had stagnated when peasants refused to cooperate because their profits were so small that they had no incentive to produce more. The new plan provided greater incentives, including ownership of land formerly nationalized by the government.

Renovation also called for more public debate and more power for the National Assembly, the main legislative branch of the government. Political prisoners were released and corrupt officials ousted from their positions. The press was allowed to criticize government policies more aggressively.

Renovation, while initially popular, met with sharp criticism when the new policies failed to improve the economy. In 1988, for example, famine was barely averted in the northern provinces, and inflation increased to almost 1,000 percent. In response, conservatives insisted that a conservative, Do Muoi, be named prime minister. Uncharacteristically, the National Assembly members demanded that two candidates be permitted to run, for the first time challenging the CPV central committee's nominee for a key government post. Do Muoi, who was unpopular in the south because of his role in introducing repressive Socialist policies, won only 64 percent of the assembly's votes against his reform-minded opponent, Vo Van Kiet, an unprecedented rebuke to the CPV. The reformers lost the vote, but the dissent allowed in the National Assembly reflected the new openness of the regime.

Renovation was also threatened by the remarkable changes in Eastern Europe, as country after country brought down Communist rulers. Of most concern to the Vietnamese party leaders was the fall of Romania's leader, who most believed was invincible. The people's revolt against the military in Burma also worried Vietnamese leaders, as there were many parallels in the two countries' bleak economic conditions. These international changes, however, only strengthened the position of the hardliners. Vietnam was one of the few nations in the world that condemned Poland's change of government and praised China's crushing of its democracy movement.

Also jeopardizing renovation was the reformers' decision to disengage from Cambodia, withdrawing troops by September 1989. The conservatives argued that Vietnam received no visible benefit, not even expressions of gratitude let alone offers from the United States to move toward normalizing diplomatic relations and ending the trade embargo put into effect by the United States during the war. This lack of positive response from the United States caused the reformers to be more orthodox and to take fewer risks.[4] Also, the reformers were more careful about indicating what beneficial responses would be forthcoming to Vietnam as a result of their more pragmatic policies.

Despite renovation, human rights violations continued in Vietnam. Amnesty International USA documented cases of detention without trial of former civil servants and members of the South Vietnamese armed forces in reeducation camps. Also documented were unfair trials of alleged opponents of the government and prisoners of conscience and reports of torture and ill treatment of prisoners in police custody and in prisons. Amnesty International concluded that improvements in the treatment of dissenters had occurred since renovation but that the record was still unacceptable.

As Vietnam entered the 1990s, the government was in transition from the old guard, revolutionary forces, who had held power in the north since independence, to younger (although still elderly), reform-minded Communists who were more willing to try new means to achieve their aims. These means fluctuated between hard-line and more open policies. While the zigs and zags of government policy remained unpredictable, the ultimate goal remained constant: perpetuating the central power of the CPV.

Institutions and Social Groups

Ho Chi Minh

On May 19, 1990, the people of Vietnam celebrated the 100th anniversary of Ho Chi Minh's birth. As the founding father of independent, Communist Vietnam, the victorious leader over the Japanese, French, and Americans, and the founder of the CPV, Ho was the most important Vietnamese in contemporary times and perhaps the most important Southeast Asian. He was and remains an important institution—the symbol of united, nationalist, Communist Vietnam. His picture is ubiquitous in the northern half of the country, and millions of people have viewed his embalmed body in the Soviet-built mausoleum in Hanoi.

Ho was the son of a Confucian scholar who was active in anti-colonial activities. His mother died when Ho was ten. Throughout his life he used numerous pseudonyms (the name Ho Chi Minh means "he who enlightens"). In his youth, he traveled to the Soviet Union, China, New

York, London, and Paris. He became a committed Communist and founded the forerunner parties of the CPV, including the Indochinese Communist party in 1930 and the Vietminh in 1941. His tastes were simple, even ascetic, yet he was tenacious and even ruthless in the means he used to achieve his goals.

Ho died six years before the nation was reunited. His last testament requested that at his death, there be a one-year moratorium on farm taxes and that his ashes be placed in urns in the three parts of Vietnam: Cochin, Annam, and Tonkin. However, these requests were not heeded by Ho's successors. Instead, taxes were raised, and his body was embalmed in a massive building similar to Lenin's mausoleum in Moscow. No leader has subsequently received the adulation Ho received during his life, although every leader has attempted to wrap himself in Ho's mantle.

Communist Party of Vietnam

Although the Communist parties of Eastern Europe were imposed from without by Soviet arms, the Communist party is indigenous to the Vietnamese and was the vehicle for the independence struggle against the French colonialists and, later, the Americans. In modern Vietnamese history, the CPV has had an almost exclusive claim to nationalism and patriotism. For many Vietnamese, the Communist party and nationalist struggle are identical.

Total membership in the party is about 1.8 million, or 3 percent of the population. In effect, the party controlled the state until the era of renovation when the state was given more authority. Vietnam's newest constitution, promulgated in 1980, gives the party the leading role in society, enforcing a unified Marxist-Leninist policy line for the state and society.

However, the party is not unified. Vietnamese politics in the politburo is best understood by analogy to the great game of *bung-di*, or faction bashing.[5] Factions, a product of Vietnamese heritage, form around individuals but traffic in issues. They are enduring but not permanent, and they can divide and reform to meet changing needs. Despite attempts to contain factionalism, factions are ubiquitous. The present politburo can be divided into four major factions: reformers, neoconservatives, military, and bureaucrats.[6] In a sense, these categories are misleading because all thirteen politburo members are "reformers"; that is, all agree that the status quo is and has been unworkable. All are "conservative" in being cautious about taking risks, all agree that national security is a top priority, and all have bureaucratic constituencies that they control.

Military

The Vietnamese army is the creation of the CPV, and the leading generals are members of the party leadership. After 1975, the 1.2 million-member People's Army of Vietnam (PAVN), initially given the mission to reunify the nation, was charged with defending the nation from external attack, such as when the Chinese crossed Vietnam's northern border in 1979. In contrast to the armies of Thailand, Burma, and Indonesia, the Vietnamese army has not threatened a coup against the Communist leadership. Its role remains subordinate to that of the party.

Mandate of Heaven

Traditional Confucianist thought remains an important institution in Vietnam, and according to traditional Vietnamese ideas, there is a universal, harmonious moral order as long as each person carries out his or her duty by fulfilling the obligations of a subordinate to a superior, and vice versa. The emperor is as obliged to rule according to moral principles as the peasant is to follow his commands. When harmony does not exist or when there are wars, pestilence, or natural calamities, the ruled may perceive that the emperor has lost the "mandate of heaven." In other words, the emperor's personal virtue is lacking, for otherwise the cosmos would not be out of harmony.

The mandate of heaven concept is important for illuminating authority relationships in Vietnam. On one hand, one can interpret the cosmological beliefs of the Vietnamese as essentially conservative, for the mandate of heaven is lost or gained by means that are beyond the control of individuals. On the other hand, the cosmological view can provide a rationale for rebellion, for if the emperor is lacking in virtue—with a consequent disharmonious effect on the cosmos and society—his mandate is perceived as lost and his rule is called into question. The rise of a new government is proof that the new revolutionary regime has taken over the mandate. Accordingly, the ruled have transferred their allegiance to the new government with a renewed sense of community.

The Communist government of April 1975 is the most recent example of such a total change. The Vietnamese had sensed the changing of the mandate during the post–World War II struggle, first against the French and then during the second Indochina War. According to Confucianist belief, Ho Chi Minh inherited the mandate when he declared Vietnam's independence in 1945, and the Communist triumph shifted authority relationships rapidly and traumatically to the new Communist rulers. The Marxist view of collective discipline is not incompatible with the Confucianist concept of societal order, and the centralized, hierarchical nature of the command structure under a vanguard class is compatible with a Confucianist mandarin state. For these reasons and because the Communist government took total control of the society, the Vietnamese are likely to carry out their duty to obey the sovereign leaders until they sense that the leadership has lost the mandate.

Democratization

In 1989 the central committee of the CPV, alarmed by developments in Eastern Europe and Burma, rejected appeals for political pluralism in Vietnam. President Nguyen Van Linh stated that the party rejected calls for "bourgeois liberalization, pluralism, political plurality, and multi-opposition parties aimed at denying Marxism-Leninism, socialism and the party's leadership."[7]

From the Vietnamese perspective, Western democracy represents all that the country's leaders have rejected: unstable regimes led by bourgeois leaders for their own interests against the interests of the masses. The Vietnamese also reject the "arrogance" of the Western world (and now the Eastern European nations as well), which criticizes the Vietnamese government. The counterrevolutionary forces in Poland were condemned by the Vietnamese when the Communist leadership there was removed. Vietnamese leaders have stated that Vietnam is not prepared for democracy, that conditions in the country are not appropriate for democracy. In this period of restoration and economic travail (according to Linh) after a destructive war, the strong leadership of the party is necessary to ensure the nation's stability and progress.

In the economic domain, democratization is not such a pejorative term. Decentralization and accountability are accepted as necessary for an effective economy. Economic principles of the market and competition, once viewed as decadent bourgeois concepts, have become the centerpieces of renovation.

Vietnam has no history of democracy. Its traditions are Confucianist, stressing hierarchy and order, and more recently Communist, emphasizing the unquestioned supremacy of the party. There have been few popular demonstrations for democratic rights, and the Vietnam War was never a struggle for civil liberties and representative government. The movement of European Communist governments toward democracy has not impelled the Vietnamese leadership or the people to a similar transformation of their government.

Economic Development

Since the end of the war in 1975, the Vietnamese economy has declined. Inflation rates have been astronomical, and unemployment has stayed at about 20 percent. Infrastructural necessities such as ports, roads, and electricity are primitive, and housing is abysmal. Vietnam's banking system is barely viable, partly because there is so little managerial expertise. Annual per capita income is estimated to be below $200, making Vietnam one of the ten poorest nations in the world. Famine, which threatened the northern provinces in 1988, affecting ten million farmers, forced Vietnam—a country once self-sufficient in rice—to appeal for international food aid. Ho Chi Minh's favorite aphorism, emblazoned on red banners strung across streets throughout Vietnam—"Nothing is more precious than independence and freedom"—has been interpreted in an ironic and sardonic sense. In unguarded moments, Vietnamese state that nothing is exactly what they have.

Given the superb natural and human resources available, the country's poverty is all the more shocking and embarrassing to Vietnamese leaders. However, there are important reasons why the country has been unable to develop in parallel fashion to its neighboring ASEAN nations. A major reason relates to extensive war damage, which has required tremendous resources to repair. In the south alone, the war is said to have produced 20,000 bomb craters, 10 million refugees, 362,000 invalids, 1 million widows, 880,000 orphans, 250,000 drug addicts, 300,000 prostitutes, and 3 million unemployed. Two-thirds of the villages and 5 million hectares of forests were destroyed.[8] Even more than a decade after the end of the war, the economic system is still mobilized for war, with 50 percent of the state's resources devoted to PAVN for military purposes such as funding the Cambodian occupation and resisting Chinese aggression in the north.

The U.S. involvement in South Vietnam created a dependent economy, and the billions of dollars spent on the war brought a surfeit of capital that ended abruptly when the United States disengaged. Hanoi had expected to receive some $3 billion in reparations aid, which was promised by Henry Kissinger but later refused when the United States maintained that North Vietnam had not carried out the terms of the Paris Peace Accords. Soviet aid has not made up for the loss of Western aid and trade lost to the Vietnamese because of the U.S.-sponsored trade embargo. Moreover, the Soviet Union's technological aid has been insufficient in many ways.

Adding to Vietnam's woes has been mismanagement by its leaders. Alternating between reform and orthodoxy, Vietnam's leaders have "displayed a paranoid world view, a low adaptability level, perfidy consistently perceived in the motives of others . . . and perpetuation of a cult-type leadership capable of believing the illogical, the irrational, even the absurd."[9] Nationalization and collectivization, thrust upon the south after reunification, were unfailingly disastrous, largely because of the refusal of southerners to adhere to Socialist policies. Peasants refused to meet their obligations to the state when the state's prices for their crops did not cover even the costs of production.

To overcome the crisis, the Sixth Party Congress in December 1986 proposed major reforms and initiatives. Rice output in 1986 was far below that in 1942, and even northern farmers (who were members of cooperatives) produced 52 percent less than private farmers. To alleviate this situation, land laws were modified to guarantee farmers a 10- to 15-year tenure on land they cultivated, although the expectation was that land could henceforth be owned in perpetuity and be inherited. This policy change signaled the end of efforts to collectivize agriculture in the south.

Since 1986, farmers have had the legal right to sell their produce on the free market after each pays a tax based on his or her output. Approximately 10 to 20 percent of the tax goes to the state for the farmers' use of cooperatively owned machinery and for fertilizer and other necessities. Under the new system, farmers can keep a far larger percentage of their output than was true under the former contract system. Although the policy took several years to make a positive impact, after nearly thirty years Vietnam reemerged in 1989 as a major rice exporter. It became the world's third-largest rice exporter after the United States and Thailand, and most of its rice was exported to West Africa, the Philippines, India, Sri Lanka, and China.

The foreign investment code was also revised to attract more foreign investors. For joint ventures, tax policies were liberalized, and guarantees were made that investment capital would not be expropriated or joint ventures nationalized.[10] The 1987 investment law offered a two-year tax moratorium for joint ventures and set up a free-export zone in which foreign companies would be free to import and assemble commodities, use low-cost local labor, and export final products. A large proportion of the new investors were overseas Vietnamese.[11] The new code increased trade with Japan, Singapore, Hong Kong, France, Indonesia, and India but did not bring in the amount of capital hoped for because of the U.S. trade embargo. More and more countries, however, broke the embargo to take advantage of the liberalized trade and investment opportunities, especially regarding offshore oil exploration.

The reforms made a dramatic difference in the everyday economy. Construction of homes, buildings, bridges, roads, and schools, for example, burgeoned throughout the country, even in the north where the economy had been stagnant for many decades. Privately run restaurants and shops were opened and flourished. Inflation dropped to more manageable levels as a result of the devaluation of the dong to the free-market rate, and government austerity measures—recommended by the International Monetary Fund with which Vietnam wanted to restore relations— were adopted in order to attract investment, credit, and technology from the West.

Vietnam remains impoverished, but for the first time since the end of the war, there is economic development. In a sense, however, the country is still divided because development is more rapid in the south than in the north (partly as a result of the millions of dollars sent back to relatives from the one million Vietnamese living abroad). Unemployment remains high, especially among those considered unreliable because of their involvement with the former regime. Peasants who continue to farm within a small margin of error risk devastation by natural disasters, such as drought or flooding, or from orthodox Socialist economics under a new administration.

Having faced up to the nation's abysmal economy, in December 1990 the Communist party set forth a plan called the Draft Strategy of Socio-Economic Stabilization and Development up to the Year 2000. The plan's goals were to double the country's per capita income, raise rice production by 50 percent, triple electricity output, and achieve a fivefold increase for exports—all by the year 2000. These goals were thought to be unattainable without significant investment from the West, which is an impossibility until the trade and aid embargoes are lifted.

As a sign of confidence in the future, Vietnam proclaimed 1990 the Year of the Tourist and began building hotels and increasing airline traffic to Ho Chi Minh City. In 1989, however, only fifty thousand tourists visited Vietnam, whereas in the same year five million tourists visited Thailand.

The Vietnamese State

Until recently, the Communist Party of Vietnam has been the state. All authoritative decisions were made by the party, then disseminated to the populace through a tightly controlled organization that allowed no dissent. Civil liberties have been curtailed to ensure that the party is uncontested. Only since 1986 have new institutions emerged that have real power, such as the National Assembly.

Vietnam is the archetypical example of a nation that endured major social disturbances that uprooted the traditional bases of social control and cleared the way for new state leaders. For Vietnam, a succession of wars and revolutions led to fundamental organizational changes in everyday life, concentrating social control into a single agency—the Communist party.

These social dislocations occurred at a time when support and shelter for Vietnamese state leaders were provided by the world Communist movement. Since World War II, Vietnam has never been free of either potential or actual aggression by outsiders. The Japanese, French, Americans, and Chinese have all intervened, causing state leaders to mobilize their forces and concentrate their power and capabilities. Vietnam is therefore a classic case of war and the threat of war, inducing state leaders to take risks to consolidate social control and thereby creating a strong state.

Vietnamese rulers have no constituencies except their party leaders, and state bureaucrats identify their ultimate interests with those of the state as an autonomous organization. Loyalties lie with the state rather than with autonomous religious, ethnic, or class interests.

Whether Vietnam has prospered from a skillful top leadership is controversial. In many respects, the Vietnamese state has not had the capacity to meet the everyday economic needs of its people. Except for Laos and Cambodia, no country in Southeast Asia is as poor, and few other countries' economies have actually deteriorated over the last several decades. On the other hand, Ho Chi Minh stands out in modern history precisely because of his skills in using conditions to concentrate social control. His successors, who have had to deal with more difficult issues than nationalism, have had to meet the needs of sixty-five million persons whose expectations were high once they achieved independence and reunification. Thus far, the state's capacity to meet these needs has been weak.

Foreign Policy

The major goal of Vietnamese foreign policy has been constant: to secure the sovereignty of the nation against all aggressors. To meet this goal, Vietnamese foreign policy has sought to ensure a cooperative, nonthreatening Indochina, firmly allied with Vietnam; to prevent an anti-Communist front from threatening Vietnamese interests; to limit the role of the United States, China, and the USSR in Vietnam's sphere of influence;

and to establish working relations with ASEAN neighbors. These latter, more specific goals have met with various degrees of success.

Since at least 1975, Vietnamese foreign policy has fallen within the context of Marxist-Leninist fundamentalism. Socialist solidarity versus the interventionist, exploitative capitalist world has narrowed the nation's options and reduced the flexibility that foreign relations require in a world of fast-moving change. Foreign policy was carried out in *dau tranh* (struggle) terms, so that foreign relations are treated strategically—like protracted military conflicts—over an extended period of time.[12] This approach made negotiations with allies and adversaries difficult because Vietnam's points were presented as statements of superior virtue, not as expressions of national interest.

After 1986, ideological fundamentalism decreased and became more nonideological, stressing the need for Vietnam to play a greater role in the world economic system. Vietnam's leaders saw that Communist governments were falling around the world, that Vietnam was economically isolated, and that the nation was increasingly dependent on the Soviet Union; thus, they moved in fundamentally new directions in their foreign policy.

Vietnam's military withdrawal from Cambodia in 1989 was one major change. Politburo liberals argued that keeping Cambodia as a friendly neighbor was important but not as important as Vietnam's economic collapse. Politburo reformers argued that withdrawal from Cambodia would end Vietnam's international isolation by leading to the normalization of ties with the United States, halting the multilateral trade embargo against Vietnam, and inviting Western aid.[13] Adding to pressure to withdraw was the restiveness of Vietnam's armed forces, demoralized by the military stalemate that had cost some fifty-five thousand Vietnamese lives.

However, the withdrawal in September 1989 did not bring the expected international gratitude. Instead, ASEAN and the United States faulted the troop withdrawal for not being part of a comprehensive peace plan for Cambodia and for not allowing the withdrawal to be monitored by an international control mechanism. It was not until July 1990, when Secretary of State James Baker announced that the United States would begin direct negotiations with Vietnam relating to the Cambodian situation, that the withdrawal elicited a positive response from the United States. Meanwhile, no moves were made toward normalization of relations, and the trade embargo continued.

Vietnam also moved to improve relations with Western nations interested in developing economic ties. Hundreds of trade and investment delegations from Japan, Taiwan, South Korea, Thailand, and various European countries arrived to set up business ventures. Relations with

China also improved, partly because of the vast border trade between the two nations.

For the United States, Vietnam and the rest of Indochina had been a low foreign policy priority since the end of the war. The United States was no longer concerned about Chinese aggression in Southeast Asia; nor did the United States see itself as the guardian of the region once thought to be vulnerable to conquest by a monolithic Communist empire. The ASEAN countries were flourishing and no longer viewed themselves as potential victims of Vietnamese aggression. In many respects, U.S. goals in Southeast Asia had been attained sufficiently to allow U.S. interests in Asia to focus more on Japan and China than on Indochina.

Nevertheless, in 1988 U.S. interests in Indochina increased when the threat of a Khmer Rouge takeover and the withdrawal of Vietnamese troops from Cambodia again brought Vietnam into the news. Memories of the war the United States had lost were fading, and Vietnam had become more cooperative on POW-MIA issues. Hanoi had accepted a standing U.S. offer to conduct joint U.S.-funded searches in provincial locations believed to have remains of MIAs. Five joint search operations have taken place in nothern Vietnamese provinces since September 1988. Of the 2,347 Americans with MIA status as of July 1989, all but one (for symbolic purposes) are listed by the Pentagon as "killed in action, body not recovered."[14]

Progress on the POW-MIA issue and the withdrawal of Vietnamese troops from Cambodia brought to the fore the question of normalization of relations between the United States and Vietnam. The issue's emotional dimension was receding as memories of the war dimmed, and arguments in favor of normalization centered on the fact that the most difficult problems had faded. Vietnam, which was no longer demanding reparations, had offered cooperation on MIAs and had withdrawn its troops from Cambodia.

A longer-term argument favoring normalization concerned the need to balance or counter the presence of the Soviet Union in Southeast Asia. The development of naval bases at Cam Ranh Bay and Da Nang was particularly troubling to ASEAN, Japan, the United States, and China, all of whom viewed the Soviet military buildup in Vietnam as a security threat. The Cam Ranh base provides potential control over vital waterways of the Pacific Ocean, South China Sea, and Indian Ocean, which are deemed indispensable for U.S. trade, Japan's access to oil, and the security of ASEAN.

As Soviet aid to Vietnam decreases and as President Gorbachev has stated the USSR's intention to give up its military bases there eventually, Vietnam is open to an alternative counter to potential Chinese aggression. Russians are not liked in Vietnam, and there is a surprising feeling of warmth for Americans in both the northern and southern areas. Moreover, it is not in the best interests of the United States to have the Soviet Union and China make the crucial decisions affecting Vietnam's present and future status. Normalization would allow the United States to act as a counterweight to Soviet and Chinese influence.

A different argument for normalization suggests that such support would help the reformers against the hard-liners. By expanding aid and trade relations, Vietnam's economy would be strengthened, thereby strengthening political liberalization as well. In non-Communist Southeast Asia, economic growth and prosperity are the underpinnings of national political stability and the movement toward democracy, and the same pattern might apply to Vietnam. By balancing pressure and normalization, the United States would help the Vietnamese end their international isolation.

Supporters of normalization note the parallel cases of Germany and Japan, two nations the United States fought in World War II. U.S. support of those nations in the postwar period encouraged them to become the closest U.S. allies in Europe and Asia, and normalization with Vietnam could produce the same outcome.

Normalization would also enable the United States better to monitor the Orderly Departure Program (ODP), a program to give Vietnamese who worked with the U.S. government an opportunity to move to the United States as refugees. In 1989, when approximately 19,500 ODP refugees came to the United States, Vietnam agreed to resettle more than 300,000 former prisoners, most of whom had been former officials associated with the U.S.-backed government in South Vietnam. In addition, a U.S. presence would encourage Vietnam to repatriate refugees.

Vietnam shifted its policy slightly later in 1989, agreeing to repatriate some refugees in order to remove an obstacle to improved relations with its neighbors that had been a source of friction since the first wave of refugees in 1975.[15] As countries of "first asylum" for Vietnamese refugees, many of Vietnam's neighbors—including Thailand, Malaysia, the Philippines, and Hong Kong—had been unduly burdened by providing refuge over the years for the enormous number of people fleeing Vietnam.[16] Normalization would facilitate discussion of this and other humanitarian issues.

The final argument for normalization relates to the perceived best interests of the United States. Vietnam is viewed by other Asian countries as the next economic frontier, and Japan, South Korea, Taiwan, and Thailand are already investing in it heavily and making use of Vietnam's inexpensive labor and famed worker discipline. With its new, liberal foreign investment code, Vietnam has become more enticing to business ventures. As the economy strengthens and the infrastructure improves, the sixty-five million Vietnamese could become an economic power in Southeast Asia. U.S. business interests are increasingly supportive of normalization so that the trade embargo can be lifted.

Arguments against normalization stress that diplomatic relations with Vietnam will legitimate a repressive government. Indeed, many Vietnamese refugees in the United States oppose normalization for that reason. In their view, the North Vietnamese brutally and illegally took control of the south, and they should not be rewarded for that action. Moreover, normalization would provide incentives to international organizations to aid Vietnam, thereby giving its Communist government resources for further repression.

Normalization could also remove the major lever the United States has to influence Vietnamese behavior. As Vietnam desires normalization, it is more willing, it is argued, to accede to U.S. demands in order to encourage the United States to end its boycott. From a geopolitical perspective, some analysts argue that normalization would cause China and the Soviet Union to seek a greater role in Southeast Asia to counter new U.S. involvement in Indochina. Also, the U.S. alliance with Vietnam might cause China to give more support to the Khmer Rouge forces in Cambodia.

From a Vietnamese perspective, normalization is desirable, notwithstanding the government's negative view of past U.S. involvement in Indochina. Vietnamese leaders believe the United States helped France attempt to restore its colonial control, helped divide the country at Geneva in 1954, bombed the nation (causing two million casualties), punished the country with a worldwide trade embargo, allied itself with Vietnam's traditional enemy, China, and condemned Vietnam for its intervention into Cambodia despite its role in ending the horrific regime of Pol Pot. Notwithstanding these negative perceptions, Vietnam has made clear its desire for normalization in order to end the blocking of U.N. aid and World Bank loans as well as U.S. opposition to investment from Japan and Western Europe. Vietnam also desires a counterbalance to its overdependent relationship with the Soviet Union.

Conclusion

Vietnam's future is linked to the outcome of factional struggles between reformers and conservatives and to the U.S. decision to normalize relations. With rich natural resources, a disciplined workforce, and a long tradition of entrepreneurial activity, Vietnam has the capacity to become the economic frontier in Asia. Until 1986, the Communist government undermined Vietnam's advantages by oppressive policies and mismanagement. Realization of that fact has brought about major economic reform, which bodes well for the nation's future.

Notes

1. Frederick Z. Brown, *Second Chance: The United States and Indochina in the 1990s* (New York: Council on Foreign Relations, 1989), p. 39.

2. David G. Marr and Christine P. White, eds., *Postwar Vietnam: Dilemmas in Socialist Development* (Ithaca: Southeast Asia Program, Cornell University, 1988), p. 2.

3. Ronald J. Cima, "Vietnam's Economic Reform," *Asian Survey,* vol. 29, no. 8, August 1989, p. 789.

4. Douglas Pike, "Change and Continuity in Vietnam," *Current History,* vol. 89, no. 545, March 1990, p. 119.

5. Douglas Pike, "Political Institutionalization in Vietnam," in *Asian Political Institutionalization,* ed. Robert A. Scalapino, Seizaburo Sato, and Jusuf Wanandi (Berkeley: Institute of East Asian Studies, University of California, 1986), pp. 49–51.

6. Pike, "Change and Continuity in Vietnam," p. 118.

7. Far Eastern Economic Review, *Asia 1990 Yearbook* (Hong Kong, 1990) p. 241.

8. Marr and White, eds., *Postwar Vietnam: Dilemmas in Socialist Development,* p. 3.

9. Pike, "Political Institutionalization in Vietnam," in *Asian Political Institutionalization,* ed. Scalapino, Sato, and Wanandi, p. 43.

10. Ronald J. Cima, "Vietnam in 1988: The Brink of Renewal," *Asian Survey,* vol. 29, no. 1, January 1989, p. 67.

11. Cima, "Vietnam's Economic Reform," p. 797.

12. Douglas Pike, "Vietnam and Its Neighbors: Internal Influences on External Relations," in *ASEAN in Regional and Global Context,* ed. Karl D. Jackson, Sukhumbhand Paribatra, and J. Soedjati Djiwandono (Berkeley: Institute of East Asian Studies, University of California, 1986), p. 240.

13. Ronald J. Cima, "Vietnam in 1989: Initiating the Post-Cambodia Period," *Asian Survey,* vol. 30, no. 1, January 1990, p. 89.

14. Brown, *Second Chance: The United States and Indochina in the 1990s,* pp. 110–111.

15. Cima, "Vietnam's Economic Reform," p. 794.

16. Ibid., pp. 794–795.

11

CAMBODIA

The many names under which Cambodia has lived in the past two decades reflect the turmoil this country has undergone. Cambodia was once known as the Kingdom of Cambodia, but the country became the Khmer Republic when the military came to power in 1970. From 1975 to 1979, the period of fanatic Khmer Rouge leadership, the country's name was changed to Democratic Kampuchea, followed by People's Republic of Kampuchea when the Khmer Rouge was overthrown. In 1989, the country became the State of Cambodia.

Cambodia traces its heritage to the great Khmer civilization, which culminated in the twelfth century when the Khmers (Cambodians) ruled over most of modern-day Cambodia, Laos, Thailand, and Vietnam. The magnificent Khmer civilization, symbolized by the great temples at Angkor, lasted over five hundred years and reached a level of military, technological, political, and philosophical achievement that was unmatched at the time in Southeast Asia. Angkor eventually fell, and the kingdom suffered from domestic instability and external invasions until 1864 when the French took over a weak Cambodia as a protectorate.

The great Khmer civilization has now become the State of Cambodia, with between six and seven million residents—mostly rural farmers—almost all of whom are Buddhists who live in deep poverty. As a nation, Cambodia personifies tragedy, its people having suffered unspeakable horrors during the era of the Khmer Rouge from 1975 to the beginning of 1979. Indeed, neither the people nor the nation have fully recovered from the horrors.

Cambodia's postwar search for identity and nationhood once it was free from French colonialism was dominated by Prince Norodom Sihanouk, whom the French had placed on the throne in 1941. In 1955, one year after Cambodia's independence was granted, King Sihanouk abdicated and entered politics as Prince Sihanouk. His unrivaled dominance of Cambodian life from the end of World War II to 1970 was based on the way he achieved leadership, which was by plebiscite, and on the unsurpassed loyalty of rural Cambodians. He was revered as a god-king in the tradition of the Angkor kings, and his authority rested on charismatic, traditional, repressive, and legal foundations.

Sihanouk, who controlled all important policymaking institutions, exhibited a remarkable capacity to keep each major sector of the society in check, thereby maintaining political stability. His overthrow on March 17, 1970, was therefore a surprise to most analysts of Cambodian politics. On that date, while Sihanouk was in the Soviet Union, the Cambodian National Assembly—charging Sihanouk with abuses of office—unanimously condemned him to death for treason and corruption. His position was assumed by General Lon Nol, the premier in Sihanouk's government.

Sihanouk's downfall stemmed from the presence of North Vietnamese and Viet Cong forces in the so-called Cambodian sanctuaries. Against his army's wishes, Sihanouk had allowed the Vietnamese to use this territory, although his trip to Moscow was to request Soviet aid in ousting the Vietnamese. The Vietnamese presence in Cambodia had become so permanent that by mid-1969 the North Vietnamese had built a base of support in a region almost equal to one-fourth the area of Cambodia. Sihanouk had also allowed shipments of Chinese arms across the country from the port at Sihanoukville.

Sihanouk's relations with the United States during this time were both acrimonious and supportive. He opposed U.S. involvement in Vietnam, although as the North Vietnamese established themselves in Cambodian territory, he changed his mind and argued the need for a U.S. force in Asia to provide a balance of power to the Communist nations. From the U.S. perspective, Sihanouk was mercurial and untrustworthy, but there is no evidence that the U.S. government gave its approval to the military's plan to overthrow Sihanouk.

From Sihanouk's perspective, his short-term changes in policy were consistent with his overall objective of a neutral and sovereign nation. Cambodia's history has been characterized by attempts by more powerful neighbors as well as Western imperialists to dominate Cambodian political life. Therefore, Sihanouk's neutralism reflected his appreciation of historical precedents and his realization of the rising influence of China and a Communist Vietnam in Asia as well as the declining influence of the United States.

The Cambodian National Assembly nevertheless deemed Sihanouk's apparent ambivalent and inconsistent policies regarding Vietnamese intrusion as an act of treason. It charged him with allowing the North

Vietnamese and Viet Cong to operate in sanctuaries on the border. It also charged that the prince had engaged in corruption and had ruined the economy by nationalizing Cambodia's few industries.

These alleged reasons for the subsequent coup must be seen, however, in a larger context. Before his fall, Prince Sihanouk had lost the loyalty of elite groups in Cambodia. The army united around General Lon Nol and agreed with his view that Sihanouk was not moving strongly enough to remove the Vietnamese from Cambodian territory. Bureaucrats resented Sihanouk's total control over policymaking and personnel decisions; intellectuals opposed his policies of press and speech censorship; and university graduates were frustrated at the lack of job opportunities. Although Sihanouk retained the loyalty of the rural masses, that group wields little influence in Cambodian politics.

Sihanouk's major failure was his inability to institutionalize the political system so that power relations were not exclusively a function of his desires and whims. Initially his charisma was the country's primary integrating force; subsequently, however, his total dominance of Cambodian political life undermined the nation's major institutions. The army became the dominant institution in Cambodian politics in March 1970, and for a short time Lon Nol had the support of many Cambodians. There was more freedom of speech and the press than under Sihanouk, and there appeared to be an opening or expansion of the economy. Lon Nol's government, therefore, appeared to be enjoying popular support. However, after a few months it became clear that the new government was not only inefficient but corrupt. By the end of April 1970, President Richard Nixon, without first informing the Cambodian government, announced an invasion into Cambodia to protect the lives of U.S. soldiers, to ensure the success of his Vietnamization program, and to gain a decent interval for U.S. withdrawal from Vietnam. He announced that the intervention would clear all major enemy sanctuaries, including the headquarters of the Communist military operation in South Vietnam. Accordingly, an estimated 550,000 tons of bombs were dropped by the United States, about 25 times the explosive force of the atomic bomb that devastated Hiroshima and three and one-half times as many bombs as were dropped on Japan during World War II. Nearly half the population was uprooted, and the people became refugees in their own country.[1] The Communist headquarters was never found.

The fall of Sihanouk precipitated five years of total war on Cambodian soil. The U.S.-backed Lon Nol government proved incapable of coping with either international or domestic crises. His regime was corrupt; there were food shortages for the first time in the country's history; inflation was out of control; and hundreds of thousands of Cambodians became refugees. Phnom Penh's population had grown from six hundred thousand to two million and one out of ten Cambodians was killed in the war—most from U.S. bombing and suicide missions sent by Lon Nol to repel the Vietnamese. From his exile in Beijing, Prince Sihanouk announced his support for the radical rebels who opposed the Lon Nol regime. The country fell into a civil war that did not end until April 1975, when the Khmer Rouge rebel forces took control of the countryside and forced Phnom Penh into submission.

The massive bombings, the social dislocation, and the corruption of the Lon Nol government attracted support to the Khmer Rouge, which many believed was made up of nationalist "peasant reformers." That myth was quickly dispelled when the Khmer Rouge ordered the complete evacuation of Phnom Penh, swollen by refugees to more than two million people, within hours of the takeover.

Pol Pot, the leader of one of several Khmer Rouge factions who eventually became the dominant individual in the new government, headed a tightly disciplined party vanguard called "the organization" (*Angka*), which ruthlessly ran the country. *Angka* represented itself as the leader of oppressed workers, farmers, and peasants against the "feudal, imperialistic, capitalist, reactionary, and oppressor classes" of former regimes. The name Cambodia was changed to Democratic Kampuchea and Prince Sihanouk was brought back as the nominal head of state, but in reality he was under house arrest.

Angka used draconian measures to silence even potential voices of opposition and to reduce to impotency every person believed to be allied with the former ruling groups. The means to this end included strict discipline, total control, terror, and isolation from "unpure" societies. The first policy, carried out immediately after the fall of Phnom Penh, was the evacuation of every person from a major city to the countryside. At first it was believed the evacuation was only for three days because the new government feared mass starvation in Phnom Penh and other cities, which had very limited supplies of rice. The evacuation, however, was meant to be permanent, to "purify" the society of decadent urban ways and to ensure internal security and rid the country of "spies, imperialists, and enemies." The evacuations led to thousands of deaths and the separation of families.

Angka also purged persons who were in any way related to the Lon Nol regime or were believed to harbor the slightest "bourgeois" values. Former residents of Phnom Penh were treated especially harshly by the regime. In places where displaced urban people settled, high death rates resulted from starvation, illness, and forced labor. An estimated one million persons were executed or worked to death between 1975 and 1979, an act of genocide that has few parallels in history. The entire intelligentsia was executed, often in hideous ways.

Further "enhancing" the Khmer Rouge's rule was the policy of forced labor, or collectivization, and total restructuring of the economy. All Cambodian entrepreneurs lost their money when the regime stopped the use of currency and nationalized private businesses. The family unit was replaced by collectives of up to one thousand households that ate and worked together. Khmer Rouge troops enforced all these harsh rules and made sure that no one resorted to the bourgeois values of privatism, hierarchy, individualism, and the nuclear family.

Refugees reported that the society was rigidly organized into separate groups of men, women, the elderly, children six to fifteen years of age, and older teenagers. Only small quantities of food were available for communal workers. No schools were open, and no money was in circulation. Buddhist temples were turned into rice storage buildings, and 80 percent of the nation's books were thrown into rivers. Under Pol Pot, Cambodia became one of the most closed societies on earth.

On Christmas day 1978, a Vietnamese-led invasion overthrew Pol Pot's regime and installed Heng Samrin as president. Heng Samrin was an unknown former Khmer Rouge division commander who had sought refuge in Vietnam when his faction was overpowered by Pol Pot's. Democratic Kampuchea became the People's Republic of Kampuchea (PRK). Vietnamese troops took Phnom Penh after less than two weeks of fighting and forced the Khmer Rouge to flee to the mountains in the west.

Following the Communist victories in Vietnam in the spring of 1975, the Cambodian Khmer Rouge had begun raiding Vietnam's border towns, thereby threatening Vietnam's important Mekong Delta and causing thousands to lose their homes. An estimated thirty thousand Vietnamese civilians were killed during the Cambodian attacks. Pol Pot may also have intended to reclaim the ancient Khmer Empire, which once covered most of southern Vietnam. The fighting reflected the long historical adversary relationship between the two nations.

Vietnam announced that the purpose of its invasion of Cambodia was to end the constant border disputes, which jeopardized Vietnamese citizens, and to expel the hated Pol Pot government. Certainly, Vietnam also desired a friendly government, not an ally of China, on its doorstep. The Khmer Rouge was viewed as Maoist and supportive of China, Vietnam's principal enemy.

The invasion has also been interpreted as a proxy war fought by surrogates of China and the Soviet Union. China provided aid to Cambodia, and the Soviet Union supported Vietnam; thus, these two world powers deliberately provoked confrontation for the purpose of increasing their own self-interests and potential control over insurgent movements and governments in Southeast Asia. This interpretation sees Cambodia and Vietnam as pawns of major powers rather than as independent nations. However, historical precedents suggest that more was at issue in these border wars than competition between the major Communist powers.

The new government moved to undo the most onerous policies of the previous government, and Phnom Penh was slowly repopulated. A market system developed, and piped or running water and electricity were made available. Marriage and family restrictions were ended, forced collectives were abolished, and Buddhism was allowed. Schools were reopened, and universal primary school education was instituted. After four years of the "killing fields," a semblance of normality appeared.

Despite reforms, the new government faced severe problems. The Cambodians disliked and distrusted the Vietnamese officials and occupation soldiers (who numbered almost two hundred thousand) but nevertheless understood that they stood between themselves and the return of the Khmer Rouge. In addition, there was an administrative vacuum caused by the absence of virtually all trained and educated Cambodians. For example, there were only forty-five doctors in the entire country. Few trained administrators survived, and the country had no currency, no markets, no financial institutions, and no industry.[2]

The new government also faced a famine from 1978 to 1980 in which hundreds of thousands starved to death, and continued fighting between the Heng Samrin and Khmer Rouge forces disrupted the harvest of what little rice was planted. Farmers were so physically weakened that they could not adequately care for their crops. International agencies were mobilized to bring food, and although thousands of people were saved from starvation, the rescue was only partially successful. As evidence of hoarding, favoritism, and corruption came to light, aid agencies were discouraged, but an even greater problem was the lack of qualified administrative personnel. In general, there was too little food, and it arrived too late.

If Cambodia had not been drawn into the Indochina War and had not suffered subsequently from its devastation, from genocide under a tyrannical regime, from famine, and from the flight of thousands seeking food and freedom, the 1980 population would have been ten million. Instead, the total population in 1980 was about five million (and has recently risen to seven million). Few societies have sustained such tremendous losses.

A visitor to Phnom Penh in 1990 is impressed by the relative normality of everyday activities after the nation suffered such an extraordinary series of tragedies. The resiliency of the Cambodians is remarkable as they move toward a semblance of stability. The Hun Sen government has liberalized the economy, allowing private shops and markets, and the goal of food self-sufficiency has been met. Nevertheless, Cambodia is one of the five poorest countries in the world, and the U.S. trade and aid embargoes have prolonged the people's suffering. As long as the CGDK is given the U.N. seat, the Phnom Penh government cannot receive needed aid.

The improved standard of living is most visible in Phnom Penh, where some eight hundred thousand people populate a city that had zero population just ten years earlier. Despite the country's remarkable economic liberalization and growth, political liberalization has been less dramatic. The Kampuchean People's Revolutionary Party, which has refused to allow competing parties, continues to dominate the country's political life. Total dominance has led to abuses of power, and the lack of progress toward settlement of the nation's civil war has diminished Hun Sen's popularity.

The more pragmatic and reform-oriented Hun Sen acts, the more his hard-line government officials are disturbed. When he attempts to appease his conservative critics, he risks losing a favorable international image and plaudits from reform-minded Cambodians. Reduced aid from the Eastern bloc, the U.S.-sponsored trade embargo, and the civil war have left the government without resources. Thus, Cambodia lurches from crisis to crisis with bleak prospects for development and peace.

Institutions and Social Groups

Prince Sihanouk

Since the 1940s, Prince Norodom Sihanouk has dominated all aspects of Cambodian society. Although placed on the throne by the French in 1941 (when he was nineteen) and thought by the French to be pliable, Sihanouk became the symbol of Cambodian independence. With his shrill voice, he rallied his people during an era when Cambodia was known as "an island of tranquility in a sea of chaos." Conversant in ten languages, the author of five books, and a stage and movie actor and director, he has been the country's most cosmopolitan citizen.

Although Sihanouk ruled autocratically, his government was supported by the overwhelming majority of the people, although he allowed only his own party to enter elections. Sihanouk kept the support of the rural people but eventually lost that of Cambodia's urban elites, who opposed his foreign and economic policies. After he was overthrown by his own premier in 1970, he allied himself with the Khmer Rouge rebels while in exile then returned to Phnom Penh as a "ceremonial" leader. Subsequently, he cooperated with the Khmer Rouge, even though it had murdered five of his sons and daughters, fourteen of his grandchildren, and more than a million of his former subjects. Sihanouk is an egotist who has been willing to prolong the civil war in order to maximize authority for himself.

During the administration of Hun Sen, Sihanouk lived in exile in Beijing and Pyongyang. His movement in and out of the CGDK has solidified his reputation as being mercurial. Sihanouk has lost much support by having been out of power for over twenty years and having allied himself with the Khmer Rouge. Nevertheless, he remains one of the country's major institutions.

Hun Sen

By 1986, the Vietnamese-installed government was running the nation's affairs. Hun Sen, the prime minister and foreign minister, had become the leading figure in the PRK although Heng Samrin, the head of state, held the highest position. Hun Sen's PRK controlled the cities and most of the countryside with the aid of Vietnamese soldiers and advisors. However, few nations recognized the PRK as the legitimate government despite its control over virtually all aspects of life in Cambodia.

The opposite of Sihanouk in many ways, Prime Minister Hun Sen is Cambodia's most important leader. He was born in a peasant family and did not finish high school. Hun Sen was twenty-four when the Khmer Rouge came to power under Pol Pot. The Khmer Rouge evacuated his family from its rural house, killed his eldest son, and imprisoned his wife. Blinded in one eye by a U.S. cluster bomb, Hun Sen joined the Khmer Rouge as a senior commander before its fanaticism became clear. He defected in 1977, as Pol Pot began his systematic execution of dissident Khmer Rouge members, and escaped to Vietnam.

As leader of the People's Republic of Kampuchea (later changed to State of Cambodia), Hun Sen has eclipsed the head of state, Heng Samrin. Hun Sen has traveled abroad to win foreign aid and support and is known to be a pragmatist more than an ideologist. His attempts to make his government independent of Vietnam have greatly improved his popularity in Cambodia and in the world.

The State of Cambodia

For seven million Cambodians, the State of Cambodia, headquartered in Phnom Penh, has been the only organization around which they could rebuild their lives after the disastrous Khmer Rouge years. The government remains weak partly because there is only a small number of experienced administrators and professionals. Its centerpiece is the People's Revolutionary Party of Kampuchea (PRPK), a Marxist-Leninist party that monopolized power until 1989 when the party lost that distinction to an elected National Assembly and executive State Council. The National Assembly, not the PRPK, renamed the country the State of Cambodia, designated Buddhism the national religion, declared Cambodian foreign policy to be based on neutrality and nonalignment, abolished the death penalty, and altered the national flag to make it look less Communist.

Coalition Government of Democratic Kampuchea (CGDK)

The CGDK, which opposed the government of the PRK, was granted the Cambodian seat at the United Nations in 1982. The three disparate factions within the coalition, which in the past were enemies, are now united solely in their opposition to the Vietnamese-sponsored regime in Phnom Penh. The largest of the factions, the Democratic Kampuchean Khmer Rouge, is headed by Khieu Sampan, who is vice president of the coalition. The military arm of the Khmer Rouge consists of some thirty-five thousand soldiers, presumably led by Pol Pot. The Khmer Rouge was seated at the United Nations from 1979 to 1981 and again, as part of the coalition, from 1982 to the present.

Based in the western mountains of Cambodia near the Thai border, the Khmer Rouge is the best-equipped, most capable, and best-organized fighting force in the country. These rebels are supplied by China with infantry weapons, rocket-propelled grenades, and mortars. In 1990 Khieu Samphan continued to function as party head, partly because his reputation was slightly better than that of Pol Pot, Ieng Sary, and other Khmer Rouge notables. Earlier, Khieu Samphan had acted for the Khmer Rouge in negotiations toward a peace settlement. Pol Pot, although he no longer holds the title of party leader (to keep the Khmer Rouge from being branded an international pariah), is considered to be the behind-the-scenes leader. By late 1990, he was rarely seen in public and was reported to be seriously ill.

With the strongest military force in the country, the Khmer Rouge controls only a small amount of land. Periodically there are reports that the Khmer Rouge has taken new territory and is threatening to take Phnom Penh. These reports are usually exaggerated by the Khmer Rouge to remind its foes that it is a force with which to be reckoned. The possibility of its return to power is one reason the U.S. policy of indirect support changed in 1990 toward excluding the Khmer Rouge.

The second faction in the coalition is the KPNLF, an anti-Communist, right-wing group with about five thousand troops under the leadership of Son Sann. Son Sann, who held numerous positions in former Cambodian administrations, is prime minister of the coalition. He is supported by the non-Communist ASEAN states and along with Prince Sihanouk's group has enjoyed funding of about $7 million per year from the United States. The KPNLF is in turn factionalized between followers of Son Sann and followers of his armed forces commander, General Sak Sutsakhan. Corruption and power struggles have weakened the KPNLF.

Prince Norodom Sihanouk, the president of the coalition, leads the third faction known as FUNCINPEC (a French acronym for the United National Front for an Independent, Peaceful, and Cooperative Cambodia). Its military arm, the *Arme Nationale Sihanoukiste*, consists of about three thousand troops on the Thai-Cambodian border. Sihanouk was named president largely because of his international fame, and his numerous "resignations" reflect his ambivalent feelings toward his coalition part-ners—especially the Khmer Rouge, which was responsible for the deaths of members of his family. His major goal has been to oust the Vietnamese from Cambodia by whatever means are necessary, including an alliance with those he loathes. Sihanouk believes the Vietnamese have system-atically destroyed Cambodian culture and must therefore be removed before Cambodians cease to exist altogether.

By 1991, no solution had emerged over resolving the impasse between the rebel forces and the PRK. One proposed formula is a quadripartite government consisting of the PRK and the three coalition groups. Those who support this formula suggest that Khmer Rouge involvement in a future government will co-opt this force, thereby preventing the Khmer Rouge from persisting in a civil war. Prince Sihanouk has been a major supporter of the quadripartite formula. The other position, a tripartite formula, excludes the Khmer Rouge on the grounds that its genocidal record precludes a legitimate role in any future government.

Refugees

On the Thai-Cambodian border, some 260,000 displaced Cambodians are still held in camps, many for several years. In 1990, an additional 1800 Cambodians fled to Indonesia where they were interred on Galang Island. Their fear of persecution by PRK authorities is judged to be poorly founded, so these Cambodians have not been given refugee status and are referred to instead as displaced persons.[3] These displaced persons came at different times: during the U.S. bombing, after Lon Nol's rise to power, in the Khmer Rouge period, during the Vietnamese invasion when famine drove thousands out of the country, and in 1990 when chances for a peace settlement were negligible. (In total, almost one million persons have fled Cambodia.) The camps were controlled by U.N. agencies as well as by Khmer Rouge and non-Communist resistance forces. In effect, the displaced became a human buffer between Thailand and Cambodia. Periodic incursions and shelling brought further devastation to people already suffering.

Refugees are still numerous in the region even fifteen years after the end of the Indochina War, and they continue to be the center of intractable warfare and conflict. The ASEAN members, while still the countries of first asylum for Cambodian and Vietnamese refugees, have threatened to stop giving asylum unless the United States reverses its position against the forced repatriation to Vietnam and Cambodia of those who are judged to be "economic migrants." Malaysia has been turning back boat people for several years, in effect condemning them to roam in the high seas. The U.S. position has been that it is unthinkable to return refugees to nations ruled by reprehensible leaders.

The refugee camps ruled by the Khmer Rouge employ the ruthless discipline of the 1975 to 1979 period as well as terror and slave labor. In 1988, for example, the Khmer Rouge forcibly removed an estimated sixteen thousand refugees from a camp and forcibly marched them into the interior for resettlement as "the vanguard of the new revolution."[4] Refugee agencies are not allowed into these camps except under conditions dictated by the Khmer Rouge.

Democratization

Cambodia has never experienced democratic rule. Since the days of ancient Angkor, Cambodian governments have been led by autocratic rulers with scarcely any accountability to the ruled. Even today in the State of Cambodia, the characteristics of democracy are absent. An important reason for this is the omnipresent threat of foreign aggression, which has encouraged strong leadership at the expense of people's involvement in governmental affairs.

Cambodians have a long history of Hindu-Buddhist notions of hierarchy, status, and deference to those in authority. Indeed, the political order is still seen as a microcosm of the universe. The king was to his kingdom as God is to the cosmos. Great monuments were built to the glory of rulers, an attitude that culminated in the great Khmer kingdoms. However, the principles of absolutism and hierarchy, introduced during the country's Hinduization, are still essential aspects of Cambodian politics.

Economic Development

In addition to being one of the five poorest countries in the world and having been ravaged by the Khmer Rouge and bombed and occupied by foreign forces, Cambodia is the only Third World nation that is denied governmental aid by most of the world's wealthy nations and the United Nations; thus, its prospects for economic development are dismal.

When the PRK took control in 1979, the government initially favored a command economy based on the Vietnamese model. Private enterprise and private property were not allowed. Since the mid-1980s, however, the PRK has instituted its own version of *perestroika* by liberalizing foreign investment laws, allowing private industries, increasing international trade, returning land to peasant ownership, permitting private transportation enterprises, guaranteeing the end of the nationalization of private enterprises, and legalizing the private sector.[5] This opening of the economy immediately improved the output of the industrial, agricultural, and private sectors, and Cambodia again became self-sufficient in rice production.

Twenty-seven nongovernmental organizations (NGOs) from Australia, Europe, and the United States provide approximately $10 million per year in relief and development assistance. These NGOs, which support nutrition centers, hospitals, and artificial limb factories, also oversee water supplies, animal welfare, sanitation, irrigation, and educational projects.[6] Only certain U.N. agencies that provide emergency relief, such as UNICEF and the World Food Program, have been allowed to operate inside Cambodia, whereas the U.N. Development Program, the World Health Organization, and other development-oriented U.N. agencies have not.[7] Even so, Cambodia's needs are far greater than what the NGOs provide.

The NGOs have built good working relations with their bureaucratic and technical Cambodian counterparts. They are also the country's main contact with the outside world. However, even the small amount of NGO aid has taxed the administrative capacity of the Cambodian government. Aid providers face problems with accommodations, communications, travel, and visa relations. Even when a peace settlement is finally negotiated and the embargo is lifted, planning, reconstruction and development will still be difficult because of severe constraints on the public sector's absorptive capacity. Today, the country's technical and administrative cadres are few in number, and they are stretched to the limit.[8]

About sixty small industries are working at half capacity in the entire nation. The major options for foreign exchange are rubber, timber, and tourism. However, there are virtually no tourists in Cambodia except for a few academic delegations. The magnificent ruins of Angkor were at one time a popular tourist attraction, but without political stability, roads, rail service, an administrative infrastructure, and airports, Cambodia will not attract visitors.

The Cambodian State

In the twelfth century the Khmer Empire, under the great warrior Jayavarman VII, dominated much of mainland Southeast Asia. It was not until the fifteenth century that the empire was reduced in size to approximately the present boundaries of Cambodia. At its height, however, the Khmer Empire was among the strongest states in the world, able to mobilize the citizenry and protect its sovereignty. Modern Cambodia, in contrast, is one of the world's weakest states.

In the analysis of the other Southeast Asian states, massive social dislocation was seen as a necessary condition for a strong state. Cambodia qualifies in this respect but nevertheless has not become strong. Again, modern Cambodian history is the story of monumental dislocation as a result of the Khmer Rouge's systematic destruction of Cambodian social, cultural, economic, and political life. Although a strong state cannot emerge until its society has been weakened, and the latter did occur in Cambodia, a strong state has not evolved because the country has been largely bereft of administrative leadership. The People's Republic of Kampuchea, installed by the Vietnamese, fulfilled state functions temporarily, but the officials did not have the wherewithal to mobilize or control in the same manner as officials in Indonesia or Vietnam, both of which also underwent major dislocations.

External support facilitates the rise of a strong state. For Cambodia, financial, administrative, and military support from Vietnam was minute compared to its needs, especially when virtually no other external support was provided by the nation's traditional sources of aid and trade. Military threats, including internal rebellion, also facilitate the emergence of a strong state. Contemporary Cambodia has faced insurgency since the 1960s, and since the 1970s that insurgency has been supported financially and militarily by outside sources. From this perspective, too, Cambodia meets the criteria of a nation with the conditions for a strong state.

The explanation for Cambodia's weakness, then, must be the lack of a grouping that is both independent of existing bases of social control and skillful enough to execute the designs of state leaders. Cambodia has few experienced technocrats whose loyalty is primarily to the state; its army is weak and undependable; and the country has few politically skillful leaders. Indeed, there is no Cambodian leader who stands out even remotely as much as Ho Chi Minh in Vietnam, Lee Kuan Yew in Singapore, Ne Win in Burma, Suharto in Indonesia, or Ferdinand Marcos in the Philippines. The closest is Prince Sihanouk, but his prestige is tainted because of his alliance with the Khmer Rouge and the fact that he has not ruled since 1970. Hun Sen began *his* rule with the perception that he was a puppet of Cambodia's traditional adversary, Vietnam. Nevertheless, his capacity to bring some normality to Cambodia has enhanced his image and moved the country toward more effective governance.

Foreign Policy

Throughout its modern history, Cambodia has been the target of aggression by its larger neighbors and by Western and Communist imperialists. The French, Americans, Soviets, Chinese, Vietnamese, and Thais have all attempted at various times to control Cambodian affairs. Since 1970, Cambodia has been the victim of U.S. and Vietnamese intervention and Chinese support for anti-government rebels. The Vietnamese intervention of December 1978 could not have occurred without significant support by the Soviets, who funded the operation and provided much of the weaponry.

The United Nations continued to recognize the Pol Pot regime despite the fact that the Khmer Rouge controlled only about 2 percent of the population and Pol Pot was branded as the world's worst violator of human rights. The vote of President Jimmy Carter's administration for Pol Pot was based on the view that his opponents, the Heng Samrin government, had achieved power by aggression. The vote also reflected Carter's desire to strengthen ties with China and his displeasure with the growing Soviet role in Southeast Asia. The PRK was viewed as a puppet of Vietnam, which in turn was seen as a surrogate for the Soviet Union.

The late 1980s brought important international changes, which affected Cambodia by advancing new opportunities for a comprehensive peace settlement after the country had floundered for a decade. Warmer relations between the United States and the Soviet Union were the primary influence on U.S. policy toward Cambodia. For many years, U.S. goals in Cambodia have included withdrawal of Vietnamese military forces; repudiation of the Khmer Rouge; a political settlement that permits Cambodians to choose their form of government; and an independent, neutral, and nonaligned Cambodia, protected from outside interference by international guarantees.[9]

These goals have been constant, but the means to achieve them have changed as the international situation has changed. President Gorbachev has explained a new Soviet policy toward Asia by emphasizing diplomacy, positive relations with ASEAN, and disengagement from Vietnam. In response to Soviet encouragement, the Vietnamese completed their withdrawal of troops from Cambodia in September 1989, and ASEAN—especially Thailand—agreed to meet with the State of Cambodia administration. Prior to 1989, the ASEAN nations and the United States had refused to talk with the Phnom Penh government and had vigorously supported the CGDK's credentials at the United Nations.

A series of conferences in Jakarta in 1988 and 1989 and the international peace conference in Paris in August 1989 failed to resolve the complex problems regarding the principal actors such as Prince Sihanouk, the Khmer Rouge, and the State of Cambodia government. In order to break the stalemate, to react to U.S. congressional criticism of U.S. policy in Cambodia, and to indicate concern that the Khmer Rouge was increasing its strength in Cambodia and threatening to win power once again, in July 1990 Secretary of State Baker announced that the United States would withdraw diplomatic recognition of the CGDK in the United Nations and would henceforth deal directly with Vietnam in resolving the Cambodian crisis. Up to this time, the United States had supported the coalition rebels and had refused to negotiate with Vietnam.

The purpose of the new policy was to isolate the Khmer Rouge and to win concessions from Hanoi and Phnom Penh that would facilitate a peace settlement. In addition, the administration of President George Bush desired to end the contradiction in U.S. policy that both supported the Khmer Rouge and opposed its return to power. While opposing a return to power by the Khmer Rouge, the United States had been supporting a coalition that was dominated by the Khmer Rouge and whose non-Communist partners had never had real autonomy, diplomatically or militarily. The coalition partners were even coordinating military forays. Both lethal and nonlethal aid for the coalition had strengthened their forces, especially the position of the Khmer Rouge against the Hun Sen government in Phnom Penh, which was the only obstacle to a return to power by the Khmer Rouge.

Before the Vietnamese withdrawal of its military from Cambodia, U.S. policymakers argued that the Hun Sen government was essentially a puppet of the Vietnamese, but that argument lost credibility once the withdrawal was accomplished. The decision to negotiate with Vietnam was a recognition of the Vietnamese withdrawal from Cambodia and an incentive to continue working toward a Cambodian peace settlement, the necessary conditions before full normalization of relations between Vietnam and the United States could occur.

Moreover, the policy change recognized that U.S. relations with China did not dictate U.S. policies in Indochina. The United States had been reluctant to clash with China because China represented a bulwark against Soviet ambition in Southeast Asia. But the Tiananmen uprising in June 1989, Gorbachev's less-threatening policies in Asia, and ASEAN's increased flexibility liberated U.S. policymakers from their dependence on China and permitted them to see Cambodia as autonomous rather than as a part of China's sphere of influence. The new policy also isolated China as the sole supporter of the Khmer Rouge. Signs of improved relations between China and Vietnam (such as increased border trade) mitigated Chinese opposition to the new U.S. policy and suggested that China may want a face-saving solution to its unpopular ties with the Khmer Rouge.

The new U.S. policy also brought the United States back into Southeast Asia as a key force. During the fifteen years following the Vietnam war, U.S. foreign policy toward Indochina had been subordinated to that toward ASEAN and China. Nevertheless, it had an important effect on Cambodia, isolating the country through the trade embargo and strengthening rebel forces. Fear of a return to power of the Khmer Rouge mandated a new policy that could not be morally or strategically faulted for supporting such a frightening possibility.

ASEAN has not been united on the best means by which to deal with Cambodia. Whereas Singapore took a hard-line stand against the Hun Sen government (while simultaneously developing trade and investment ties), Thailand desired to turn Indochina from a battlefield into a marketplace, with Thailand taking the leading economic role in mainland Southeast Asia. Prior to the change in U.S. policy, Prime Minister Chatichai met with Prime Minister Hun Sen on numerous occasions to negotiate trade programs and a settlement of the Cambodian imbroglio. Initially, ASEAN leaders protested the U.S. withdrawal of support for U.N. recognition of the CGDK, but the protests were short-lived as it became clear that the United States would continue to provide economic aid to the non-Communist resistance.

The future of Cambodia can be presented with alternative scenarios. The most unacceptable—but not impossible—outcome is the return of the Khmer Rouge to power. With the strongest military force, through terrorist campaigns the Khmer Rouge could slowly take power in the countryside and eventually strangle Phnom Penh, just as it did in April 1975. The unknown variable is the willingness of Vietnam and the international community to stop the Khmer Rouge and the support provided to it by China. In 1975, neither the Cambodians nor the rest of the world knew the kind of horror that awaited the country when the Khmer Rouge prevailed, something everyone knows in the 1990s.

The second alternative is continuation of the stalemate with no settlement of the civil war, perhaps for years. China would continue to support the Khmer Rouge, and the United States would support the non-Communist resistance. The country would become increasingly split, as if partitioned between areas controlled by the Hun Sen government and areas controlled by factions of the CGDK. This state of permanent war would continue to destroy the Cambodian culture and would lead to the flight of even more of the country's most educated people.

Prince Sihanouk has supported the third scenario, a quadripartite settlement with the Hun Sen administration and each of the three coalition members sharing equally in the running of the government until there are free, internationally supervised elections. Sihanouk has insisted on the dismantling of the Hun Sen administration before elections as well as on equal-sized armies and a four-way leadership of key ministries.

The Hun Sen regime has dismissed the quadripartite plan as unacceptable, as tantamount to bringing jackals into the tent in order to tame them. Also, the PRK leaders assert that there is no evidence that the Khmer Rouge would not disrupt an interim or long-term coalition government. If Hun Sen were to allow a role for the Khmer Rouge in a future administration, such toleration would demolish the basis of his legitimacy as the liberator of Cambodia from the genocidal Khmer Rouge regime. Moreover, the other two factions of the CGDK are weak and could not withstand a highly organized and disciplined Khmer Rouge involvement. It is unlikely that the monarchical Sihanouk, the anti-Communist Son Sann, and the fanatical Khmer Rouge would be willing to negotiate a plan for power sharing.

A tripartite settlement is closer to the wishes of the United States, as it excludes the Khmer Rouge. In this scenario the Khmer Rouge would be isolated, assuming the end of Chinese support. Sihanouk, Hun Sen, and Son Sann would work together, with Sihanouk as head of state, Hun Sen the prime minister, and Son Sann in some significant position of power. Hun Sen, moreover, has agreed to free, multi-party elections and has accepted Sihanouk's return as head of state. Elections would be supervised by an international commission, and resumed diplomatic relations between Cambodia and the United States would lead to the end of the trade embargo and to larger aid programs.

The tripartite formula has been criticized, however, for excluding one of the main forces in Cambodia. Prince Sihanouk in particular has argued that integrating the Khmer Rouge into the government will co-opt it, while excluding it will perpetuate its insurgency. Also, the formula requires a stable and capable administration, a condition not yet met by any of the proposed tripartite groups. Even the Hun Sen administration, which has been in power since 1979, has not yet been able to fashion a government that is effective throughout the countryside.

In August 1990, the five permanent members of the U.N. Security Council announced an agreement aimed at ending the civil war by transferring temporary control of the country to the United Nations. The proposal involved employing some ten thousand U.N. peacekeeping troops and ten thousand civilian personnel to virtually control the Cambodian government, from foreign affairs to public security. The plan called for a Supreme National Council (SNC) to represent Cambodia during the interim period before elections, with each faction having one-fourth of the representation. The SNC would fill Cambodia's seat in the United Nations. The United Nations would supervise elections; provide for internal security; administer foreign, finance, and defense affairs; and guarantee human rights during the transition period. Each of the three factions of the CGDK agreed to the U.N. plan, but Hun Sen was reluctant to give up power, especially to a coalition that included the Khmer Rouge. The fact that the United States, the Soviet Union, and China agreed to the proposal put pressure on Hun Sen to accept the plan.

Prospects for a stable, free, and independent Cambodia are bleak in both the short and the long run. The contending factions have not even been able to agree on their representation on the SNC, let alone on their role in a future government.

Conclusion

No country in Southeast Asia has undergone the horrific trauma suffered by Cambodia during the decades of the 1960s, 1970s, and 1980s. War, famine, and oppression have devastated the society once known as an oasis of tranquility. With virtually its entire educated class decimated, Cambodia is attempting to rebuild. However, it is still buffeted by the world's great powers and by its neighbors. The phenomenal resilience of the Cambodians, as shown by the high degree of normality in Phnom Penh and the food self-sufficiency achieved in the rural areas, is the most hopeful sign that the killing fields will never return and that Cambodia can develop and remain independent.

Nevertheless, for the foreseeable future Cambodia will continue under a weak state, threatened by external aggressors and internal rebels. Without trained administrators, infrastructures, or external aid, the immediate outlook is bleak. The problems of governing Cambodia and bringing it peace are among the most vexing issues facing contemporary Southeast Asia in the new international era. The demise of the cold war has thus far not made the crises in Cambodia less intractable.

Notes

1. Eva Mysliwiec, *Punishing the Poor: The International Isolation of Kampuchea* (Oxford: Oxfam, 1988), p. 2.

2. Ibid., p. 11.

3. Robert J. Muscat, *Cambodia: Post-Settlement Reconstruction and Development* (New York: East Asian Institute, Columbia University, 1989), p. 98.

4. Frederick Z. Brown, *Second Chance: The United States and Indochina in the 1990s* (New York: Council on Foreign Relations, 1989), p. 71.

5. Muscat, *Cambodia: Post-Settlement Reconstruction and Development*, pp. 88–89.

6. Mysliwiec, *Punishing the Poor: The International Isolation of Kampuchea*, p. 66.

7. Muscat, *Cambodia: Post-Settlement Reconstruction and Development*, p. 2.

8. Ibid., p. 83.

9. Brown, *Second Chance: The United States and Indochina in the 1990s*, p. 11.

12

LAOS

Laos might best be described as a quasi-nation, having emerged from maps drawn by European colonialists rather than from a sense of territory and nationhood among a united people. The history of Laos is one of constant warfare among contending forces within the region as well as among external powers—mainly Thailand, Vietnam, China, France, and the United States. The present government faces the same problems as the governments of centuries ago: relocating the large refugee population stemming from past wars, uniting ethnic groups that fought each other for decades, decreasing the gap between urban and rural peoples, educating a citizenry that is overwhelmingly illiterate, and protecting the nation's sovereignty against encroachments by neighbors and by the major powers.

Contemporary Laos has changed little over the decades. It is still a rural, subsistence, agrarian society of some four million people divided among over forty ethnic groups, with the dominant lowland Lao consisting of just under two million people.[1] Most Laos are isolated from both their neighbors and the world and from the hill or lowland people who are also their neighbors. Almost all Laos are poor. The household economy is based on rice and the use of water buffalo. High technology has not reached the Lao farmers. About 90 percent of the population is Buddhist.

The present crises in Laos are prolongations of centuries-old problems, when ancient Lan Xang—the Kingdom of a Million Elephants—was a battleground for the expansionism of neighboring states. It was not until the fourteenth century that a semblance of national unity emerged. However, dynastic quarrels in the eighteenth century undermined this unity, and the area was divided into the kingdoms of Luang Prabang in the north, Champassak in the south, and Vientiane in the central region.

Vietnam and Thailand periodically plundered Laos until the French colonized the area beginning in the late 1880s. In 1899, the French claim of suzerainty brought Laos into a single political unit, but French rule did little to modernize or integrate the nation. On the contrary, a small group of elite Laotian families was allowed to consolidate its power; thus, Laotians emerged from colonial rule (after World War II) more divided, isolated, and backward than ever.

From 1941 to 1945 the Japanese ruled Laos, although the collaborating Vichy French administered many governmental affairs. At the end of the war in 1945, the Gaullist French recaptured Vientiane, the administrative capital, and fought a group called the *Lao-Issara* (Free Laos), which established a government in Bangkok and became the forerunner and nucleus of the pro-Communist, anti-French, nationalist *Neo Lao Hak Sat* (NLHS)—the so-called patriotic front. *Lao-Issara* was led by Prince Souvanna Phouma and his half-brother, Prince Souphanouvong, who later broke with his half-brother and joined the NLHS in geographic areas held by the Vietnamese Vietminh. By 1953 the NLHS's military force, known as the Pathet Lao, had seized control of the nation's northeastern provinces. In 1954 France accorded self-government to Laos at the Geneva Conference, which gave Laos complete independence.

The aftermath of the Geneva Conference was a period of disarray for Laos, as the competing sides vied for control of the populace and the countryside. Also in 1954, when the Pathet Lao was making significant military gains in large areas of the countryside, the United States sponsored a coup by anti-Communists against Premier Souvanna Phouma, who was considered too much a neutralist by the U.S. government. The coup failed, but Souvanna Phouma was given notice that left-wing or even neutralist policies were considered intolerable by the United States. When a right-wing government appeared in 1955, the United States immediately began a $45 million annual aid program.

In 1957 the neutralists, led by Souvanna Phouma—this time with backing from the United States—set up a government of national union, with cabinet posts for leftists and rightists. In special elections as called for in the Geneva Agreements, NLHS candidates won the majority of seats, an outcome deemed intolerable by Souvanna Phouma's government and U.S. diplomats. To overturn the results of the election and reverse the apparent trend toward a Communist government, the United States—principally through the Central Intelligence Agency—extended massive support to right-wing military officials. For the next five years, Laos was governed by right-wing regimes that excluded NLHS representation. There were numerous coups d'etat during this period as anti-Communist leaders jockeyed for power. However, the major beneficiary of governmental chaos was the NLHS movement, which continued to expand its control as it received increasing amounts of military supplies and support from the Soviet Union.

At the second Geneva Conference in 1961, neutralist Souvanna Phouma, leftist Souphanouvong, and rightist Boun Oum agreed on coalition rule. The United States reversed its support of right-wing rule and supported Souvanna Phouma's appointment as prime minister (after he gave secret permission to the United States to bomb Pathet Lao areas). The coalition collapsed almost immediately, however, as factions maneuvered for power. The NLHS broke from the coalition, and Souvanna Phouma's government became a virtual client of the United States.

Escalation of the Vietnam War changed the nature of the struggle between the NLHS and Royal Lao government forces. Hanoi's interest in Laos increased as its need for sanctuaries from U.S. bombing became paramount. Thus, Laos was swept up in the war as Hanoi, in violation of the Geneva Agreements, escalated its presence in the northeastern provinces of Laos and as the United States, also in violation of the agreements, began its secret bombing missions in 1964. In the following years, the landlocked nation became one of the most heavily bombed countries in history; some 2.1 million tons of bombs were dropped between 1964 and 1972 (about two-thirds of a ton per Laotian).[2] Despite this ferocity, the strategic effect was minimal so that the Central Intelligence Agency trained and supplied hill peoples, introduced military advisors, and used the Agency for International Development as a front for intelligence and training purposes. Laos became the battleground for a neighboring war fought by surrogate powers.

The Laos Peace Accords came in 1973 as the Vietnam War was brought to a close. The accords called for stopping the bombing, disbanding foreign-supported forces, removing of all foreign troops, and developing a coalition Provisional Government of National Unity (PGNU). The new ministries were divided between the Royalists and the Pathet Lao. At the time of the signing of the accords, the NLHS controlled about three-fourths of all the land and one-half of the population. Both sides were allowed to keep their zones of control until elections were arranged. The bombing ended.

The well-organized Pathet Laos (now called the Lao People's Liberation Army) prevailed over the Royal Lao government, which lacked discipline, was enervated by feudal-like family feuds, and was considered a puppet of the United States. The Pathet Laos spoke convincingly to the rural people of Laos who had seen their agricultural base destroyed, their population dislocated, and their villages destroyed.[3] No family was unscathed by the civil war and the U.S. bombing.

In December 1975 the Lao Communists dissolved the PGNU, abolished the 622-year-old monarchy, and established the Lao People's Democratic Republic. The change in government was preceded by Communist victories in Vietnam and Cambodia and by pro-Communist demonstrations throughout Laos. The rightist ministers fled, and all power was eventually placed in the hands of the Communists. Souvanna Phouma resigned and Kaysone Phomvihan, the Communist party general-secretary, became the new prime minister. A Supreme People's Council was set up with Prince Souphanouvong as president and chief of state, while Kaysone Phomvihan—virtually unknown to all but a handful of Communist leaders before 1975—assumed political and administrative control of the Lao People's Democratic Republic. In contrast to Vietnam and Cambodia, where Communists came to power as a result of a military victory, the change of government in Laos came about peacefully.

The Communist victory changed Lao politics fundamentally. For centuries the region had been dominated by a small group of wealthy families that combined great political and economic influence. Today, most of those families have fled to Thailand, Europe, or the United States. and those that remained have undergone "reeducation" programs to rid them of their "bourgeois mentality." For example, an estimated four hundred thousand persons, many of them the most educated in Laos, fled to Thailand following the change in government. Thus, the escape of educated Laotians and the systematic expunging of civil servants of the former administration have created a leadership vacuum that has seriously impaired the government's ability to administer and implement new programs.

Another major change was the departure of the United States as a principal player in Laotian politics. Most Western aid, which had funded over 90 percent of the Royal Lao government budget, ended when the Communists took power, although the countryside was still devastated from the war.

The new government moved quickly to eradicate the worst vestiges of bourgeois society by banning nightclubs, massage parlors, and dance halls. Private enterprise was stifled, and the government attempted to collectivize farms despite the peasants' resistance. Moreover, the government's attempt to reeducate thousands of Laotians made the populace wary of the new regime. Refugees reported stories about arrogant bureaucrats and repressive rules and regulations.

The virtual cessation of U.S. influence in Laos was also a fundamental change. Although the United States did not break diplomatic relations with Laos even after the Communist takeover in 1975, U.S. involvement became peripheral as the Soviet Union and Vietnam filled the vacuum. In 1979 the leaders of Laos and Vietnam signed a joint revolutionary declaration, a Treaty of Friendship and Cooperation, granting Vietnam approval to maintain some forty thousand troops in Laos. Vietnam's increased economic influence came about partially because Thailand initially refused to allow imports and exports both into and out of Laos. The fact that the port of Haiphong in Vietnam became the only outlet for Laotian goods also gave Vietnam leverage and influence over Laotian policies. China's role in Laos declined in rough correspondence to Vietnam's larger role. China soon accused Vietnam of creating an Indochinese federation dominated by the Vietnamese and withdrew its aid for numerous development projects. The Soviet Union, supplying some two thousand advisors and $50 million in annual aid, became the superpower in Laos.

In 1982, pragmatic policies were set forth at the third congress of the Lao People's Revolutionary Party. The government's control over the economy was loosened; agriculture was decollectivized as the right to private property was restored; and agricultural technology was introduced, resulting in larger crop output and self-sufficiency in rice for the first time since the revolution. These reforms are called *chin tanakan may* (new thinking), Lao's version of the Soviet Union's *perestroika* or Vietnam's *Doi Moi*.

By the late 1980s, the Lao economy had returned to where it had been in the early 1970s. In 1990, the capital of Laos, Vientiane, looked like the same sleepy village of 1960. Indeed, a visit to today's Vientiane, with its dusty roads, water buffalo roaming the streets, and shabby French-style buildings, is akin to stepping back into the nineteenth century. There are virtually no new buildings except for an occasional Soviet-built clinic.

Institutions and Social Groups

The United States

Until 1975, the United States played the leading institutional role in Laos. By dominating the policies of the Vientiane administrations and financing the Laotian military, the United States became the patron and the Lao government became a client of U.S. interests. To minimize opposition to U.S. involvement, the Central Intelligence Agency was given the principal responsibility to ensure—by clandestine measures—the continuation of U.S. interests. One example of CIA involvement was its secret support of an army of Hmong hill people, who became the most important fighting force against Communist Pathet Lao troops.

To secure continuation in power of pro-U.S. forces, the United States engaged in a secret war in Laos in the 1960s, which cost $2 billion annually. The purpose of the bombing raids over Laos was to strengthen the anti-Communist government in Vientiane, demolish the Pathet Lao infrastructure, and interdict soldiers from North Vietnam. In the long run, however, none of these goals was achieved.

After 1975, the United States no longer had influence on the Lao People's Democratic Republic. In the decade prior to the change in governments, however, the Lao government was so dependent on U.S. aid that U.S. institutions in Vientiane had become the real government.

Lao People's Revolutionary Party (LPRP)

Since 1975, the country's dominant institution has been the LPRP, the Communist party that emerged from the Pathet Lao leadership. Led by elderly revolutionaries who fought against the French, Japanese, and Americans, the party practices democratic centralism requiring unanimous support of all decisions by the leadership. Policy is made and implemented by the party politburo led by Kaysone Phomvihan, the general-secretary of the party and prime minister. He, like the other Laos leaders, has for years led a spartan life, not the ostentatious lifestyle so typical of other Southeast Asian leaders.

The LPRP, with about forty thousand members—having failed to achieve popular support for its Socialist policies—launched a series of reform policies in 1986 to decentralize economic decision-making and to liberalize, both economically and politically. In 1989—for the first time—the LPRP allowed elections for the Supreme People's Assembly, Laos's nominal parliament. Some 121 government-approved candidates ran for 79 seats, and 65 of the victors were party members. As chairman, the assembly elected Pouhak Phoumsavan number two leader of the LPRP politburo.[4]

There is no national constitution, so the LPRP is able to rule without guidelines or limits. Devoid of a constitution as well as codified legislative, electoral, and criminal justice procedures, Laos remains a government of men and not of law.[5] All the key men, moreover, are LPRP members.

Kaysone Phomvihan

In December 1975 Kaysone emerged from the caves of a northern province where he and his Pathet Lao colleagues hid to escape U.S. bombing. He became the head of the Communist party and the leader of Laos, a position he still held in 1991. Outside of the inner circle of the Pathet Lao, few Laotians knew him or knew about him, and Kaysone still eschews a cult of personality, living quietly and making himself available to very few visitors except Communist allies. Little is known about his past except for his close association with Vietnam, where he studied at the University of Hanoi.

Kaysone holds the positions of prime minister and LPRP general-secretary. Surrounded by colleagues from his revolutionary days in the 1950s, his rule has changed little since 1975. Continuity and stability were the themes of governmental leadership until 1979, when reforms were instituted that significantly changed the hard-line policies of the government.[6] Since that time, and especially since 1986 when "new thinking" was instituted, Kaysone has visited non-Communist countries, and his activities have even been reported in the press. Nevertheless, he remains one of the world's least-known leaders.

Democratization

There is no semblance of democracy in Laos, nor has there ever been. Its Communist leadership has not instituted reforms that permit a representative system or numerous civil liberties. Testimony to the Lao people's view that their government is not legitimate is the fact that fully one-tenth of the population has chosen to leave the country since 1975. Indeed, the regime's insecurity regarding its legitimacy is shown by its refusal to allow any kind of opposition or free elections. Furthermore, the major hill tribes, especially the Hmong, have not pledged allegiance to the Communist regime and have even participated in national resistance movements.

Democracy is difficult even under the best of circumstances but especially in nations whose culture and traditions are antithetical to democratic practices. Laos was further disadvantaged by its severe war damage and its former economy, which had depended heavily on U.S. support. When that support suddenly ended in 1975, the country's economic collapse was not unexpected; the government's subsequent moves to collectivize farms, nationalize the few industries, and rid the country of administrators who were part of the former regime exacerbated the siege mentality that made open politics impossible.

The fall of Communist governments in Eastern Europe has not affected the Laotian people because they do not have access to information about such changes. Following the democratization processes in Eastern Europe and the Philippines and the people's revolt in Burma, the Lao government made no moves to liberalize its rule.

Economic Development

Laos, like Cambodia and Vietnam, is one of the world's poorest countries. With an estimated annual per capita income of $160, life expectancy of 45 years, and infant mortality at 117 per 1,000 births, the standard of living is low. Less than 6 percent of the economy is industrial, and rice production, although largely subsistence, is poorly coordinated with any market or distribution system. Four out of ten children contract malaria, and diarrhea is a constant part of life.

Although such extreme poverty is not new to Laos, the contrast with economic standards in the ASEAN countries is more obvious than in the past when all the nations of Southeast Asia were poor. Laos people watch Thai television programs in Vientiane and other border towns and see the great differences in economic conditions. Desperate conditions persist in Laos despite the fact that the country has not been at war for over fifteen years.

After four years of rule, LPRP leaders discovered that their agricultural and industrial policies had failed to revive the economy. In 1979, therefore, a process of decentralization was begun, but the most fundamental changes did not begin until 1986 at the fourth congress of the LPRP. These changes, known as the New Economic Mechanism, allowed family farms to replace the unpopular agricultural cooperatives. Also, market mechanisms replaced centralized planning. In 1988, Kaysone admitted that the party's policy of putting private traders out of business, collectivizing farmers, and nationalizing industry had caused the production and circulation of goods to come to a halt, grievously affecting the people's livelihood.[7] The World Bank had been critical of the government's policy and cited Laos's agricultural inefficiency, decline in industrial output, dependency on the loans of Socialist nations (on poor terms), stagnant exports, and huge balance of payment deficits, all of which were compounding underdevelopment.[8]

The 1986 reforms included a new foreign investment code designed to bring in outside investment to finance the Laotian infrastructure, but the results have been disappointing. Most foreign investor's interest has been on small-scale manufacturing, notably textiles. Thus, the new code generated only a small amount of new investments, partly because Laos does not have a constitution or a civil code, a fact that scared off potential participants. Corruption has also discouraged foreign investors, who are reluctant to pay "tea money" to officials whose salaries are insufficient for bare subsistence. An equally important problem is administrative capacity: There is no absorptive capability that allows follow-through on investment and aid projects.

In 1989 the United States granted its first assistance to Laos since 1975 by supporting a $1 million anti-narcotics project. Australia, meanwhile, has provided satellites for international telephone calls and will finance the first bridge across the Mekong River between Thailand and Laos. Also in 1989 the World Bank and the Asian Development Bank pledged $238 million in no-interest loans. (Laos is not included in the trade embargo against Vietnam and Cambodia.)

The reforms placed emphasis on grassroots economic units including factories, merchant's shops, and construction projects.[9] Rather than move directly from subsistence to large-scale collective farming, peasant families were encouraged to join the small goods economy, trading their surplus production for commodities. In this way, Laotians were encouraged to become small-scale capitalists and consumers. State land was distributed to individual families on a long-term basis and might even become inheritable.[10]

Following the reforms, there was a noticeable improvement in the standard of living of many Laos, including more bicycles and house construction as well as more consumer goods in the major towns. However, the reforms did little to benefit rural people, who have very few roads on which to transport their farm products.

Ecologically, Laos is suffering from deforestation because of timber exported to Thailand. Laos's forests fell from 70 percent of the country's area 100 years ago to 30 percent in 1990.

The Laotian State

Laos, like Cambodia, is an example of a state with little capacity to meet the needs of its citizenry or to mobilize its collective strength. Like most Southeast Asian states, it has dual elements of strength and weakness. Certainly, it meets the criterion for all strong states: massive social dislocation. Laos has been exploited by a self-serving colonial regime, occupied by the Japanese and later becoming a client state of the United States, bombed to a greater extent even than Japan in World War II, and finally taken over by a hard-line Communist government; thus, it qualifies as a nation whose society has been weakened by massive social dislocation.

Although the United States has provided financial and military support to its client regimes, administrations in Laos never achieved stability.

However, massive Soviet aid to the LPDR helped strengthen the state's stability by undermining potential societal threats to the regime. The LPRP dominated every aspect of Laotian political life, having co-opted virtually the entire administrative class.

Laos does not have a social grouping that is independent of social controls and skillful enough to execute the designs of state leaders. Its bureaucrats and technocrats are not independent of the LPRP authorities. Those who were autonomous left the country for Thailand. There is no intellectual class in the entire country capable of competing with the state leaders. The Lao government has purposely precluded the rise of autonomous groups; thus, the Lao state can be considered strong. This lack of autonomy, however, has reduced the regime's legitimacy and its ability to meet the needs of the people, thereby undermining state strength. Whereas Thailand enjoys the symbolic importance of the king to provide legitimacy, Laos has no parallel institution.

Weakening the Lao state is the absence of a charismatic and skillful leader such as Suharto, Ho Chi Minh, or Ne Win (in an earlier era). Kaysone Phomvihan's leadership has resulted more from his control of the LPRP and from repression than from his capacity to gain the approbation of the Laotian people.

Foreign Policy

As a landlocked nation, Laos has always had to rely on its neighbors for security and for its international relations. Traditionally, Thailand, China, and Vietnam have had the greatest impact on Laotian political affairs because these nations share long borders with Laos and control its access to the oceans. After World War II, however, the United States became the paramount power, with almost total control over every aspect of Laotian political and economic life.

The United States supported the series of right-wing regimes that ruled Laos after the war, but after the Communist takeover in 1975, the United States no longer played an important role in Laotian affairs. Vietnam, which had approximately fifty thousand troops in Laos, became the major influence on foreign and domestic policies. Although there was fear in the 1980s that Laos and Cambodia would be assimilated into a greater Indochina federation under Vietnamese dominance, such a confederation never occurred. For some time Laos was dependent upon Vietnam and echoed Vietnam's line on most international questions. By 1990, however, all Vietnamese troops had been withdrawn, and Laos was asserting a more independent policy as well as strengthening its relations with Western powers, China, and Thailand.

Relations with the United States have been low-key since 1975. The United States has diplomatic relations with Vientiane but none at the ambassadorial level. The two nations have negotiated such issues as MIAs in Laos, drug trafficking, and human rights. Laos has worked with the United States on MIAs and has agreed to cooperate in narcotics control; however, the United States decertified Laos because of alleged government involvement in the illicit drug trade. Decertification meant that Laos was no longer eligible for aid and that U.S. officials were required to vote against loans to Laos from international institutions such as the World Bank. Laos was recertified in 1990.

In 1989 Laos moved to end its near-total dependence on the Soviet Union and Vietnam. Prime Minister Kaysone traveled to Japan, China, and France to request aid and investment.[11] Australia agreed to build a bridge over the Mekong River, which would link Thailand with Laos for the first time in history.

Laos's relations with Thailand have been tense since the Laotian Communists formed their government because the Thais view Laos as a base for support of insurgency and because the hundreds of thousands of Laotian and Cambodian refugees who have crossed to Thailand are viewed as an economic burden. In 1988, a ceasefire ended a bloody three-month war over a disputed border area. Later as relations warmed, Thai businessmen took advantage of the economic reforms in Laos to set up businesses, and border towns became market centers for Thailand. Indeed, in 1990 Prime Minister Chatichai visited Vientiane, the first trip to Laos by a Thai prime minister in a decade.

Improved relations did not resolve the centuries-long problem of a strong Thailand versus a weak Laos. Semiofficial commentaries noted that having failed to destroy Laos with its military, Thailand had employed a new strategy: attacking Laos by trying to turn the Indochinese battlefield into a marketplace. Although the Lao government later distanced itself from that view, many Laotians feared that Thailand—with more than ten times the population of Laos and a history of aggression against its smaller neighbor—might once again intervene. The Laotian government was particularly concerned about Thai support for right-wing insurgent forces, which were formed to oust the Kaysone administration.

Conclusion

Laos is the "forgotten country" of Southeast Asia because it is small and is no longer strategically important to the world's major powers. Its population is far smaller than that of the city of Bangkok. Laos's leadership is unknown throughout the world, and its military capacity is nil. In contrast to Thailand, and fundamentally different from the Thailand of just a decade ago, Laos has changed little over several decades. Its towns, available resources, and level of development have also not changed appreciably over the years. Thus, the prospects for Laos in terms of improving the standard of living of its people are bleak.

Notes

---

1. W. Randall Ireson and Carol J. Ireson, "Laos," in *Coming to Terms: Indochina, the United States, and the War*, ed. Douglas Allen and Ngo Vinh Long (Boulder, Colo.: Westview Press, 1991).
2. Ibid., p. 66.
3. Ibid.
4. Geoffrey C. Gunn, "Laos in 1989: Quiet Revolution in the Marketplace," *Asian Survey*, vol. 30, no. 1, January 1990, p. 84).
5. Charles A. Joiner, "Laos in 1987," *Asian Survey*, vol. 28, no. 1, January 1988, p. 104.
6. Macalister Brown and Joseph J. Zasloff, *Apprentice Revolutionaries: The Communist Movement in Laos, 1930–1985* (Hoover Institution, Stanford University, 1986), p. 165.
7. Far Eastern Economic Review, *Asia 1990 Yearbook* (Hong Kong, 1990), p. 161.
8. Joiner, "Laos in 1987," p. 19.
9. Ibid., p. 96.
10. Martin Stuart-Fox, "Laos in 1988," *Asian Survey*, vol. 29, no. 1, January 1989, pp. 81–82.
11. Far Eastern Economic Review, *Asia 1991 Yearbook* (Hong Kong, 1991), p. 151.

13

CONCLUSION

The U.S. involvement in Southeast Asia during the region's postindependence period was traumatic. The United States, which had carried out a long, costly, and controversial war in Indochina and developed patron-client relationships (and all the attending obligations) with the non-Communist nations, was integrally involved in the region's affairs.

Thus, the subordination of Southeast Asia in U.S. foreign policy during the 1980s was a striking change in the new international era. Analysts of Southeast Asia during the Vietnam era did not predict the breadth or direction of this change. At that time, every ASEAN nation was deemed susceptible to Communist-inspired insurgencies; the region's economies were among the poorest in the world; authoritarian governments ruled virtually every country; and Vietnam, Cambodia, and Laos were overwhelmed by war. Although the United States was the only superpower with tremendous influence in Southeast Asia, its failure to achieve its aims in Vietnam led to a pessimistic evaluation of the region's future.

In many respects, the present era in Southeast Asia suggests that the pessimistic view was unwarranted and that U.S. aims have been achieved. The area is dominated by economically vital, anti-Communist nations, and it shelters no adversarial superpower that threatens U.S. interests. With varying success, the ASEAN nations have moved toward democratic rule. In the new international era, Vietnam and Laos are no longer at war, and both countries have launched economic reforms to involve themselves more intimately with the world capitalist system. Except for the Philippines, the ASEAN nations have terminated their insurgent threats and are now an anti-Communist bastion in the Third World. Again excepting the Philippines, rather than falling as dominoes the ASEAN countries are dynamic models for successful development. U.S. interests in the region have correspondingly changed, becoming primarily economic rather than military.

Rather than relying exclusively on the United States for support as in preceding decades, the ASEAN countries have widened their relations with the old Soviet bloc, Western Europe, China, and Japan. At the same time, there is movement toward the normalization of relations between Vietnam and the United States as the Soviet Union reduces its involvement in Indochina. It is conceivable that Vietnam as well as Laos and Cambodia will join ASEAN as the cold war mentality continues to dissipate.

The most salient unresolved issue is the Cambodian civil war, which has thus far resisted reconciliation despite the movement toward reform and the end of the genocidal Khmer Rouge regime. The major difficulties are Vietnam's distrust of China and vice versa in terms of their intentions in Cambodia, the ongoing insurgency of the rebel forces led by the Khmer Rouge, and the trade and aid embargoes established by the United States.

Another difficult issue concerns the refusal of the Burmese military to respect the desire of the populace for democratization by turning the government over to the winners of the 1990 election. The possibility of a civil war makes this an issue of great importance both for the Burmese and for the stability of Southeast Asia.

A third unresolved issue is the enduring instability of the Philippines, which is caused by a democratic but weak government, an insurgency that continues to feed upon widespread poverty (and the large gap between the few rich and the many poor), the feudal nature of the society, and the gross corruption of officials. These problems are exacerbated by negotiations over the U.S. use of military bases in the Philippines.

The future role of Vietnam in Southeast Asia and in the international system is another problem. Viewed as a pariah by the United States and the ASEAN nations since the end of the Vietnam War, Vietnam has since made clear its desire to participate in the new international arena. That aim, however, will remain impossible as long as the United States and Vietnam cannot agree to normalize relations. Until there is a comprehensive settlement in Cambodia, the United States prefers to isolate Vietnam. Japan, Korea, Taiwan, and Thailand have nevertheless established economic ties with Vietnam, a country they view as the new economic frontier in Asia.

The success of the ASEAN nations in improving their citizens' standard of living and in opening their political systems is an important change for Southeast Asia in the new international era. Virtually every social-political indicator (life expectancy, infant mortality, number of doctors, and literacy) shows improvement in the citizens' standard of living compared with ten years ago. Nevertheless, economic inequality in the ASEAN nations has become greater even while per capita income increases. The elites live in urban areas and tend to neglect the rural peasantry. Economic development priority is given to urban industrial centers in the expectation that resources will eventually "trickle down" to the masses. This change stems in part from the ASEAN nations' integration into the world economic system and the international division of labor in which ASEAN provides cheap labor for export products to the West. Moreover, the rapid growth of ASEAN's primary cities has led to overcrowding and insufficient services, resulting in gigantic slums and urban alienation.

Vietnam, Cambodia, Laos, and Burma have made significant strides toward economic and political development. Since around 1986, the Indochinese countries have initiated reforms that are beginning to show results. Despite these reforms, the Indochinese people are still impoverished, the nations' infrastructures are dilapidated, and the bureaucracy is oppressive. In Vietnam, the government is led by an elderly generation of Communists who are sometimes out of touch with the needs of the citizenry. The outcome of factional disputes between reformers and hard-line conservatives will determine Vietnam's capacity to participate in the new international era.

The analysis of the role of the state in explaining high economic growth rates does not indicate a clear pattern. Where the states have acted autonomously, independent of societal groups, economic development has both flourished and deteriorated. For example, Singapore is a strong state with a flourishing economy, whereas Vietnam is also a strong state but with a stagnant economy. In Thailand, the state has been strong enough to allow the private sector to propel economic growth, but in Burma the authorities increased the state's role in economic policymaking with disastrous results. Weak and inefficient governments hinder economic growth; however, strong states do not necessarily realize rapid development and often cause as many problems as they solve.

The clearest explanation for economic growth is the pattern of openness in a state's polity. Democratization correlates positively with high growth rates. The semidemocracies of Thailand (until 1991) and Malaysia have the highest rates of growth in contrast to Vietnam, Laos, Cambodia, and Burma, all of which have relatively closed polities and the region's lowest growth rates. Indonesia's controlled democracy is in the middle in terms of economic growth. Singapore, because of its city-state character, and Brunei, because of its oil revenues and small population, cannot be compared with other Southeast Asian countries. It seems, therefore, that no country in the region is likely to develop economically if it is ruled by a closed political system, whereas an open system committed to a market economy is necessary for development.

The future of Southeast Asia is inextricably tied to the policies of the great powers. Southeast Asia is of secondary interest to the United States compared to U.S. interest in the Middle East, the Soviet Union, Europe, China, and Japan. While the United States and the Soviet Union retain their security interests in Southeast Asia, the reduction in tensions between the two nations portends the diminution of an active U.S. presence.

The obvious potential national power in Southeast Asia is Japan, which already has a significant involvement in the economic affairs of the region. Although the United States will continue to pressure Japan to do more in terms of burden-sharing, the memories of the Japanese occupation during World War II are strong enough to cause fear about a Japanese return to militarism.

At the same time, the nations of Southeast Asia are moving in the direction of greater national resilience and self-reliance. Their prospects rest on each nation's internal capacity to meet the needs of its people and to assure them of a higher standard of living. Each nation must strike its own bargain between its requirements for growth and stability, authority and freedom, regional interdependence and nationalism, and modernization and cultural integrity.

Southeast Asia in the New International Era suggests that the region is diverse, with political systems as varied as any region of the world. The new international era is influencing each nation in different ways, with some nations—such as Singapore and Thailand—moving rapidly toward westernization and others—such as Burma—moving toward isolation. Each nation, however, is coping with change in ways that create difficult problems and choices. The choices should not be evaluated against Western standards but against each nation's past. In short, Southeast Asia is worthy of consideration on its own terms.

BIBLIOGRAPHY

For up-to-date analyses of politics in Southeast Asia, consult the following journals: *Asian Survey, Pacific Affairs, Far Eastern Economic Review, Asian Thought and Society, The Journal of Asian Studies, Asiaweek,* and *Indochina Chronology.* Each year the January and February issues of *Asian Survey* feature articles that summarize the previous year's events in each Southeast Asian nation.

Following is a selected bibliography of books written since 1980, organized according to country.

General Southeast Asia

Clad, James. *Behind the Myth: Business, Money and Power in Southeast Asia.* London: Unwin Hyman, 1989.

Diamond, Larry, Juan J. Linz, and Seymour Martin Lipset, eds. *Democracy in Developing Countries: Asia.* Boulder: Lynne Rienner Publishers, 1989.

Djiwandono, J. Soedjati, and Yong Mun Cheong, eds. *Soldiers and Stability in Southeast Asia.* Singapore: Institute of Southeast Asian Studies, 1988.

Ghee, Lim Teck. *Reflections on Development in Southeast Asia.* Singapore: Institute of Southeast Asian Studies, 1988.

Kallgren, Joyce K., Noordin Sopiee, and J. Soedjati Djiwandono, eds. *ASEAN and China: An Evolving Relationship.* Berkeley: Institute of East Asian Studies, University of California, 1988.

Jackson, Karl D., Sukhumbhand Paribatra, and J. Soedjati Djiwandono, eds. *ASEAN in Regional and Global Context.* Berkeley: Institute of East Asian Studies, University of California, 1986.

Mauzy, Diane K., ed. *Politics in the ASEAN States.* Kuala Lumpur: Maricans, 1986.

Robison, Richard, Kevin Hewison, and Richard Higgott, eds. *Southeast Asia in the 1980s: The Politics of Economic Crisis.* Sydney: Allen and Unwin, 1987.

213

Scalapino, Robert A., Seizaburo Sato, and Jusuf Wanandi, eds. *Asian Economic Development—Present and Future.* Berkeley: Institute of East Asian Studies, University of California, 1985.

Scalapino, Robert A., Seizaburo Sato, and Jusuf Wanandi, eds. *Asian Political Institutionalization.* Berkeley: Institute of East Asian Studies, University of California, 1986.

Scalapino, Robert A., Seizaburo Sato, and Jusuf Wanandi, eds. *Internal and External Security Issues in Asia.* Berkeley: Institute of East Asian Studies, University of California, 1986.

Scalapino, Robert A., Seizaburo Sato, Jusuf Wanandi, and Sung-joo Han, eds. *Asia and the Major Powers: Domestic Politics and Foreign Powers.* Berkeley: Institute of East Asian Studies, University of California, 1988.

Snitwongse, Kusuma, and Sukhumbhand Paribatra, eds. *Durable Stability in Southeast Asia.* Singapore: Institute of Southeast Asian Studies, 1987.

Steinberg, David Joel, ed. *In Search of Southeast Asia.* Honolulu: University of Hawaii Press, 1985.

Wurfel, David, and Bruce Burton, eds. *The Political Economy of Foreign Policy in Southeast Asia.* London: Macmillan, 1990.

Yoshihara, Kunio. *The Rise of Ersatz Capitalism in South-East Asia.* New York: Oxford University Press, 1988.

Thailand

Girling, John L. S. *Thailand: Society and Politics.* Ithaca: Cornell University Press, 1981.

Jackson, Karl D., and Wiwat Mungkandi, eds. *United States–Thailand Relations.* Berkeley: Institute of East Asian Studies, University of California, 1986.

Laothamatas, Anek. *From Bureaucratic Polity to Liberal Corporatism: Business Associations and the New Political Economy of Thailand.* Boulder: Westview Press, 1991.

Morell, David, and Chai-Anan Samudavanija. *Political Conflict in Thailand: Reform, Reaction, Revolution.* Cambridge: Oelgesclager, Gunn and Hain, 1981.

Muscat, Robert. *Thailand and the United States.* New York: Columbia University Press, 1990.

Neher, Clark D., and Wiwat Mungkandi, eds. *U.S.–Thailand Relations in a New International Era.* Berkeley: Institute of East Asian Studies, University of California, 1990.

Ramsay, Ansil, and Wiwat Mungkandi, eds. *Thailand–U.S. Relations: Changing Social, Political and Economic Factors.* Berkeley: Institute of East Asian Studies, University of California, 1988.

Randolph, Sean. *The United States and Thailand: Alliance Dynamics, 1950–1985.* Berkeley: Institute of East Asian Studies, University of California, 1986.

Xuto, Somsakdi, ed. *Government and Politics of Thailand.* Oxford: Oxford University Press, 1987.

The Philippines

Bonner, Raymond. *Waltzing with a Dictator.* New York: Times Books, 1987.
Broad, Robin. *Unequal Alliance: The World Bank, the International Monetary Fund, and the Philippines.* Berkeley: University of California Press, 1978.
Greene, Fred, ed. *The Philippine Bases: Negotiating for the Future.* New York: Council on Foreign Relations, 1988.
De Guzman, Raul P., and Mila A. Reforma, eds. *Government and Politics of the Philippines.* Singapore: Oxford University Press, 1988.
Hawes, Gary. *The Philippine State and the Marcos Regime: The Politics of Export.* Ithaca: Cornell University Press, 1987.
Johnson, Bryan. *The Four Days of Courage.* New York: The Free Press, 1987.
Kerkvliet, Benedict. *Everyday Politics in the Philippines.* Berkeley: University of California Press, 1990.
Kessler, Richard J. *Rebellion and Repression in the Philippines.* New Haven: Yale University Press, 1989.
Lande, Carl H. *Rebuilding a Nation: Philippine Challenges and American Policy.* Washington D.C.: The Washington Institute, 1987.
Steinberg, David Joel. *The Philippines: A Singular and Plural Place.* 2d ed. Boulder: Westview Press, 1990.
Wurfel, David. *Filipino Politics: Development and Decay.* Ithaca: Cornell University Press, 1988.

Indonesia

Crouch, Harold A. *The Army and Politics in Indonesia.* Ithaca: Cornell University Press, 1988.
Jackson, Karl D., and Lucian Pye, eds. *Political Power and Communications in Indonesia.* Berkeley: University of California Press, 1978.
MacAndrews, Colin, ed. *Central Government and Local Development in Indonesia.* Oxford: Oxford University Press, 1986.
Robison, Richard. *Indonesia: The Rise of Capital.* Sydney: Allen and Unwin, 1986.

Malaysia

Jomo, Kwame Sundaram. *A Question of Class: Capital, the State, and Uneven Development in Malaya.* New York: Oxford University Press, 1986.
Mauzy, Diane K. *Barisan Nasional: Coalition Government in Malaysia.* Kuala Lumpur: Marican and Sons, 1983.

Scott, James C. *Weapons of the Weak: Everyday Forms of Peasant Resistance.* New Haven: Yale University Press, 1983.

Singapore

Rodan, Garry. *The Political Economy of Singapore's Industrialization: National, State, and International Capital.* New York: St. Martin's Press, 1989.

Negara Brunei Darussalam

Leake, David, Jr. *The Modern Southeast Asian Islamic Sultanate.* Jefferson, N.C.: McFarland and Co., 1989.

Burma

Lintner, Bertil. *Outrage.* Hong Kong: Review Publishing Co., 1989.
Silverstein, Josef. *Independent Burma at Forty Years: Six Assessments.* Ithaca: Cornell University Press, 1989.
Steinberg, David I. *Burma: A Socialist Nation of Southeast Asia.* Boulder: Westview Press, 1982.
_____. *The Future of Burma: Crisis and Choice in Myanmar.* Lanham, Md.: University Press of America, 1990.
Taylor, Robert. *The State in Burma.* Honolulu: University of Hawaii Press, 1987.

Vietnam

Brown, Frederick Z. *Second Chance: The United States and Indochina in the 1990s.* New York: Council on Foreign Relations, 1989.
Cima, Ronald, ed. *Vietnam: A Country Study.* Washington, D.C.: Library of Congress, 1989.
Duiker, William J. *China and Vietnam: The Roots of Conflict.* Berkeley: Institute of East Asian Studies, University of California, 1986.
Goodman, Allan E. *The Search for a Negotiated Settlement of the Vietnam War.* Berkeley: Institute of East Asian Studies, University of California, 1986.
Kahin, George McT. *Intervention: How America Became Involved in Vietnam.* New York: Alfred A. Knopf, 1986.

Marr, David G., and Christine P. White, eds. *Postwar Vietnam: Dilemmas in Socialist Development.* Ithaca: Cornell University, Southeast Asia Program, 1988.

Tai, Ta Van. *The Vietnamese Tradition of Human Rights.* Berkeley: Institute of East Asian Studies, University of California, 1988.

Turley, William S. *The Second Indochina War.* Boulder: Westview Press, 1986.

Vu, Tran Tri. *Lost Years: My 1,632 Days in Vietnamese Reeducation Camps.* Berkeley: Institute of East Asian Studies, University of California, 1986.

Cambodia

Chanda, Nayan. *Brother Enemy: The War After the War.* New York: Macmillan Publishing Co., 1986.

Chandler, David P., and Ben Kiernan. *Revolution and Its Aftermath in Kampuchea: Eight Essays.* New Haven: Yale University, Southeast Asia Studies, 1983.

Kiernan, Ben, and Chanthou Boua, eds. *Peasants and Politics in Kampuchea: 1942–1981.* New York: M. E. Sharpe, 1982.

Muscat, Robert J. *Cambodia: Post-Settlement Reconstruction and Development.* New York: Columbia University, East Asian Institute, 1989.

Mysliwiec, Eva. *Punishing the Poor: The International Isolation of Kampuchea.* Oxford: Oxfam, 1988.

Laos

Brown, Macalister, and Joseph J. Zasloff. *Apprentice Revolutionaries: The Communist Movement in Laos, 1930–1985.* Stanford: Hoover Institution, Stanford University, 1986.

ABOUT THE BOOK AND AUTHOR

In an era of rapid change in the world environment, Southeast Asia is a key, yet often overlooked, region. This is the first book available that comprehensively assesses Southeast Asia both regionally and in terms of individual nations struggling to fit into a changing global context. Within a framework that combines comparative and international approaches, Neher considers the increasingly vital issues of modernization, democratization, economic development, U.S.–Southeast Asian relations, and the role of the state. Interweaving historical, political, and cultural themes, he enables readers to understand the region from a Southeast Asian rather than a Western perspective. This text's readable style and comparative structure will make it valuable for courses in international relations, Third World politics, Asian politics, and comparative politics at both the undergraduate and graduate levels.

Clark D. Neher is professor of political science at Northern Illinois University and has also taught for seven years in Thailand and the Philippines. He has written several books, including *Politics in Southeast Asia* (1987) and *Modern Thai Politics* (1979), and many articles that analyze Southeast Asian politics.

INDEX

Abdul Rahman, Tunku, 104, 117, 122
Absolute loyalty (*taat setia*), 107
Absolute monarchy, 3, 20, 23, 152. *See also* Brunei
Absolutism, 187
Academic freedom, 143
Afghanistan. *See under* Soviet Union
AFP. *See* Armed Forces of the Philippines
AFPFL. *See* Anti-Fascist People's Freedom League
Agency for International Development (U.S.), 199
Agriculture, 2, 3, 17. *See also under individual countries*
AIDS (acquired immune deficiency syndrome), 72, 82
Air conditioners, 115
Air pollution, 18
Alienation, 17, 18
Alliance party (Malaysia), 105, 108, 113, 116, 117, 122
American Chamber of Commerce (Bangkok), 33
Amnesty International USA, 164
Anand Panyarachun, 31
Angeles City (Philippines), 82
Angka (Khmer Rouge faction), 180
Angkatan Perpaduan Umnah (APU) (Malaysia), 107, 109
Angkor (Cambodia), 177, 187
Anglo-Malaysian Defence Agreement, 110
Animism, 2
Annam area (Vietnam), 157, 158

Anti-Fascist People's Freedom League (AFPFL) (Burma), 142
Anti-narcotics project (Laos), 205
APU. *See Angkatan Perpaduan Umnah*
Aquino, Benigno, Jr., 57, 58, 66, 69
  assassinated (1983), 57, 63, 67, 76
Aquino, Corazon (Cory) Cojuangco, 1, 4, 5, 19, 20, 58, 59, 60–63, 64, 65, 66, 67, 68, 69, 70, 73, 74, 76, 78, 79, 83, 149, 150
  and Catholic church, 71, 72
  family wealth, 61–62
  reconciliation policy, 70–71
Armed Forces of the Philippines (AFP), 57, 67. *See also* Philippines, military
Armed Forces of the Republic of Indonesia, 91. *See also* Indonesia, military
Arme Nationale Sihanoukiste (Cambodia), 186
ASEAN. *See* Association of Southeast Asian Nations
Asian-Americans, 12
Asian Development Bank, 205
Asian Human Rights Commission, 61
Assimilation, 37
Association of Southeast Asian Nations (ASEAN) (1967), 6, 17, 100, 192, 209
  economies, 13, 16, 17, 18, 74, 173, 209–211
  and Indochinese refugees, 187
  quality of life, 17–18, 210
  security, 10, 117–118, 173
  See also under individual countries

Athit Kamlangek, 32
Aung Gyi, 148
Aung San, 141–142, 145, 148
  assassinated (1947), 142
Aung San Suu Kyi, 145, 146, 148–149,
  150, 155
Australia, 81, 110, 127, 152, 155, 205, 207
Authoritarian-pluralist systems, 4
Authoritarian political systems, 9, 10, 29,
  38, 56, 57, 89, 94, 122, 124, 151
Automobiles, 18
Ayutha period (Thailand), 23–24
Azahari revolt (1962) (Brunei), 133, 137

Baker, James, 172, 191
Balance of power, 11, 15
Bandar Seri Begawan (Brunei), 134
Bangkok (Thailand), 24, 29, 35, 40
Bank of Thailand, 44
Bao Dai, 158
Barangay, 69. *See also* Philippines, people's
  assemblies
Bargain, the (Malaya), 104, 105, 118
Barisan Nasional. See National Front
Barisan Sosialis. See Socialist Front
Bicycles, 205
Bipolar world, 9
Birth control, 17, 41, 72. *See also* Family
  planning
Blue-collar class, 18
Borneo (Malaysia), 103, 104, 133
Boun Oum, 199
Brahmanism, 23, 24
Brezhnev doctrine, 10
Brunei (Negara Brunei Darussalam)
  agriculture, 136
  and ASEAN, 6, 135, 138
  bureaucracy, 134
  capital. *See* Bandar Seri Begawan
  constitution (1959, 1984), 133, 135
  democratization, 135
  dissidents, 137
  economic growth and development, 134,
    136
  economy, 4, 136, 137, 211
  education program, 19, 134, 136, 137
  ethnic groups, 133, 137
  Fifth National Development Plan (1986–
    1990), 136
  fisheries, 136
  food dependency, 136

foreign aid to, 137
foreign investment in, 138
foreign policy, 133, 138
forestry, 136
GDP, 136
GNP, 17
government, 3, 4, 5, 19, 134. *See also*
  Sultan of Brunei
  and Great Britain, 104, 133, 135, 137
  health care, 134, 136
  housing, 134, 136
  income, 128, 133
  independence (1984), 4, 19, 133
  and Indonesia, 137, 138
  industry, 136
  infrastructure, 136
  location, 133
  and Malaysia, 137, 138
  military, 133, 135, 137, 138
  name, 133
  nationalism, 3, 135
  natural gas, 134, 136
  and non-Communist, 6, 138
  oil, 4, 17, 19, 134, 136, 138, 211
  political party, 135
  population, 4, 5, 133, 211
  press, 135
  recession (1985), 136
  religion, 5, 133
  security, 133, 137
  state autonomy, 136–137
  and U.S., 138
  welfare program, 19, 134, 136, 137
Brunei National Democratic Party (*Partai
  Kebangsaan Demokratik Brunei*) (1985),
  135
BSPP. *See* Burmese Socialist Program
  Party
Buddhism, 2, 5, 16, 23, 44, 142, 151, 157,
  177, 182, 185, 187, 197
Bureau of the Budget (Thailand), 44
Burma, 17
  agriculture, 152
  and Australia, 152, 155
  black market, 142, 143–144, 151
  bureaucracy, 142, 148, 152, 153
  capital. *See* Rangoon
  and China, 152, 154
  colonialism, 141, 153
  Communist party, 145, 149, 154
  constitution (1947), 146, 150

corruption, 142
Council of State, 147
coup (1962), 142–143
coup attempt (1988), 4, 141, 145, 147, 154, 155
currency demonetization, 143, 144
democratization, 144, 146, 150–151, 153, 155, 210, 211
economic growth and development, 143, 151–152, 211
economy, 141, 142, 144, 150, 153, 155, 211
ethnic groups, 141, 142, 145, 149, 153, 154
exports, 142
foreign aid to, 152, 154, 155
foreign investment in, 152
foreign policy, 143, 154–155, 212
forests, 154–155
GNP, 17, 151
government, 3, 4, 19, 141, 142, 143, 145, 146, 149, 150, 152
and Great Britain, 141, 142, 151, 155
human rights, 145, 155
independence (1948), 141
and India, 155
inflation, 152
and Japan, 141, 142, 152, 153, 154, 155
as least-developed nation, 143, 152
life expectancy, 17, 97
martial law (1988), 141, 145, 146
military, 1, 3, 4, 6–7(n1), 19, 91, 141, 142, 143, 144–145, 146, 147, 149, 150, 153, 155, 156, 210
name change, 6–7(n1), 141, 156(n1)
nationalism, 3, 141
nationalization, 143, 153
natural resources, 141, 143
neutrality, 6, 143, 154
oil exploration agreements, 152
opposition groups, 19, 142, 143, 145, 146, 148–149, 155
parliament, 143, 152
patron-client politics, 147, 155
People's Assembly (*Pyithu Hluttaw*), 145–146, 147
political culture, 150, 155–156
political parties, 19, 142, 143, 145, 146, 148, 152
population, 141
press, 144

prodemocracy demonstrations (1988), 1, 19, 141, 143–144, 151, 152
religion, 5, 142
relocations, 145
repression, 5, 141, 143, 145, 153
security, 142, 154
security police, 144
Socialist policy, 142, 143, 144, 151
and South Korea, 152
state autonomy, 152–154, 211
students, 144, 145
television, 146
and Thailand, 24, 149, 152, 154–155
and UN, 143, 152
universities, 143
urban, 145
and U.S., 144, 145, 152, 155
Westernization, rejection of, 143, 151, 154
and West Germany, 155
women, 149–150
and World War II, 141, 142
Burmans, 141
Burmese Socialist Program Party (BSPP), 143, 144, 146, 147, 148, 152
Burmese Way to Socialism, 143, 144
Bush, George, 191

Cambodia
agriculture, 16, 182, 188
anti-Communists, 16, 185–186, 187, 193
and ASEAN, 16, 186, 191, 192, 210
automobiles, 18
bureaucracy, 16, 179, 185, 188, 189
capital. *See* Phnom Penh
and China, 11, 16, 178, 181, 185, 190, 194, 210
civilization, 177, 189
civil war, 11, 16, 180, 184, 193, 194, 210
colonialism, 177
as Communist, 6, 16, 25, 185
corruption, 179, 180, 182
death penalty abolished, 185
democratization, 179, 185, 187, 211
economic growth and development, 179, 182, 183, 188–189, 211
economy, 15, 16, 181, 188
education, 182, 188
electricity, 182
expansionism, 6, 181

exports, 188
famine (1978–1980), 182
flag, 185
food aid to, 182, 188
food self-sufficiency, 182, 188, 194
food shortages, 179, 180, 181, 182
foreign aid to, 183, 188, 191
foreign investment in, 16, 188
foreign policy, 185, 190–194
and France, 177
GNP, 17
government, 4, 16, 177, 178, 179, 181,
    182, 183, 184–186, 190, 191, 193, 194
health care, 188
human rights, 190
independence (1954), 178
industry, 16, 179, 188
inflation, 179
infrastructure, 16, 189
intellectuals executed, 180, 194
and Khmer Rouge (1975–1979), 4, 14,
    16, 51, 175, 177, 180–181, 182, 183–
    184, 185, 186, 187, 188, 189, 190,
    191, 192–193, 210
life expectancy, 17, 97
military, 177, 179, 185, 186, 190
monarchy, 178, 183, 187
name changes, 6–7(n1), 177, 180, 181,
    184
National Assembly, 178, 185
nationalism, 179, 188
neutralism, 178, 185
political parties, 183, 185
politics, 18, 179, 187
population, 177, 182
poverty, 171, 177, 182
press, 179
private sector, 182, 188
purges, 180
religion, 5, 16, 177, 182, 185
rural, 177, 179, 184, 188, 194
and South Vietnam, 159, 178, 179
state autonomy, 189–190
State Council, 185
television sets, 18
tourism, 188–189
trade, 16
and UN, 16, 183, 185, 188, 190, 191,
    192, 194
unemployment, 179
urban, 183, 184

and U.S., 16, 159, 178, 182, 183, 185,
    186, 190–191, 192, 193, 194
U.S. bombing of (1970), 179
and Vietnam, 4, 6, 10, 11, 14, 16, 161,
    178, 179, 180, 181–182, 184, 186, 189,
    190, 192, 210
Vietnam invasion of (1978), 110–111,
    161, 168, 181
Vietnam troop withdrawal (1989), 11,
    14, 163, 172, 173, 191
water, 182, 188
See also under Indonesia; Singapore;
    Thailand
Cam Ranh Bay (Vietnam), 10, 15, 80, 173
Canada, 12
Cao Dai sect, 157
Capital flow, 12, 17
Capital markets, 13
Carter, Jimmy, 190
Catholics, 5, 157. See also Philippines,
    Catholic Church
Cebu City/Province (Philippines), 72
Censorship, 56, 124, 179
Central Intelligence Agency, U.S. (CIA),
    145, 198, 199, 201
Centralized state monopoly (Burma), 143
Centrist-reform administration
    (Philippines), 67
CGDK. See Coalition Government of
    Democratic Kampuchea
Chakri dynasty (Thailand), 24
Chamlong Srimuang, 35
Champassak kingdom (Laos), 197
Chatichai Choonhavan, 15, 20, 26–27, 30–
    31, 32, 33, 34, 37, 38, 39, 49, 50, 51,
    52, 192, 207
Chat Thai Party (Thai Nation), 32, 34, 35
Chavalit Yongchaiyut, 27, 29, 33, 34, 37,
    38, 39, 154
China, 11, 13, 46, 47, 131, 151, 154, 157,
    163, 173, 175
    and ASEAN, 11, 15
    economy, 11
    GNP, 17
    and Khmer Rouge, 14, 175, 185, 192,
    193
    and Soviet Union, 10, 11, 15
    trade, 9, 11, 152
    and U.S., 173, 190, 192, 212
    See also under individual countries

Chinese
  in Brunei, 133, 137
  in Burma, 153, 154
  economic power, 2, 34, 36, 40, 43, 96–
    97, 103
  in Indonesia, 88, 96–97, 98, 161
  in Malaysia, 103–104, 106, 108, 111,
    114, 117, 118, 161
  in Philippines, 74, 78
  in Singapore, 121, 122, 126, 161
  in Thailand, 23, 34, 36–37, 40, 43, 45,
    48, 161
  in Vietnam, 157, 161
Chin tanakan may (new thinking) (Laos),
  201
Christianity, 2, 5
CIA. *See* Central Intelligence Agency
Citizens' Consultative Committees (PAP),
  126
City-state. *See* Singapore
Civil disobedience campaign (1986)
  (Philippines), 59
Civil liberties, 3, 4, 19, 52, 56, 60, 65,
  88, 94, 105, 112, 113, 124, 143, 170
Civil society, 46
Clark Air Force Base, U.S. (Philippines),
  68, 80, 81, 82, 83
Coalition Government of Democratic
  Kampuchea (CGDK), 16, 183, 184,
  185–186, 191, 192, 193, 194
Cochin China (Vietnam), 158
Coconuts, 75, 76
Coffee, 40
Cojuangco, Eduardo "Danding," 62
Cojuangco, Jose "Peping," 62
Cojuangco family, 61–62
Cold war, 48, 51, 122, 129, 131, 195, 210
Collectivization, 16, 169, 181, 200
Communalism, 103, 104–105, 111, 113
Communications, 10, 18, 114, 137
Communism, 6, 9, 10, 11, 14, 15, 47
Communist authoritarian political
  category, 3–4. *See also* Cambodia;
  Laos; Vietnam
Communist parties. *See* Malaysia,
  Malayan Communist Party; *under
  individual countries*
Compadrazgo/compadre system, 73
Comprehensive Agrarian Reform Program
  (Philippines), 62
Confucianism, 5, 126, 157, 166, 167

Consensus, 21, 88, 94, 118
Constitutional monarchy (Thailand), 20,
  24
Consultation, 21
Containment policy (U.S.), 14
Continuity, 129
Contraceptives, 72
Contract system (Vietnam), 163, 169
Contras (Nicaragua), 138
Cooperatives, 16
"Co-prosperity sphere" (Japan), 12
Copyrights, 49
Corruption, 17, 18, 20. *See also under
  individual countries*
Council of Academic Advisors (Thailand),
  49
CPP. *See* Philippines, Communist Party of
  the
CPV. *See* Vietnam, Communist Party of
Crime, 17, 18
Crony capitalism (Philippines), 57, 77
Cronyism, 5, 20, 60
Cuba, 46, 47
Cukong system (Indonesia), 97

Dakwah (Muslim youth groups, Malaysia),
  111
Da Nang (Vietnam), 10, 80, 173
DAP. *See* Democratic Action Party
Decentralized planning, 16, 167, 204
Deforestation, 18, 26, 41, 205
Democratic Action Party (DAP)
  (Malaysia), 108, 109, 111, 113
Democratic centralism, 4, 202
Democratic Kampuchean Khmer Rouge,
  185
Democratization, 2, 9, 13, 19, 20, 174,
  211. *See also under individual countries*
Democrat party (*Prachatipat*) (Thailand),
  34, 35
Diarrhea, 204
Diego Garcia, 80
Dislocation, 46–47, 78, 98–99, 116, 129,
  137, 171, 189, 205
Displaced persons, 186–187
Doi Moi (Vietnamese renovation), 11,
  162–163, 164, 165
Do Muoi, 163
Dong (Vietnamese currency), 170
DPR. *See* Indonesia, parliament

Draft Strategy of Socio-Economic
   Stabilization and Development up to
   the Year 2000 (Vietnam), 170
Drug trade, 51, 149, 154, 205, 207
Dutch East Indies (now Indonesia), 98

Eastern Europe, 10, 151, 163, 165, 167,
   203
East Timor, 100
Economic competition, 6
Education, 17, 18. *See also under*
   individual countries
Electricity, 36, 63, 114, 170, 182
Elite, 18, 211. *See also under* Malaysia;
   Philippines; Thailand
Elitist-centered political order, 3, 4
English (language), 56, 79
Enrile, Juan Ponce, 59, 67, 68
Environmental problems, 17, 18, 205
EOI. *See* Export-oriented industrialization
European Community, 9, 13
Export-oriented economies, 13, 40, 41,
   127
Export-oriented industrialization (EOI), 75,
   115

Faction constitutionalism, 28
Family-operated farm, 3
Family planning, 17, 62, 71
Farm Act (U.S.), 50
Federation of Malaysia (1963–1965), 104–
   105, 116, 122
Fertility rates, 17–18
Five-Power Defence Arrangement
   (Malaysia), 110
Flooding, 41
Flowers, 40
Food canning, 96
Footwear, 96, 115
Fort Bonifacio (Philippines), 68
Four Tigers. *See* Hong Kong; Singapore;
   South Korea; Taiwan
France, 12. *See also under* Cambodia;
   Laos; Vietnam
Free-export zone (Vietnam), 169
Free Laos. *See* Lao-Issara
Free-market economies, 40
French-Indochinese War (1946–1954), 158
Fruits, 40
FUNCINPEC. *See* United National Front
   for an Independent, Peaceful, and
   Cooperative Cambodia

Galang Island (Indonesia), 186
GDP. *See* Gross domestic product
Generalized System of Preferences (GSP),
   50, 131
Geneva Agreements
   1954, 158, 159, 198
   1961, 199
Genocide, 180, 182
Glasnost, 9, 10, 11
GNP. *See* Gross national product
God-kings, 24, 178
Goh Chok Tong, 123
Golden Land/Peninsula. *See Suwanabhum*
Golkar (Indonesia government party), 21,
   89, 91, 92, 93, 96, 98, 116
Gorbachev, Mikhail, 9, 10, 11, 15, 173,
   191, 192
Gotong rojong (mutual benefit), 88, 94
GRCs. *See* Group Representation
   Constituencies
Great Britain, 103, 104. *See also under*
   Brunei; Burma; Malaysia; Singapore
Green Northeast project (Thailand), 29
Green revolution, 97
Gross domestic product (GDP), 44. *See*
   also under individual countries
Gross national product (GNP), 12, 17. *See*
   also under individual countries
Group of 50 Petition. *See Petisi Kelompok*
   50
Group Representation Constituencies
   (GRCs) (Singapore), 125
GSP. *See* Generalized System of
   Preferences
Guam, 80, 81
Guam Doctrine (Nixon), 14
Guided democracy, 87, 88, 94, 126
Gurkhas, British Army (Brunei), 135, 137,
   138

Haiphong (Vietnam), 201
Haji Hassanal Bolkiah Mu'izzaddin
   Waddaulah. *See* Sir Muda Hassanal
   Bolkiah
Haji Omar Ali Saifuddien Sa'adul Khairi
   Waddien, ibni Almarhum Sultan
   Mohammad Jamulul Alam. *See* Seri
   Begawan
Hanoi
   as Tonkin capital, 157
   U.S. bombing of (1972), 159

as Vietnam capital, 161, 164
Hawaii, 80
Health facilities, 17, 18
Hedonism, 121
Hierarchical patterns, 21, 24, 28, 38, 52, 55, 64, 94, 143, 150, 166, 167, 187
High-tech industries, 127
Hinduism, 2, 187
Hmong, 201, 203
Hoa Hao sect, 157
Ho Chi Minh, 123, 158, 161, 162, 164–165, 166, 168, 171
  death (1969), 162, 165
Ho Chi Minh City (formerly Saigon), 161
Homosexuality, 72
Honasan, Gregorio, 68
Hong Kong, 96
  trade, 12, 40, 127, 131, 169
Hue (Annam capital), 157
Human rights, 145, 155, 164, 190
Hungary, 114

Ilocanos, 67
Imperialism, 2
Import substitution industrialization (ISI), 13, 75, 96
India, 154, 155, 169
  GNP, 17
Indian Ocean, 10, 80, 173
Indians
  in Burma, 154
  economic power, 2
  in Malaysia, 103, 104, 108
  in Singapore, 121
  in Thailand, 23
Indochina, 3, 6, 14, 15, 17. *See also* Cambodia; Laos; Vietnam
Indochina Federation proposal, 6
Indochinese Communist party (1930), 165
Indochinese refugees, 1, 51, 161, 168, 174, 179, 181, 186–187, 207
Indonesia
  agriculture, 5, 90, 97
  and ASEAN, 6, 100
  automobiles, 18
  bureaucracy, 89, 91–92, 98
  and Cambodia, 100, 186
  and China, 100
  colonialism, 87, 91, 94, 98, 116
  Communist Party of (PKI), 47, 88, 99, 100

constitutions, 90
corruption, 88, 92, 94, 96, 97, 98, 101
debt, 96
democratization, 87–88, 92, 93, 94–95, 101, 211
dissidents, 91
diversity in, 87, 97
duty-free zones, 96
and East Timor, 100
economic growth and development, 89–90, 92, 93, 95–97, 99, 101, 211
economy, 88, 89, 90, 95, 98, 99
education, 92, 96, 101
ethnic groups, 88, 101. *See also* Chinese, in Indonesia
exports, 96
fertility rate, 18
five-year plan, 95, 97
food self-sufficiency, 90, 97
foreign aid to, 99, 100
foreign investment in, 96, 100
foreign policy, 99–100
Gestapu coup (1965), 88–89, 98
GNP, 17, 90, 95, 97
government, 3, 4, 20–21, 47, 88, 89, 92–93, 99
and Hong Kong, 96
income, 90, 96, 97, 101
independence (1949), 20, 87
infant mortality, 97
inflation, 89–90
infrastructure, 95, 96
internationalism, 92
ISI, 96
islands, 87
and Japan, 98, 100
joint ventures, 96
life expectancy, 90, 97
literacy rate, 17
and Malaysia, 89, 100, 110
manufacturing assembly area, 96
mass executions (mid-1960s), 47, 89, 98–99
middle class, 101
military, 4, 20, 21, 47, 88–89, 91, 92, 93, 96, 98, 99, 101
military dual-function role, 29, 91
Muslims in, 87, 88, 89, 92–93, 98, 101
nationalism, 3, 88, 92, 100
as non-Communist, 6, 92, 99, 100
oil, 90, 95, 96

opposition parties, 89, 93, 98
parliament (DPR), 88, 90, 94, 95
People's Consultative Assembly (MPR),
    89, 90, 92
political culture, 94
political parties, 88, 89, 92–93, 94, 95,
    98
political system, 87–88, 89, 90, 91, 95,
    97, 99, 101
population, 5, 87, 90, 100, 101, 129
poverty, 90
private sector, 95
religion, 5, 87, 92
repression in, 5, 21
rural, 94, 97
security, 98, 99
and Singapore, 96
size, 129
and South Korea, 96, 100
state autonomy, 97–99, 101
state ideology, 92, 98
students, 88
and Taiwan, 96, 100
television sets, 18
and UN, 89
unemployment, 88
universities, 92
urban, 101
and U.S., 81, 99, 100
and Vietnam, 100, 169
wages, 96
and Western Europe, 100
women, 93
See also under Brunei
Indonesian Democratic Party (PDI), 89, 92
Industrialization, 13, 40, 41, 75
Industry, 2, 13, 18, 96
Infant mortality rate, 97, 204
Infrastructure, 16, 17, 18. See also under
    individual countries
Insurgencies, 14. See also Cambodia, and
    Khmer Rouge; Malaysia, Communist
    insurgents; Philippines, Communists;
    under Thailand
Intellectual property rights (IPR), 49–50
Internal Securities Act (Malaysia), 107,
    113
International division of labor, 13, 211
International Monetary Fund, 170
Interventionist model, 98
IPR. See Intellectual property rights

Irangate (U.S.), 138
Iraq, 13, 63
Irrigation, 29
ISI. See Import substitution
    industrialization
Islam, 2, 5, 104, 109, 111, 112, 133, 135.
    See also Muslims
Isolationism, 143, 151, 154, 155, 172, 174,
    212
Israel, 46, 47
Italy, 12

Jakarta (Indonesia), 129
Jakarta Informal Meetings (1989, 1990),
    100
Japan, 2, 11, 46, 115, 141, 142, 152, 212
    and ASEAN, 12, 15, 18
    banks, 12
    consumer goods, 13
    defense budget, 12
    demilitarization, 12
    economy, 11, 13
    GNP, 12, 17
    trade, 9, 10, 11, 12, 127
    and U.S., 11, 12, 173, 174, 212
    U.S. military bases in, 80, 81
    See also under individual countries
Java (Indonesia), 87, 101
Jayavarman VII (Khmer emperor), 189
Johnson, Lyndon, 159, 160

Kachins, 149
Kampuchea, 6–7(n1), 177, 181. See also
    Cambodia
Kampuchean People's Revolutionary Party,
    183
Karens, 142, 149
Kaysone Phomvihan, 200, 202–203, 204,
    206, 207
KBL. See New Society Movement
Kennedy, John F., 159
Khmer People's National Liberation Front
    (KPNLF) (Cambodia), 16, 185, 186
Khmer Republic (1970–1975), 177. See also
    Cambodia
Khmer Rouge. See under Cambodia; China
Khmers, 23, 177
Khorat Province (Thailand), 30
Killing fields. See Cambodia, and Khmer
    Rouge

Kingdom of a Million Elephants (Laos).
  See Lan Xang
Kissinger, Henry, 168
Kit Sangkhom. *See* Social Action party
Konfrontasi. *See* Indonesia, and Malaysia
Korpri (Indonesian civil servants), 92
KPNLF. *See* Khmer People's National
  Liberation Front
Kraisak Choonhavan, 32
Kuala Lumpur (Malaysia), 105
Kuwait, Iraqi invasion of (1990), 13, 63,
  74
Kyat (Burmese currency), 143

LABAN! (Filipino political party), 66
Laban ng Demokratikong Pilipino, 62
Laissez-faire model, 98
Land scarcity, 18
Landslides, 41
Lan Xang (Kingdom of a Million
  Elephants), 197
Lao-Issara (Laotian political group), 198
Lao People's Democratic Republic (1975),
  199–200. *See also* Laos
Lao People's Liberation Army, 199
Lao People's Revolutionary Party (LPRP),
  201. *See also* Laos, Communist party
Laos, 207–208
  agriculture, 197, 199, 200, 201, 204, 205
  anti-Communists, 198
  and ASEAN, 16, 210
  and Australia, 205, 207
  automobiles, 18
  bureaucracy, 200
  capital. *See* Vientiane
  and China, 197, 201, 206, 207
  colonialism, 197, 198, 205
  as Communist, 6, 16, 25, 199–200, 207
  Communist party (LPRP), 199–201,
    202, 203, 204, 206
  constitution, lack of, 202, 204
  corruption, 204
  democratization, 203
  economic development, 204–205, 211
  economic liberalization, 4, 16, 201, 202,
    204, 209
  economy, 15, 16, 201, 203
  education, 197
  elite, 200
  ethnic groups, 197, 201, 203
  foreign aid to, 198, 200, 201, 202, 205,
    206, 207
  foreign investment in, 16, 204–205, 207
  foreign policy, 206–207
  forests, 205
  and France, 197, 198, 207
  GNP, 17
  government, 4, 198–200, 202, 205–206
  housing, 205
  income, 204
  independence (1954), 198
  industry, 16, 204, 205
  infant mortality, 204
  and Japan, 198, 205, 207
  kingdoms, 197
  life expectancy, 17, 204
  military, 198, 199, 201, 208
  monarchy, 199
  nationalism, 3, 198
  patron-client relationship, 201, 205
  political parties, 201
  politics, 18, 198
  population, 197, 207
  poverty, 171, 204
  private sector, 200, 201, 204, 205
  reforms, 201, 202, 203, 205, 211
  religion, 5, 197
  repression, 200, 206
  rice self-sufficiency, 201
  Royalists, 199
  rural, 197, 199, 205
  security, 197, 206, 207
  and Soviet Union, 199, 200, 201, 206,
    207
  standard of living, 204, 205, 208
  state autonomy, 205–206
  Supreme People's Assembly, 202
  Supreme People's Council, 200
  television sets, 18
  trade, 16
  underdevelopment, 204
  urban, 197, 205, 208
  and U.S., 197, 198, 199, 200, 201–202,
    203, 205, 206, 207
  U.S. bombing of (1964), 199, 202
  and Vietnam, 197, 198, 199, 200–201,
    206, 207
  and World War II, 198, 205
  See also under Thailand
Laos Peace Accords (1973), 199
Laurel, Salvador, 58, 59, 66, 67, 68, 70
League for the Independence of Vietnam.
  See Vietminh

Le Duan, 162
Le Duc Tho, 162
Lee Hsien Loong, 123
Lee Kuan Yew, 21, 104, 122, 123–124,
126, 128, 129, 130, 132
Leninist single-party dictatorships, 4
Liberal party (Philippines), 56, 66
Life expectancy, 17, 90, 97
Literacy, 17
Livestock, 40, 197
Logging, 26, 44, 154–155
Lon Nol, 178, 179, 180
Look East policy (Malaysia), 106, 115
LPRP. *See* Lao People's Revolutionary
Party
Luang Prabang kingdom (Laos), 197
Luisita hacienda (Tarlac Province), 62
Luzon (Philippines), 62, 67

Machismo, 62–63
Mahathir bin Mohamad, Datuk Seri, 20,
106–108, 109, 111, 113, 115, 117
MAI. *See* Multilateral Aid Initiative
Maize, 40
Malacanang palace (Philippines), 68
Malaria, 204
Malay (language), 104, 105
Malaya (now Malaysia), 103, 104, 122
Malayan Chinese Association, 108, 111
Malayan Indian Congress, 108
"Malay Malaysia," 122
Malays
in Brunei, 133
in Singapore, 121, 122
See also Malaysia
Malaysia, 103
agriculture, 115, 122
and ASEAN, 6, 117–118
and Australia, 110
bureaucracy, 109, 116, 117
capital. *See* Kuala Lumpur
and China, 118
colonialism, 103, 104, 116
communal riots (1969), 105, 114, 116
Communist insurgents, 110, 111, 118
constitution, 104, 107
courts, 107, 116
democratization, 112–113, 116, 211
dissidents, 107
diversity, 103
economic growth and development, 106,
108, 114–115, 116, 118, 211

economy, 4, 103, 104, 105, 116
education, 114
electricity, 114
elites, 112, 116
Emergency, the, 110, 111, 118
EOI, 115
ethnic groups, 4, 20, 103–105, 106, 114,
117, 118. *See also* Chinese, in
Malaysia; Indians, in Malaysia
exports, 115
fertility rate, 18
foreign investment in, 114–115
foreign policy, 117–118
GNP, 17, 106, 114
government, 3, 4, 5, 20, 104, 105–108,
113, 116, 117. *See also* Communalism;
Sultans
and Great Britain, 104, 110, 112, 118
income, 103
independence (1957), 20, 104, 112, 114,
115
and Indochinese refugees, 187
industry, 103, 115
infant mortality, 97
language, official, 104, 105
life expectancy, 97
Malayan Communist Party (MCP), 111
media, 113, 116
middle class, 106
military, 110–111, 118
Muslims in, 103, 111
nationalism, 3
and New Zealand, 110
as non-Communist, 6
opposition parties, 105, 106, 107, 109,
111, 113, 116
parliament, 105, 106, 107, 108, 110, 112,
113, 116, 118
and Philippines, 117, 118
political parties, 20, 104, 105, 106, 107,
108–109, 111, 112, 116, 118
politics, 20, 104, 106–107, 113
population, 103
poverty, 114, 118
press, 107, 113
privatization, 106, 115
recession, 106, 114
religion, 5, 104, 111
roads, 114
rural, 103, 110, 114, 115
security, 107, 110, 111, 116–117

and Singapore, 104, 110, 116, 122, 127, 129
standard of living, 103, 114
state autonomy, 116–117
state of emergency (1969–1971), 104, 105, 112, 113, 117
television sets, 18, 114
and Thailand, 117, 118
twenty-year plan, 114, 115
and UN, 118
urban, 103
and U.S., 81
water supply, 114
women, 93, 111–112
and World War II, 111, 116
See also under Brunei; Indonesia
Malaysia Incorporated, 106
"Malaysian Malaysia," 122
Malay way, 113, 118
Malolos constitution (1899) (Philippines), 64
Mandalay (Burma), 144
Mandarin class, 158, 167
Mandate of heaven concept, 166–167
Manila (Philippines), 63, 68, 75, 78
archbishop of, 71
Manoon Rupkachorn, 32
Manufacturing, 2, 17. *See also* Industry
Maoists, 181
Mao Zedong, 11
Marcos, Ferdinand, 4, 5, 17, 19, 20, 56–58, 60, 62, 64, 65, 66, 67, 69, 71, 74, 75, 77, 78, 79, 81, 93, 117
death (1989), 59
and 1986 election, 58–59
wealth, 59, 76
as World War II hero, 58–59
Marcos, Imelda, 69, 70
Marines (Philippines), 68
Market-oriented economies, 15, 31, 45, 115, 211
Marxist-Leninist fundamentalism, 172
Mass party (*Muanchon*) (Thailand), 34
Materialism, 17, 18, 121, 128
Maung Maung, 144, 145
MBA. *See* Military Bases Agreement
MCP. *See* Malaysia, Malayan Communist Party
Mekong River
bridge, 52, 205, 207
Delta, 157, 181

Meritocracy, 121
MIAs. *See* POW-MIA issues
Micronesia, 81
Middle class, 18. *See also under* Indonesia; Thailand
Middle East crisis (1990–1991), 13, 74
Military authoritarian political category, 3. *See also* Burma
Military Bases Agreement (MBA), 79, 82. *See also* Philippines, U.S. military bases in
Mindanao (Philippines), 59
Modernization, 2, 17, 21, 23, 36, 48, 101, 212
Money economy, 2
Mons, 23
Mosques, 114
Motorcycles, 36
MPR. *See* Indonesia, People's Consultative Assembly
Muanchon. See Mass party
Mufakat. See Consensus
Multilateral Aid Initiative (MAI), 76
Multinational corporations, 74, 75
Multipolar world, 9
Musjawarah. See Consultation
Muslims, 30, 56, 78, 87, 88, 89, 92–93, 98, 101, 103, 111
Myanmar, 6–7(n1), 141, 156(n1). *See also* Burma

Nacionalista party (Philippines), 56, 66, 67
Nahdatul Ulama (Indonesian Muslim organization), 93
NAP. *See* New Aspirations Party
Narcotics. *See* Drug trade
National Democratic Front (NDF) (Burma), 149
National Economic and Social Development Board (Thailand), 44
National Front (*Barisan Nasional*) (Malaysia), 20, 105, 106, 107, 108, 109, 111, 113, 116, 117, 118
Nationalism, 2–3, 6, 212
new, 15, 37, 49, 51
See also under individual countries
National League for Democracy (NLD) (Burma), 19, 145, 146, 148
National Liberation Front (NLF) (South Vietnamese Communists), 159
National Operations Council (NOC) (Malaysia), 105

National Peace Keeping Council (NPKC)
  (Thailand), 31
National Unity Party (NUP) (Burma), 19,
  146, 148
Natural gas. *See under* Brunei
Natural resources, 18, 128, 141, 175
NDF. *See* National Democratic Front
NEFOS. *See* Newly emerging forces
Negara Brunei Darussalam. *See* Brunei
Neocolonialism, 74, 88
Neoimperialist states, 100
Neo Lao Hak Sat (NLHS) (Laos), 198, 199
NEP. *See* New economic policy
Netherlands, 87, 91, 98
New Aspirations Party (NAP) (Thailand),
  27, 33
New Economic Mechanism (Laos), 204
New economic policy (NEP) (Malaysia),
  114–115, 116, 117, 118
New Hope projects (Thailand), 29
Ne Win, 19, 123, 142, 143, 144, 145, 147,
  148, 150, 152, 153, 154, 155
  biographer of, 144
New international era, 11, 13–15, 22, 48,
  49, 209, 210
Newly emerging forces (NEFOS)
  (Indonesia), 100
Newly industrialized countries (NICs), 9,
  13, 31, 103, 115, 131
New order (Indonesia), 88, 89, 91, 95, 98,
  99, 100, 101
New People's Army (NPA) (CPP), 57, 61,
  70–71
New Society Movement (KBL)
  (Philippines), 57, 66, 67, 70, 75
New Zealand, 110
Ngo Dinh Diem, 158–159
  death (1963), 159
NGOs. *See* Nongovernmental
  organizations
Nguyen Van Linh, 162, 167
Nicaragua, 138
NICs. *See* Newly industrialized countries
Nixon, Richard M., 14, 159, 160, 179
NLD. *See* National League for Democracy
NLF. *See* National Liberation Front
NLHS. *See* Neo Lao Hak Sat
NOC. *See* National Operations Council
Nongovernmental organizations (NGOs),
  188
North Borneo (now Sabah), 104

North Korea, 47
North Vietnam, 159–160. *See also*
  Vietnam
NPA. *See* New People's Army
NPKC. *See* National Peace Keeping
  Council
Nu, U, 142, 146, 147, 150
Nuclear weapons, 82
NUP. *See* National Unity Party

ODP. *See* Orderly Departure Program
Official Secrets Act (Malaysia), 113
Oil, 10, 152, 169
  prices, 74, 75, 96, 127, 136
  See also under Brunei; Indonesia
OLDEFOS. *See* Old established forces
Old established forces (OLDEFOS)
  (Indonesia), 100
Oligarchy, 55, 56, 60, 61, 77, 83, 155
Olongapo (Philippines), 82
Operation Lallang (Malaysia), 107
Opium, 149
Orderly Departure Program (ODP), 174
Osmeña family, 72
Overseas Vietnamese, 169, 170, 175

Pacific Ocean, 10, 173
Pacific Rim, 11, 79
Palang Dharma party (Thailand), 35
Pancasila (Indonesian state ideology), 92,
  98
PAP. *See* People's Action Party
Pariah entrepreneurship, 48
Paris Peace Accords (1973), 159–160, 168
Parliamentary-democratic system, 5, 87,
  94, 105, 112
Partai Islam Se-Malaysia (PAS), 108, 109,
  113
Partai Kebangsaan Demokratik Brunei. See
  Brunei National Democratic Party
Partido ng Bayan (Philippines), 67
PAS. *See Partai Islam Se-Malaysia*
Patents, 49
Paternalistic authority, 150
Pathet Lao (NLHS military), 198, 199,
  201, 202. *See also* Lao People's
  Liberation Army
Patronage, 44–45, 64, 65, 73, 77, 122, 153
Patron-client relationship, 2, 3, 28, 35,
  147, 155, 201, 209. *See also under*
  individual countries

PAVN. *See* People's Army of Vietnam
PDI. *See* Indonesian Democratic Party
Peace Corps, 51
Peasants, 2, 18, 36, 70, 158, 163, 211. *See also individual countries,* rural
People's Action Party (PAP) (Singapore), 122, 123, 124–125, 126, 127, 129, 130
  factionalism, 124, 126, 130
  grassroots organizations, 126
People's Army of Vietnam (PAVN), 166. *See also* Vietnam, military
People's party (*Rasadorn*) (Thailand), 34
People's Revolutionary Party (South Vietnam), 159
People's Revolutionary Party of Kampuchea (PRPK), 185
Perestroika, 9–10, 11
Persian Gulf, 80, 81
  war (1991), 9, 83. *See also* Kuwait, Iraqi invasion of
Personalism, 18, 19–20, 24, 27, 28, 30, 39, 46, 52, 55, 60, 61, 67, 179
Pertamina (Indonesian state oil company), 96
Petisi Kelompok 50 (Indonesia), 98
PGNU. *See* Provisional Government of National Unity
Pham Van Dong, 162
Phibun Songkran, 47
Philippine American Cooperation Talks, 83
Philippine Assistance Program. *See* Multilateral Aid Initiative
Philippines, 1, 2
  agriculture, 57, 62, 63, 74, 75, 76
  AIDS in, 72, 82
  and ASEAN, 6
  automobiles, 18
  bureaucracy, 69, 78
  capital flight, 57, 60, 76
  Catholic church, 57, 59, 62, 71, 78
  colonialism, 55, 56, 72, 74, 78, 79, 98
  Communist Party of the (CPP), 57, 70–71
  Communists, 56, 59, 61, 67, 68, 209
  constitutions, 56, 60, 64–65, 82
  corruption, 56–57, 59, 60, 61, 64, 69, 75, 77, 210
  coup attempts, 60, 63, 68, 70
  democratization, 55, 56, 60, 65, 72–73, 78

dissidents, 56, 57, 60
earthquake (1990), 63
economic growth and development, 55, 56, 57, 60, 61, 71, 74–77
economy, 17, 55, 56, 57, 59, 60, 64, 74, 75, 77, 83, 98
education, 56, 77
electrical blackouts, 63
elite, 55, 56, 61, 67, 73, 74, 78, 83
ethnic groups, 74, 78
exports, 56, 60, 74, 75
fertility rate, 18, 62–63, 71
food shortages, 56
foreign aid to, 76, 80, 83
foreign investment in, 75, 76
foreign policy, 79–83
GNP, 17, 69, 74, 80
government, 3, 4, 5, 14, 19–20, 55, 56–58, 59, 60–63, 64, 67, 72, 78, 83, 210
health care, 71
imports, 74
independence (1946), 56
industry, 60
infant mortality, 97
inflation, 57, 60, 61, 74
and Japan, 56, 76, 78
land-owning class, 55, 56, 62, 72, 74, 83
language, national, 56, 79
legislature, 65–66
life expectancy, 97
literacy, 56, 77
manufacturing, 75
martial law (1972–1981), 56, 57, 58, 65, 67, 78
media, 56, 60
military, 56, 57, 59, 60, 61, 67–68, 70, 83
military coup attempts (1989), 63
Muslims, 56, 78
National Assembly, 59, 62, 67
nationalism, 3, 68, 81
as non-Communist, 6, 57
oil imports, 74, 75
opposition groups, 57, 58, 59, 66, 68
patron-client relationships, 56, 61, 63–64, 67, 72–73, 77, 78
people's assemblies (1973), 65
"people's power" (1986), 19, 58, 59–60, 72
political parties, 56, 58, 60, 61, 62, 66–67, 109, 116

political system, 55, 56–57, 58, 60, 61, 64, 65, 67, 72–73, 77, 83
population, 62, 71–72, 74
poverty, 61, 62, 71, 210
press, 56
private armies, 56, 57, 61
private sector, 69
recession (1970s), 75
religions, 5
rural, 57, 61, 69, 72, 75–76
security, 67, 78, 81
socioeconomic system, 19–20, 56, 57, 60, 61, 62–63, 76
standard of living, 71, 74, 75, 77, 83
state autonomy, 77–79, 83
television sets, 18
typhoon (1990), 63
underemployment, 57, 74
undernourishment, 57
unemployment, 57, 74, 75
and U.S., 14, 55–56, 58, 59, 64, 66, 68, 69, 74–75, 76, 79–83
U.S. military bases in, 14, 15, 59, 68, 79–83, 102
vigilantism, 61
violence, 56, 68, 71
wages, 57, 76
water shortages, 63
women, 69–70
and World War II, 56, 59, 75, 78
See also under Malaysia; Vietnam
Phnom Penh (Cambodia), 16, 179–180, 182, 183
Phumiphol Adunyadej (king of Thailand), 24, 25, 31, 32, 35–36
PKI. *See* Indonesia, Communist Party of
Pluralist political systems, 10, 18–19, 167
Poland, 163, 167
Political participation, 18, 36, 52, 65, 93
Political repression, 5
Political stability, 40, 42, 44, 46, 56, 90, 99, 101, 174, 178
Pollution, 17, 18
Pol Pot, 161, 180, 181, 184, 185, 190
Population growth, 17
Ports, 2, 201
Portugal, 114
Pouhak Phoumsavan, 202
Power, 3, 9. *See also individual countries,* state autonomy
POW-MIA (prisoner of war-missing in action) issues, 173, 207

PPP. *See* United Development Party
Prachatipat. See Democrat party
Prem Tinsulanond, 25–26, 32, 34, 36
Price controls, 16
Privatization, 44, 106
Protectionism, 13, 49, 50, 75, 96, 127
Provisional Government of National Unity (PGNU) (Laos), 199
PRPK. *See* People's Revolutionary Party of Kampuchea
Puan Rafidah, 112
Pyidawtha, 141
Pyithu Hluttaw. See Burma, People's Assembly

Quadripartite plan (Cambodia), 193
Quality of life indicators, 17–18

Radios, 36
Railways, 2
RAM. *See* Reform of the Armed Forces Movement
Ramos, Fidel, 59
Rangoon (Burma), 6–7(n1), 144
Rangoon Spring (1988), 144
Rasadorn. See People's party
Razak, Tun, 105
death (1976), 106
Razaleigh Hamzah, Tunku, 106, 107, 109
RBAF. *See* Royal Brunei Armed Forces
Reagan, Ronald, 14, 131
Red River Delta, 157
Reeducation camps/programs, 161, 164, 200
Reforestation, 29
Reform of the Armed Forces Movement (RAM) (Philippines), 68
Refugees. *See* Indochinese refugees
Regional integration, 5, 6. *See also under* Thailand
Rice, 16, 36, 40, 90, 97, 136, 152, 168, 169, 180, 181, 188, 197, 201
Roads, 2, 36, 114
Romania, 163
Royal Brunei Armed Forces (RBAF), 135
Rubber, 2, 40, 188

Sabah (Malaysia), 103, 104, 116, 117, 122
Saigon
captured by North Vietnamese (1975), 160

as Cochin China capital, 158
as Ho Chi Minh City, 161
as South Vietnam capital, 159
Sakdi na rankings (Thailand), 24
Samphan, Khieu, 185
Samrin, Heng, 161, 181, 182, 184
Sann, Son, 185–186, 193
Sarawak (Malaysia), 103, 104, 116, 122, 133
Sarit Thanarat, 25, 47
Sary, Ieng, 185
Satellite towns (Burma), 145
Saw Maung, 19, 144, 145, 147
Scout Rangers (Philippines), 68
SEATO. *See* Southeast Asia Treaty Organization
Second Industrial Revolution (1979) (Singapore), 127
Secret ballot, 56
Security, 9, 14. *See also under individual countries*
Sedition Act (Malaysia), 113
Sein Lwin, 144
Self-centeredness, 121
Semangat '46 (Spirit of '46) (Malaysia), 107
Semiconductors, 115
Semidemocracy, 3, 29, 34, 37, 38, 39, 49, 52, 56, 113, 120, 211. *See also* Indonesia; Malaysia; Philippines; Singapore; Thailand
Sen, Hun, 15, 16, 26, 51, 182, 183, 184, 190, 191, 192, 193, 194
Seri Begawan (sultan of Brunei), 134
17th parallel, 158
Shans, 142, 149
Shevardnadze, Eduard, 11
Ship repairing and building, 128
Siddhi Savetsila, 50
Sihanouk, Norodom (Cambodian king/prince), 16, 123, 177–179, 180, 183–184, 186, 190, 191, 193
exile in Beijing, 180, 183, 184
exile in Pyongyang, 184
overthrown (1970), 178, 179, 183
Sihanoukists, 16
Sihanoukville (Cambodia), 178
Sin, Jaime Cardinal, 59, 71
Singapore, 6, 131–132
agriculture, 121, 127
and ASEAN, 6, 131

and Australia, 127
automobiles, 18
bureaucracy, 124, 129
and Cambodia, 192
and China, 131
colonialism, 104, 122, 125, 129
Communists, 124
corruption, 122
democratic structure, 21, 123
democratization, 126
dissidents, 124, 131
economic growth and development, 123, 127–128, 211
economy, 127, 128
education, 121, 128, 130
emigration, 121, 128
ethnic groups, 104, 121, 125, 129
exports, 127
family incentives, 128
and Federation of Malaysia, 104, 116, 122, 129
fertility rate, 18
financial and business services, 128
foreign aid to, 129
foreign investment in, 127, 131
foreign labor force in, 127
foreign policy, 130–131, 212
GDP, 127, 128
GNP, 17, 128
government, 3, 4–5, 21, 122, 123
and Great Britain, 104, 122, 127
and Hong Kong, 127, 131
housing, 127, 128
income, 128
independence (1959, 1965), 21, 122, 123, 129
inflation, 127
infrastructure, 128
and Japan, 127, 131
life expectancy, 97
literacy, 121
manufacturing, 127, 128
medical care, 128
military, 129, 131
nationalism, 3
as NIC, 131
as non-Communist, 6, 122, 129
one-party system, 21, 123–124, 126. *See also* People's Action Party
opposition party, 124
parliament, 125–126

politics, 121, 122, 125
population, 121
press, 124
regulations, 121, 122, 128, 129, 130
religions, 5
repression, 5, 124, 130
savings, 128
security, 122, 131
size, 129
standard of living, 103, 121, 128
state autonomy, 128–130, 211
television sets, 18
and Thailand, 127
unemployment, 127
as urban entrepot, 121
and U.S., 12, 81, 118, 127, 131
and Vietnam, 131, 169
wages, 127
and West Germany, 127
See also under Indonesia; Malaysia
Sino-Soviet border, 10
Sirikit (queen of Thailand), 32
Sirindhorn (crown princess of Thailand),
    36, 39
Sir Muda Hassanal Bolkiah (sultan of
    Brunei), 19, 134, 135, 137
SLORC. *See* State Law and Order
    Restoration Council
SNC. *See* Supreme National Council
Social Action party (*Kit Sangkhom*)
    (Thailand), 34
Socialist camp, 10
Socialist economies, 15, 151, 161
Socialist Front (*Barisan Sosialis*)
    (Singapore), 124
Socialist Republic of Vietnam, 161. *See
    also* Vietnam
Socialist solidarity, 172
Socioeconomic change, 18
Souphanouvong (Laotian prince), 198,
    199, 200
South Africa, 118
South China Sea, 10, 103, 133, 173
Southeast Asia, 1–5, 10, 12, 13, 15, 212
    and ASEAN, 6, 17
    diversity, 3, 6, 212
    independence struggles, 2, 3, 16
    political culture, 21
    political structure, 3–5, 21
    religions, 2, 5
    See also individual countries

Southeast Asia Treaty Organization
    (SEATO), 14, 160
South Korea, 13, 18, 44, 46, 47, 96, 115,
    152
    trade, 40, 41, 172, 174
    and U.S., 12, 80, 81
South Vietnam, 158–159, 160
    Communist guerrillas, 159, 179
    Communist party (People's
        Revolutionary Party), 159
    coup (1963), 159
    and U.S., 14, 158, 159, 160, 168
    See also under Cambodia
Souvanna Phouma (Laotian prince), 198,
    199, 200
Soviet Union, 9–11, 131
    and Afghanistan, 10
    and ASEAN, 10, 11, 15, 191
    Communist party, 10
    economy, 10
    expansionism, 11
    military, 10, 13
    nationalism, 10
    and Southeast Asia, 10, 11, 13, 14, 175,
        191, 192, 194, 210, 212
    trade, 10, 11
    See also under individual countries
Spain, 55, 72, 74
Spirit of '46. *See Semangat '46*
Sri Lanka, 169
Standard of living, 17, 18. *See also under
    individual countries*
State Law and Order Restoration Council
    (SLORC) (Burma), 145, 146, 152
Status, 3, 150, 187
Strategic Army Reserve (Indonesia), 89
Strong states, 46, 47–48, 78, 98, 99, 116,
    117, 129–130, 137, 153, 171, 189, 205,
    206, 211
Subic Bay Naval Station, U.S.
    (Philippines), 79–80, 81, 82, 83
Subsidies, 16, 134
Suchinda Kraprayoon, 31, 32
Sugar, 40, 56, 75, 76
Suharto, 20–21, 89–90, 91, 92, 93, 94–95,
    96, 98, 99, 100, 101, 123
Sukarno, 20, 21, 87, 88, 90, 94, 100, 110,
    123, 126
    death (1970), 89
Sukhothai Kingdom (Thai), 23
Sukhumbhand Paribatra, 37–38

Sultan of Brunei, 19, 133, 134, 135, 137, 138
Sultans (Malay), 104, 110
Sundhara Kongsompong, 31, 32
Supreme National Council (SNC) (Cambodia), 194
Sutowo, Ibnu, 96
Sutrisno, Try, 91
Sutsakhan, Sak, 186
Suwanabhum, 5, 30, 49

Taiwan, 13, 18, 44, 46, 47, 96, 172, 174
  and Japan, 12
  and U.S., 12
  trade, 12, 40, 41
Tapioca, 40
Tarlac Province (Philippines), 62
Tatmadaw. *See* Burma, military
Teak, 154
Team A (UMNO faction), 106
Team B (UMNO faction), 106, 107
Team Member of Parliament (MP) scheme (Singapore), 125
"Tea money," 204
Technocrats, 25, 33, 37, 40, 41, 43, 47, 69, 78, 89, 91, 92, 95, 96, 99, 106, 109, 117, 130, 189
Technology, 10, 12, 13, 40, 97, 201
Telephone lines, 114
Television sets, 18, 36, 114
Tenant farmers, 75
Tet offensive (1968), 159
Textiles, 96, 115, 204
  quotas (U.S.), 50
Thailand, 2, 3, 151
  agriculture, 36, 40
  arms purchases, 15
  and ASEAN, 6, 51
  automobiles, 18
  bureaucracy, 24, 26, 28, 33, 42, 45, 46, 47, 48, 49, 52, 77
  Burmese invasion of (1767), 24
  and Cambodia, 15, 16, 26–27, 37, 51, 187, 191, 192
  capital. *See* Bangkok
  centralized administrative system, 43
  and China, 11, 15, 51, 100, 118
  and communism, 47
  Communist party, 30, 47
  constitutions, 25, 26, 28–29, 31
  corruption, 25, 27, 32, 33, 37

currency devaluation, 43
democratization, 20, 24, 25, 26, 27, 28–29, 33, 34, 37, 38–39, 43, 52, 211
domestic policies, 44–45, 46
economic growth and development, 1, 25, 27, 29–30, 31, 32, 38, 39–41, 43, 44, 45, 46, 48, 49, 52, 55, 75, 151, 192, 211
economy, 31, 38, 39, 40–41, 50, 98
education, 41, 44
elite, 23, 24, 28, 34, 42, 45, 48, 52
environmental policy, 26, 29, 41, 44, 154
ethnic groups, 23. *See also* Chinese, in Thailand
exports, 40, 41, 50, 169
factionalism, 27, 30, 46
fertility rate, 18
foreign aid to, 12, 51
foreign investment in, 12, 40–41
foreign policy, 48–51, 212
forests, 26, 29, 41, 44
GDP, 44
GNP, 17, 40, 74, 151
government, 3, 4, 5, 20, 24, 25–27, 29, 30, 31–33, 37, 38, 42, 43, 49, 52
"great tragedy." *See subentry* student-led revolt
health care, 44
history, 23–24
and Hong Kong, 40
imports, 50
infant mortality, 40, 97
inflation, 25
infrastructure, 32, 33, 36, 44
insurgencies, 25, 30, 47
intellectuals, 37–38, 45, 48
and Japan, 12, 24, 40, 41, 46
and Laos, 27, 37, 51–52, 197, 198, 201, 205, 206, 207
life expectancy, 97
literacy, 41
manufacturing, 40
martial law, 25, 52
middle class, 31, 37
military, 3, 4, 20, 24–25, 27, 29–33, 34, 37, 38, 42, 46, 47, 49, 51, 52, 77
military coup (1976), 25
military coup (1991), 3, 20, 26, 27, 28, 30, 31–33, 36, 39, 40

military coup attempts (1981, 1985), 30, 31, 36
monarchy, 24, 25, 29, 31, 32, 35–36, 39, 43–44, 47, 52, 206
Muslims, 30
National Legislative Assembly, 31
national slogan, 29
as NIC, 31
as non-Communist, 6, 30
opposition groups, 27, 34
parliament, 20, 25, 26, 28, 30, 31, 33–34, 42, 43, 46, 52
patron-client relationship, 28, 35, 44, 45, 46
personal ranking system, 24
political culture, 29, 38, 39
political parties, 20, 25, 26, 27, 30, 31, 32, 34–35, 42, 43, 46, 52, 109, 116
population, 41
press, 27, 32, 36
private sector, 44, 211
and regional integration, 5, 30, 49
religions, 5, 23, 24, 44
repression, 5
revolt (1932), 24
rural, 36, 40, 42
security, 25, 29, 31, 33, 38, 39, 47, 48, 49, 51
and South Korea, 40, 41
standard of living, 41
state autonomy, 42–48, 77, 153, 211
student-led revolt (1973), 20, 25, 37, 42
and Taiwan, 40, 41
taxes, 44
television sets, 18, 36
tourism, 170
uncolonized, 23, 46
urban, 40
and U.S., 14, 25, 26, 40, 47, 49–51, 116
and U.S. military bases, 80, 81
and Vietnam, 11, 15, 26, 27, 37, 51, 118, 172, 174
wages, 26
women, 38
and World War II, 24, 46
See also under Burma; Malaysia; Singapore
Thai Nation. *See Chat Thai* Party
Thankin movement (Burma), 141–142
Thanom Kittikachorn, 25, 47
Third World, 100, 151

Tiananmen Square (China) massacre (1989), 11, 154, 192
Timber, 88, 205
Time of Troubles (1948–1958) (Burma), 142
Tin, U, 146, 148
Tin mines, 2, 103
Tonkin area (Vietnam), 157
Trade relations, 9, 10, 11–12, 13
Traffic, 17, 18, 63
Tripartite plan (Cambodia), 193–194
Truong Chinh, 162

UMNO. *See* United Malay Nationalist Organization
UNICEF. *See* United Nations Children's Fund
UNIDO. *See* United Nationalist Democratic Organization
Union of Burma, 149
United Development Party (PPP) (Indonesia), 89, 92
United Malay Nationalist Organization (UMNO), 106, 107, 108–109, 113, 116
New, 107, 108
United National Front for an Independent, Peaceful, and Cooperative Cambodia (FUNCINPEC), 186
United Nationalist Democratic Organization (UNIDO) (Philippines), 58, 66
United Nations, 16, 89, 118, 143, 175, 183, 185, 186, 188, 190, 191, 192, 194
United Nations Children's Fund (UNICEF), 188
United Nations Development Program, 188
United States, 9, 11
and ASEAN, 11, 14, 15, 187
and Communism, 14, 160
de-Europeanization, 12
GNP, 12, 17
and Northeast Asia, 80
Seventh Fleet, 80
and Southeast Asia, 10, 11, 13–14, 48, 79–81, 173, 192, 209–210, 212
trade, 11–12, 50
trade deficit, 12
trade embargo. *See* Cambodia, and U.S.; Vietnam, and U.S.
See also under individual countries

Urbanization, 18, 211
Urine detection devices, 130

Vachiralongkorn (crown prince of
  Thailand), 36, 39
Value-added tax, 44
Vanguard class, 167
Vegetables, 40
Ver, Fabian, 67
Vientiane (Laos), 197, 198, 201
Vietcong (South Vietnamese Communists),
  159, 178, 179
Vietminh (League for the Independence of
  Vietnam), 158, 165, 198
Vietnam, 46, 47
  agriculture, 16, 157, 163, 169, 170
  and ASEAN, 15, 16, 172, 210
  automobiles, 18
  bureaucracy, 165, 171
  capital. *See* Hanoi
  and China, 157, 161, 168, 169, 171, 173,
    174, 175, 192
  and Chinese invasion of (1979), 161–
    162, 166
  collectivization, 169
  colonialism, 157–158, 162
  as Communist, 6, 16, 25, 99, 161, 164,
    167, 172
  Communist Party of (CPV), 19, 162,
    163, 164, 165, 166, 167, 169, 170, 171,
    172, 211
  constitution (1980), 165
  corruption, 163
  currency, 170
  democratization, 167
  economic development, 168–170, 174–
    175, 211
  economic liberalization, 4, 11, 16, 162,
    163, 167, 169, 174, 176, 209
  economy, 14, 15, 16, 161, 162, 167, 170,
    171, 211
  electricity, 170
  emigration, 161, 169, 174
  ethnic groups, 158. *See also* Chinese, in
    Vietnam
  expansionism, 6
  factions, 165, 175
  farm taxes, 165, 169
  food self-sufficiency (1989), 16, 168
  and foreign aid, 172
  foreign investment in, 169, 170, 172,
    174

  foreign policy, 171–175
  forests, 168
  and France, 3, 157, 158, 169, 171
  GNP, 17
  government, 4, 164, 166–167, 169, 176,
    211
  and Hong Kong, 169
  housing, 168, 170
  human rights, 164
  income, 168, 170
  independence (1945, 1955, 1959), 157
  and India, 169
  industry, 16
  inflation, 163, 168, 170
  infrastructure, 168, 170, 174
  and Japan, 3, 157, 158, 169, 171, 172,
    174, 210
  joint ventures, 169
  land laws, 169
  life expectancy, 17, 97
  military, 161, 162, 166, 168, 172
  National Assembly, 163, 170
  nationalism, 157, 158, 160, 165
  nationalization, 163, 169
  natural resources, 175
  opposition parties, 19, 163
  and Philippines, 169
  political prisoners, 163
  politics, 18, 19, 162
  population, 157
  poverty, 168, 171
  press, 163
  private sector, 169
  regions, 157–158
  religion, 5, 157
  renovation. *See Doi Moi; subentry*
    economic liberalization
  rice exports, 16, 169
  rural, 158, 163, 168, 169, 170
  security, 162, 165, 171
  and South Korea, 172, 174, 210
  and Soviet Union, 11, 14, 15, 161, 168,
    171, 173, 174, 175, 181, 190, 191
  standard of living, 162
  state autonomy, 170–171
  and Taiwan, 172, 174, 210
  television sets, 18
  tourism, 170
  trade, 16, 169
  unemployment, 168, 170
  urban, 158

and U.S., 3, 14, 80, 157, 159, 163–164,
     168, 169, 171, 172, 173–174, 175, 191,
     192, 210
  and the West, 167, 172, 175
  and World War II, 157, 158
  See also South Vietnam; Vietnam War;
     under Cambodia; Indonesia; Laos;
     Singapore; Thailand
Vietnamization, 159, 179
Vietnam War (1965–1975), 1, 14, 129,
     159–161, 167, 173, 199
  damage, 168, 179–180
Villages, 36, 94, 143
  hierarchical structure, 3
  identity, 2, 3
Vo Van Kiet, 163

Wan Maha Wipayok. See Thailand, student-
     led revolt
Water buffalo, 197
Wealth, 3, 17, 121
  gap, 17, 18, 92, 210–211
West Africa, 169

Westernization, 17, 112, 121, 212
West Germany, 12, 127, 155, 174
Westminster model, 112
Wolfowitz, Paul, 101
Wood processing, 96
World Bank, 13, 75, 76, 175, 204, 205,
     207
World capitalist system, 10, 11, 17, 50, 74,
     209
World Food Program, 188
World Health Organization, 188
World recession, 25
World War II (1939–1945), 2, 12, 13, 24,
     212. *See also under individual
     countries*

Yang diPertuan Agong (king of Malaysia),
     110

Zone of Peace, Freedom, and Neutrality
     (ZOPFAN), 100, 117–118
ZOPFAN. *See* Zone of Peace, Freedom,
     and Neutrality